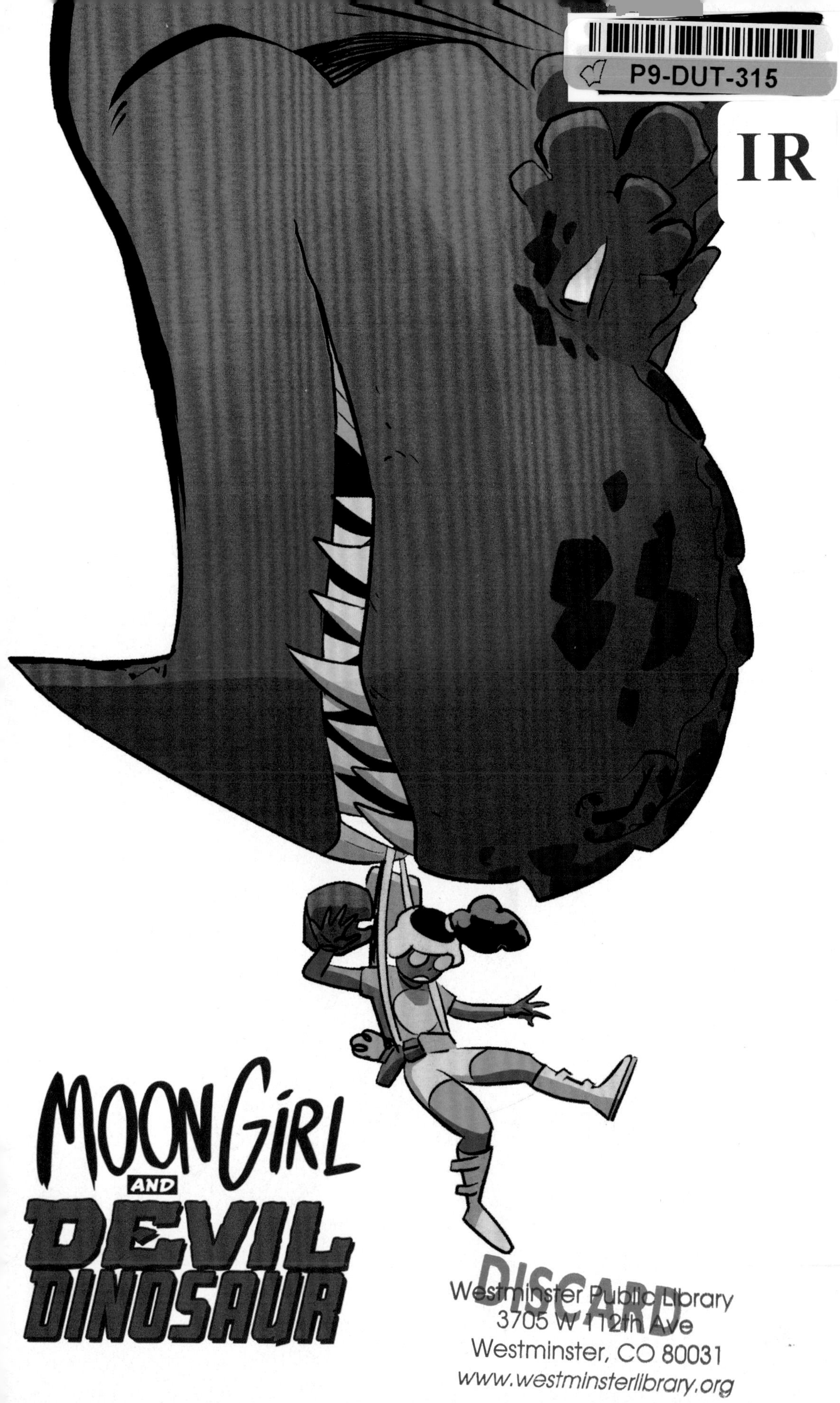

MOON GIRL AND DEVIL DINOSAUR

LUNELLA LAFAYETTE IS A 9-YEAR-OLD PRODIGY LIVING WITH HER MOM AND DAD IN MANHATTAN'S LOWER EAST SIDE. DEVIL DINOSAUR IS A BRIGHT RED TIME-DISPLACED *TYRANNOSAURUS REX*. THEY ARE SHUNNED AND IGNORED BY MOST, BUT FOR BETTER OR WORSE, THEY HAVE EACH OTHER! AFTER GOING THROUGH TERRIGENESIS, LUNELLA DISCOVERED THAT DURING THE FULL MOON LUNAR PHASE, SHE AND DEVIL WILL SPONTANEOUSLY SWITCH BRAINS.

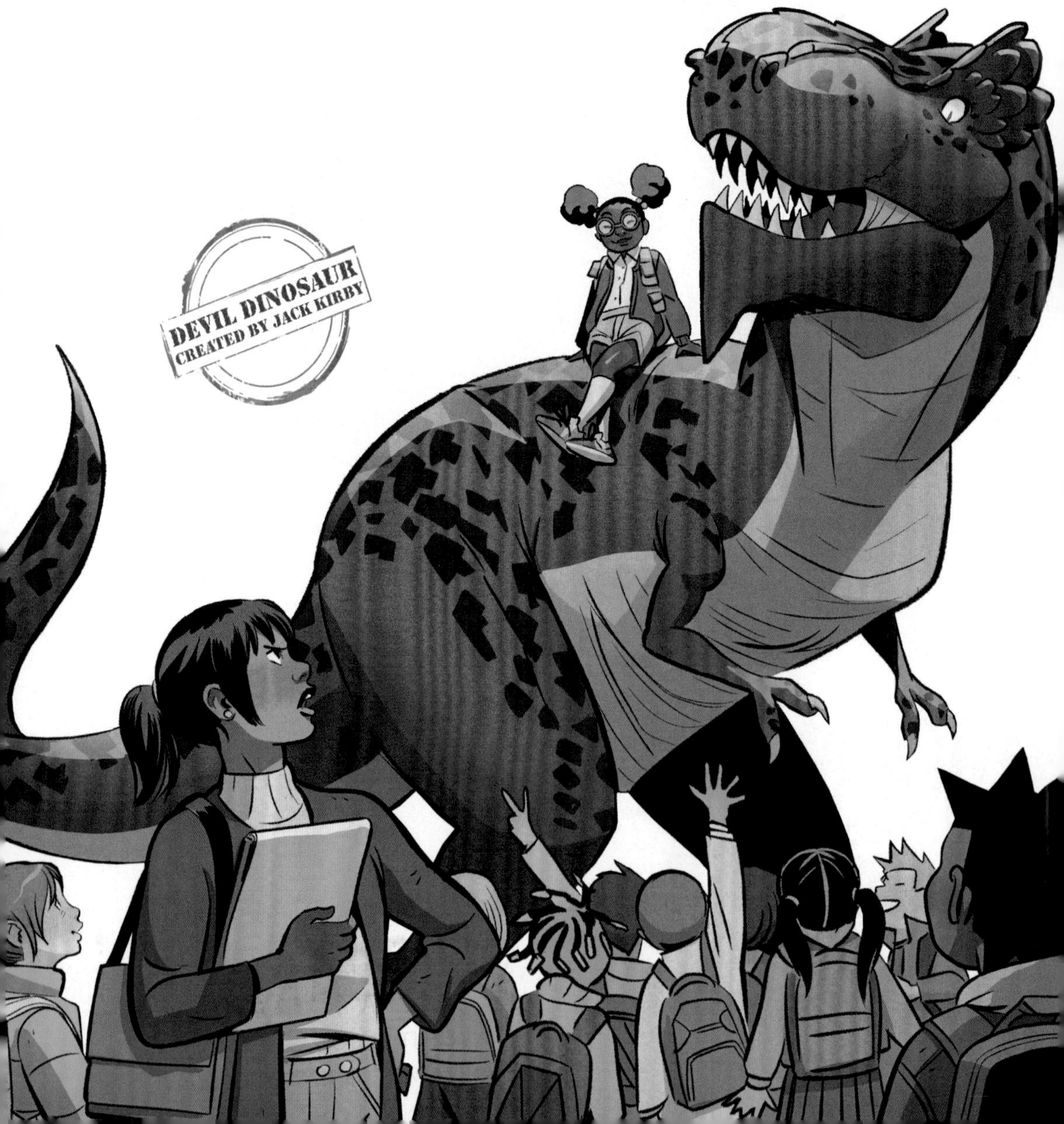
DEVIL DINOSAUR
CREATED BY JACK KIRBY

MOON GIRL AND DEVIL DINOSAUR
SAVE OUR SCHOOL

Brandon Montclare
WRITER

Natacha Bustos
ARTIST

Tamra Bonvillain
COLOR ARTIST

VC's Travis Lanham
LETTERER

Natacha Bustos
with Rachel Orlo (#32, #34-36) & Judy Stephens (#33)
COVER ART

Chris Robinson
EDITOR

Jordan D. White
SUPERVISING EDITOR

SPECIAL THANKS TO MARK PANICCIA

COLLECTION EDITOR: Jennifer Grünwald
ASSISTANT EDITOR: Caitlin O'Connell
ASSOCIATE MANAGING EDITOR: Kateri Woody
EDITOR, SPECIAL PROJECTS: Mark D. Beazley
VP, PRODUCTION & SPECIAL PROJECTS: Jeff Youngquist
SVP PRINT, SALES & MARKETING: David Gabriel
BOOK DESIGNER: Jay Bowen

EDITOR IN CHIEF: C.B. Cebulski
CHIEF CREATIVE OFFICER: Joe Quesada
PRESIDENT: Dan Buckley
EXECUTIVE PRODUCER: Alan Fine

MOON GIRL AND DEVIL DINOSAUR VOL. 6: SAVE OUR SCHOOL. Contains material originally published in magazine form as MOON GIRL AND DEVIL DINOSAUR #32-36. First printing 2018. ISBN 978-1-302-91100-3. Published by MARVEL WORLDWIDE, INC., a subsidiary of MARVEL ENTERTAINMENT, LLC. OFFICE OF PUBLICATION: 135 West 50th Street, New York, NY 10020. Copyright © 2018 MARVEL No similarity between any of the names, characters, persons, and/or institutions in this magazine with those of any living or dead person or institution is intended, and any such similarity which may exist is purely coincidental. **Printed in Canada.** DAN BUCKLEY, President, Marvel Entertainment; JOHN NEE, Publisher; JOE QUESADA, Chief Creative Officer; TOM BREVOORT, SVP of Publishing; DAVID BOGART, SVP of Business Affairs & Operations, Publishing & Partnership; DAVID GABRIEL, SVP of Sales & Marketing, Publishing; JEFF YOUNGQUIST, VP of Production & Special Projects; DAN CARR, Executive Director of Publishing Technology; ALEX MORALES, Director of Publishing Operations; DAN EDINGTON, Managing Editor; SUSAN CRESPI, Production Manager; STAN LEE, Chairman Emeritus. For information regarding advertising in Marvel Comics or on Marvel.com, please contact Vit DeBellis, Custom Solutions & Integrated Advertising Manager, at vdebellis@marvel.com. For Marvel subscription inquiries, please call 888-511-5480. **Manufactured between 10/26/2018 and 11/27/2018 by SOLISCO PRINTERS, SCOTT, QC, CANADA.**

10 9 8 7 6 5 4 3 2 1

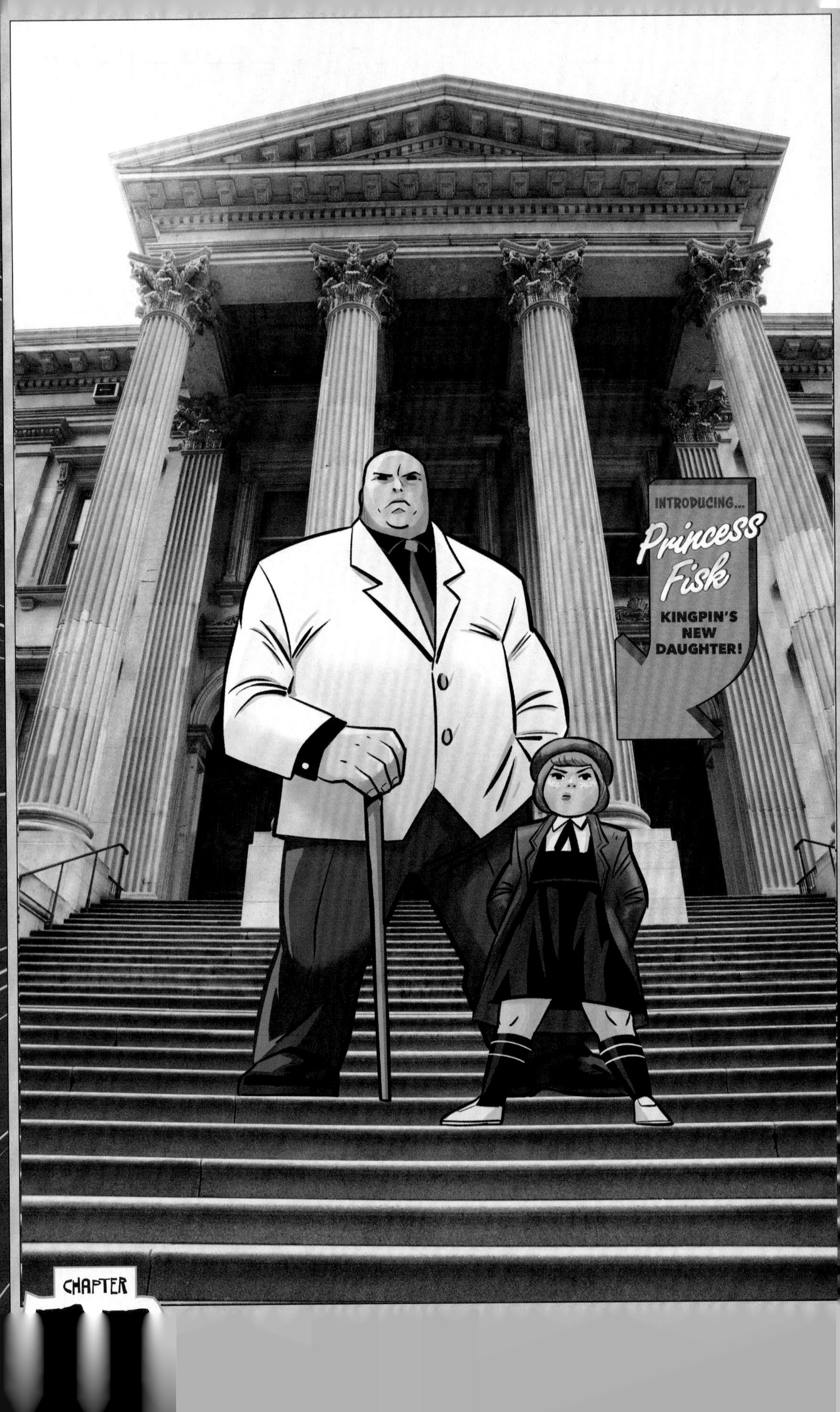
INTRODUCING...
Princess Fisk
KINGPIN'S NEW DAUGHTER!
CHAPTER

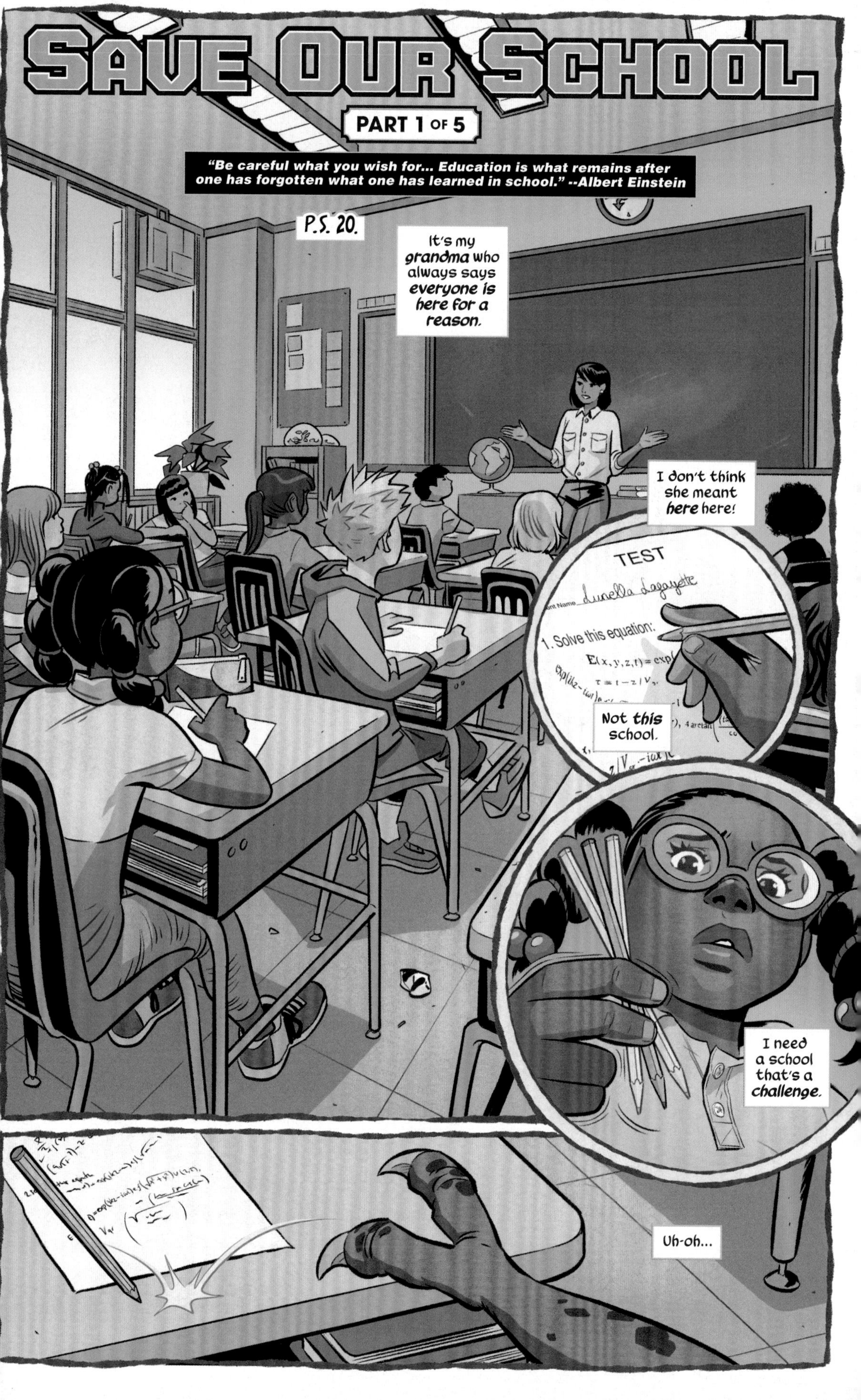
SAVE OUR SCHOOL
PART 1 OF 5
"Be careful what you wish for... Education is what remains after one has forgotten what one has learned in school." --Albert Einstein
P.S. 20.
It's my grandma who always says everyone is here for a reason.
I don't think she meant here here!
TEST
1. Solve this equation:
Not this school.
I need a school that's a challenge.
Uh-oh...

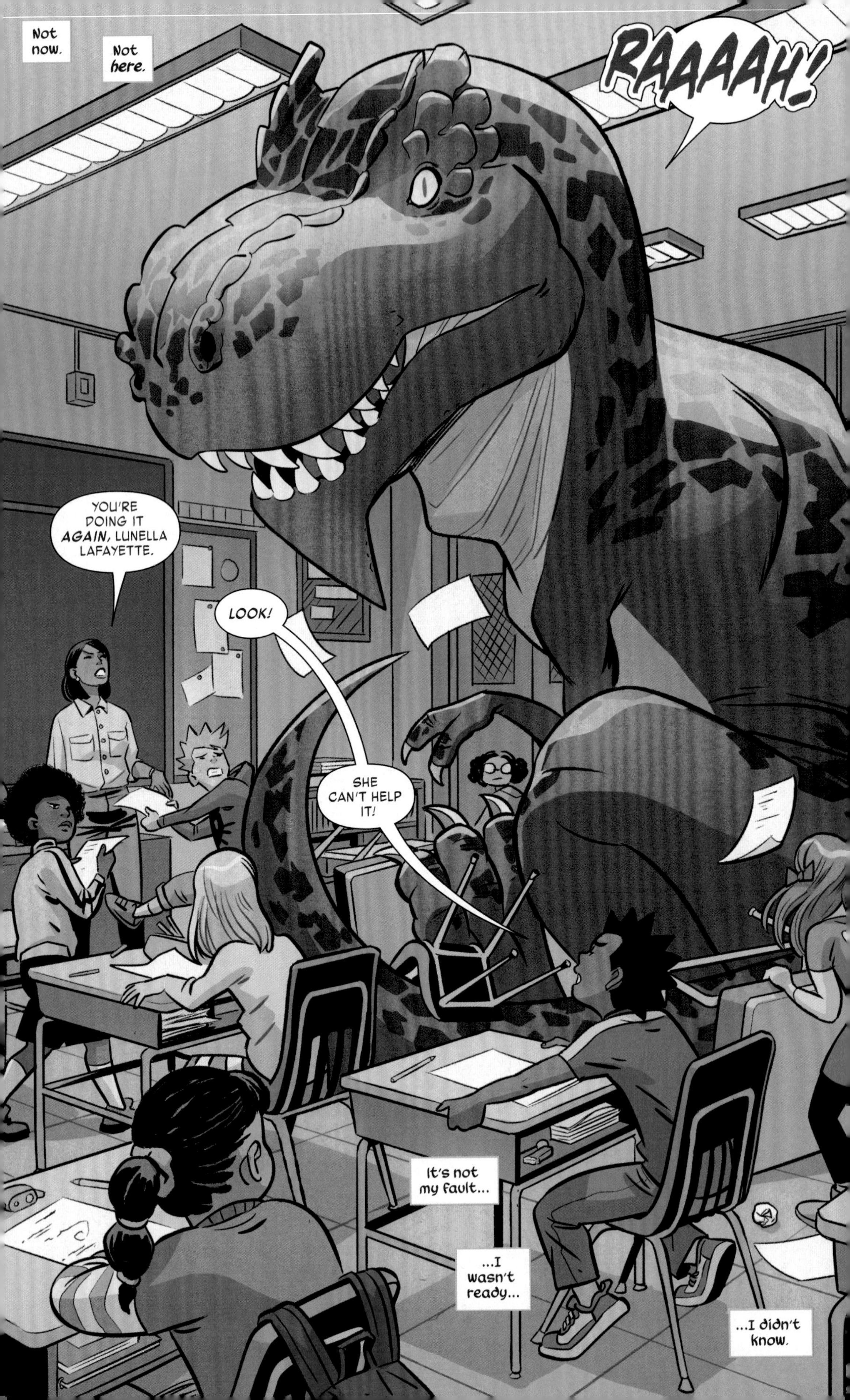

Not now.
Not here.
RAAAAH!
YOU'RE DOING IT AGAIN, LUNELLA LAFAYETTE.
LOOK!
SHE CAN'T HELP IT!
It's not my fault...
...I wasn't ready...
...I didn't know.

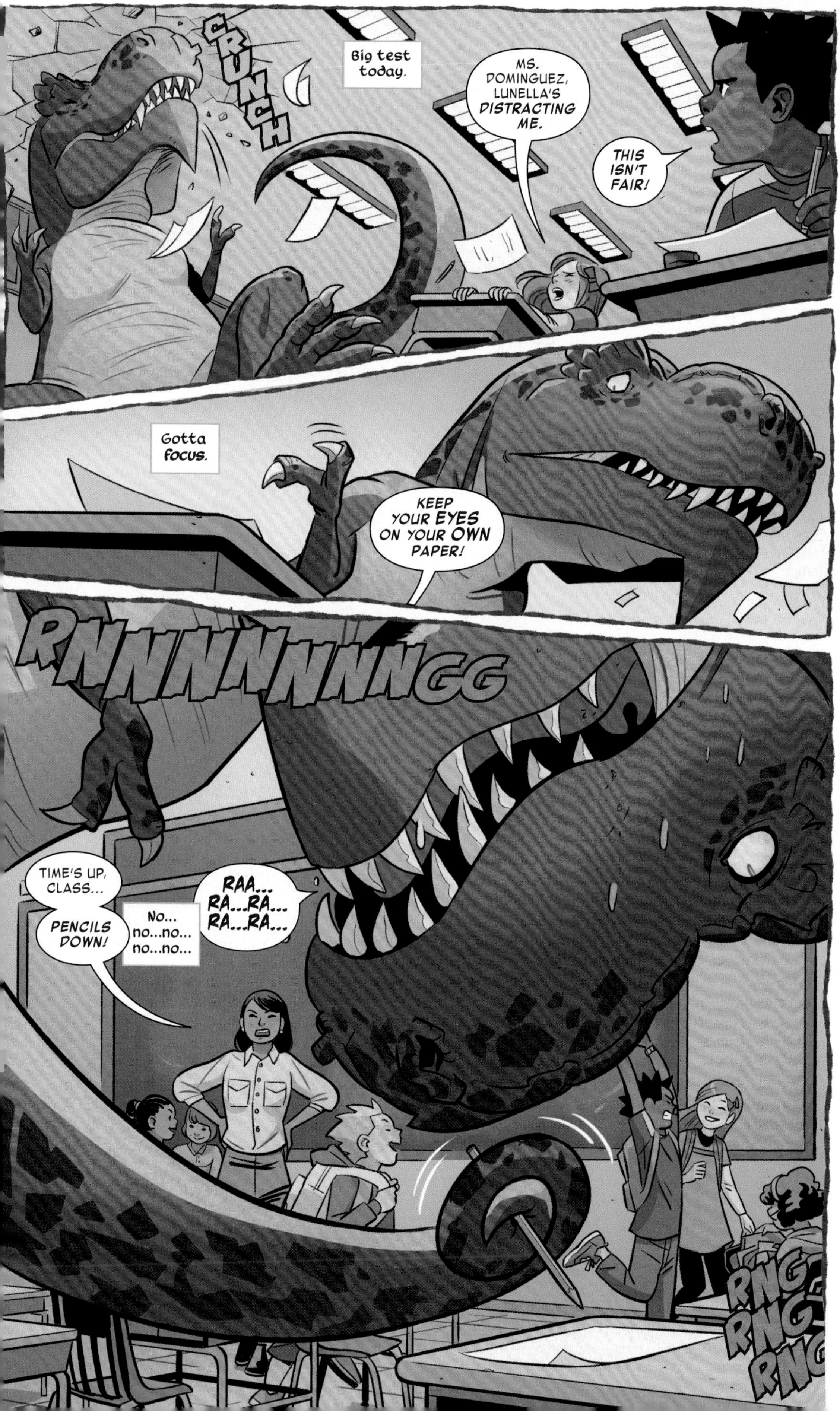
CRUNCH
Big test today.
MS. DOMINGUEZ, LUNELLA'S DISTRACTING ME.
THIS ISN'T FAIR!
Gotta focus.
KEEP YOUR EYES ON YOUR OWN PAPER!
RNNNNNNNNGG
TIME'S UP, CLASS...
PENCILS DOWN!
No... no...no... no...no...
RAA... RA...RA... RA...RA...
RNG RNG RNG

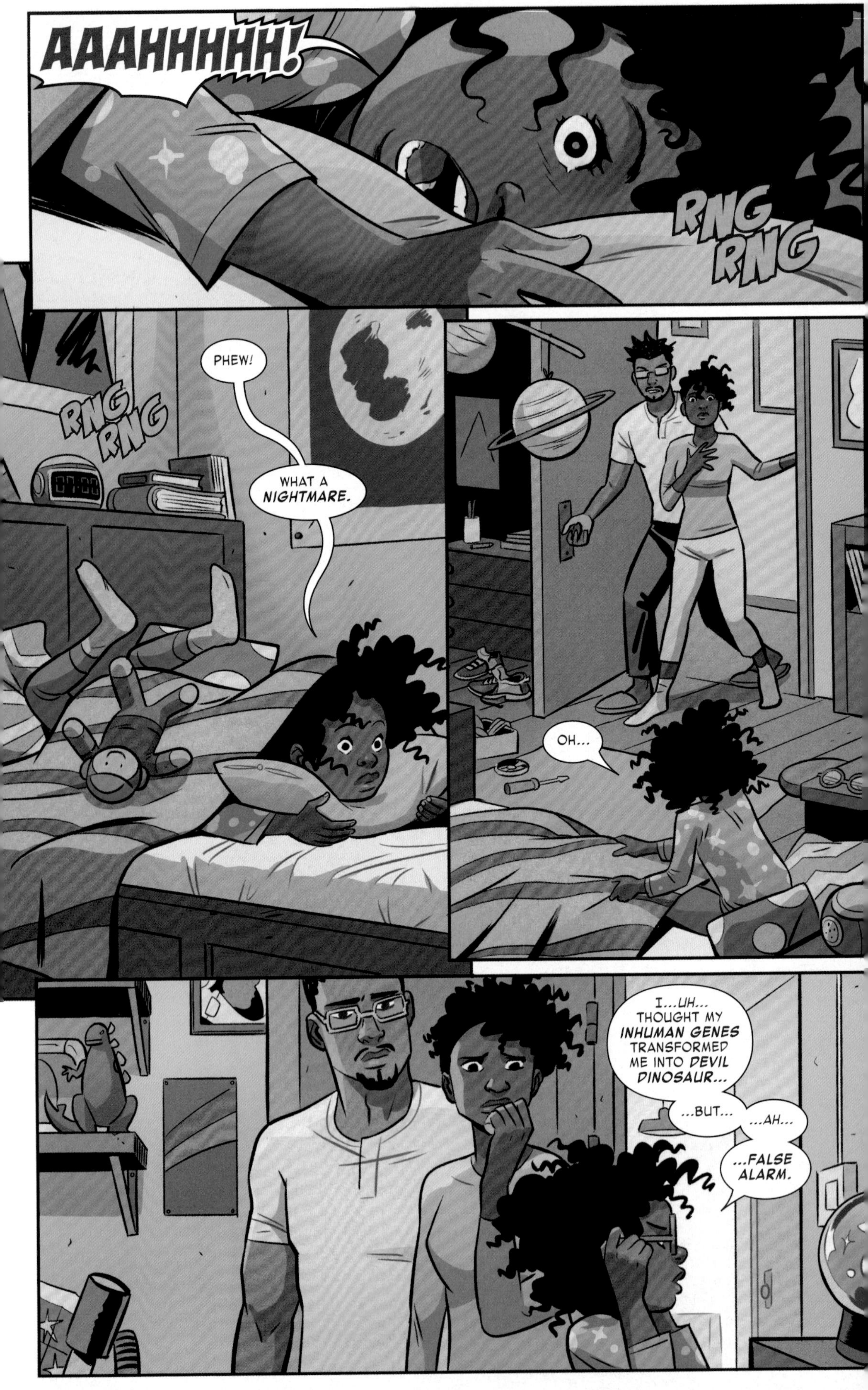
AAAHHHHH!
RNG RNG
RNG RNG
PHEW!
WHAT A NIGHTMARE.
OH...
I...UH... THOUGHT MY INHUMAN GENES TRANSFORMED ME INTO DEVIL DINOSAUR...
...BUT...
...AH...
...FALSE ALARM.

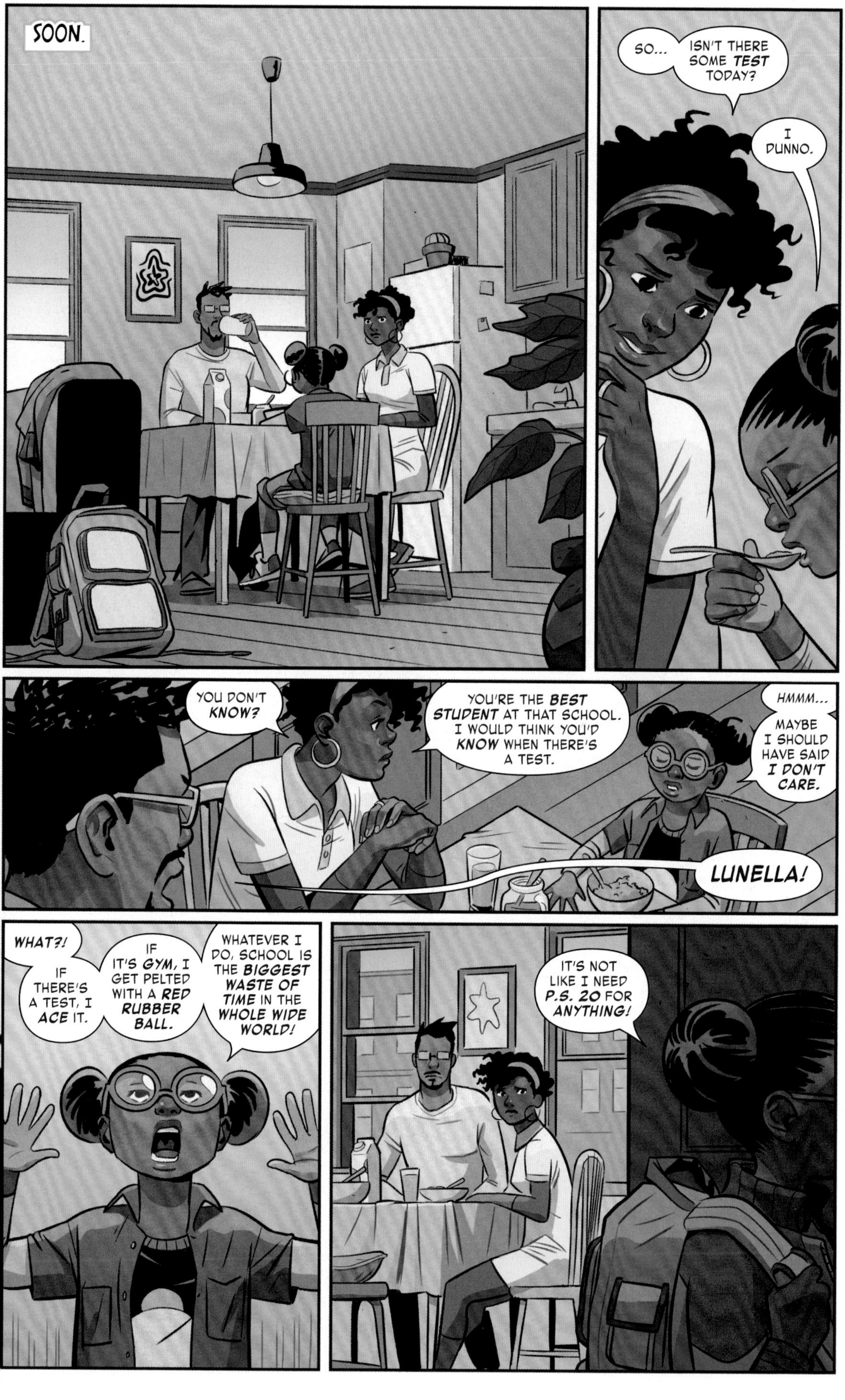
SOON.
SO...
ISN'T THERE SOME TEST TODAY?
I DUNNO.
YOU DON'T KNOW?
YOU'RE THE BEST STUDENT AT THAT SCHOOL. I WOULD THINK YOU'D KNOW WHEN THERE'S A TEST.
HMMM...
MAYBE I SHOULD HAVE SAID I DON'T CARE.
LUNELLA!
WHAT?!
IF THERE'S A TEST, I ACE IT.
IF IT'S GYM, I GET PELTED WITH A RED RUBBER BALL.
WHATEVER I DO, SCHOOL IS THE BIGGEST WASTE OF TIME IN THE WHOLE WIDE WORLD!
IT'S NOT LIKE I NEED P.S. 20 FOR ANYTHING!

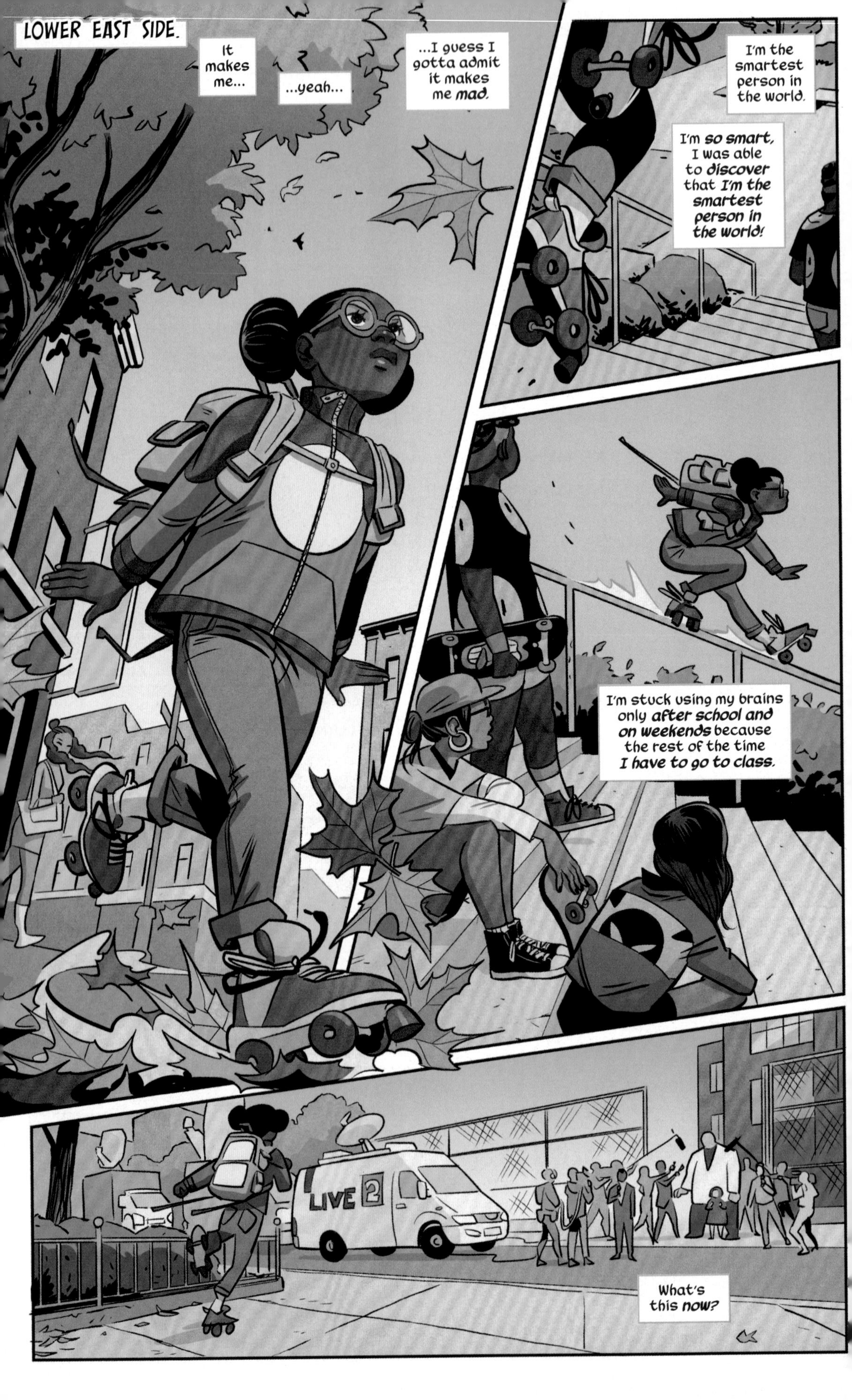
LOWER EAST SIDE.
It makes me...
...yeah...
...I guess I gotta admit it makes me *mad*.
I'm the smartest person in the world.
I'm *so smart*, I was able to *discover* that *I'm the smartest person in the world!*
I'm stuck using my brains only *after school and on weekends* because the rest of the time *I have to go to class*.
LIVE 2
What's this *now?*

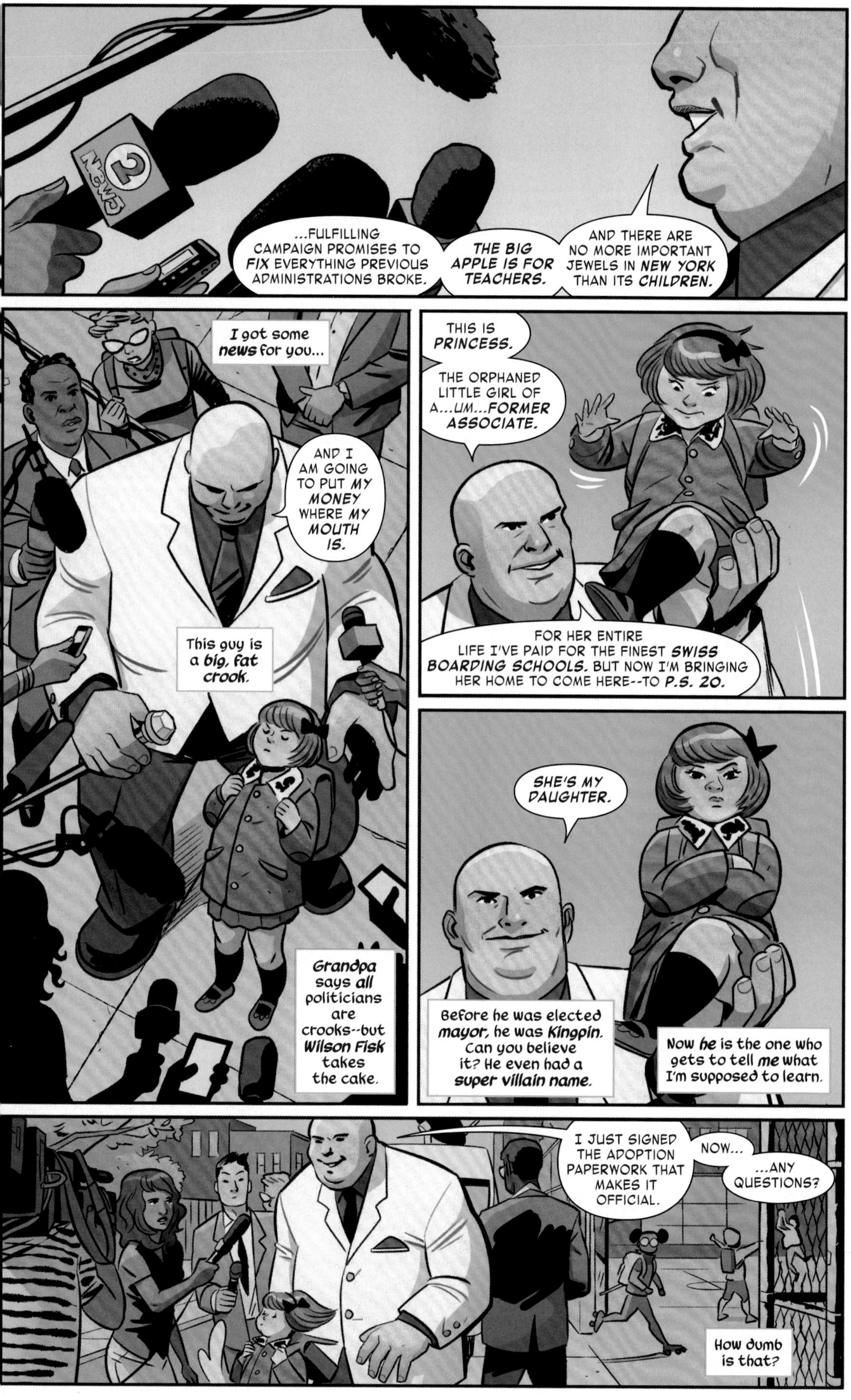

...FULFILLING CAMPAIGN PROMISES TO FIX EVERYTHING PREVIOUS ADMINISTRATIONS BROKE.
THE BIG APPLE IS FOR TEACHERS.
AND THERE ARE NO MORE IMPORTANT JEWELS IN NEW YORK THAN ITS CHILDREN.
I got some news for you...
AND I AM GOING TO PUT MY MONEY WHERE MY MOUTH IS.
This guy is a big, fat crook.
Grandpa says all politicians are crooks--but Wilson Fisk takes the cake.
THIS IS PRINCESS.
THE ORPHANED LITTLE GIRL OF A...UM...FORMER ASSOCIATE.
FOR HER ENTIRE LIFE I'VE PAID FOR THE FINEST SWISS BOARDING SCHOOLS. BUT NOW I'M BRINGING HER HOME TO COME HERE--TO P.S. 20.
SHE'S MY DAUGHTER.
Before he was elected mayor, he was Kingpin. Can you believe it? He even had a super villain name.
Now he is the one who gets to tell me what I'm supposed to learn.
I JUST SIGNED THE ADOPTION PAPERWORK THAT MAKES IT OFFICIAL.
NOW...
...ANY QUESTIONS?
How dumb is that?

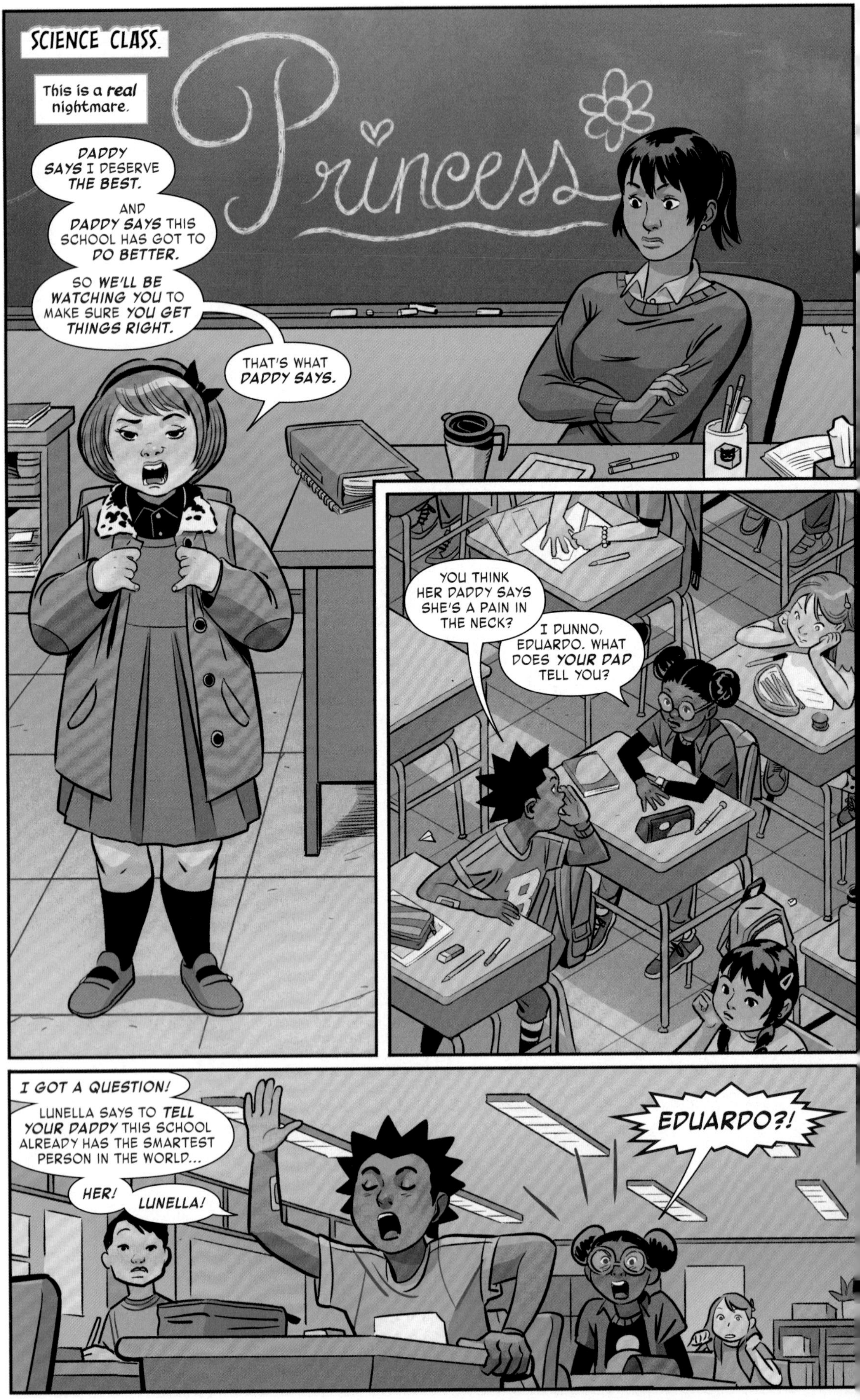
SCIENCE CLASS.
This is a *real* nightmare.
Princess
DADDY SAYS I DESERVE *THE BEST.*
AND *DADDY SAYS* THIS SCHOOL HAS GOT TO *DO BETTER.*
SO *WE'LL BE WATCHING YOU* TO MAKE SURE *YOU GET THINGS RIGHT.*
THAT'S WHAT *DADDY SAYS.*
YOU THINK HER DADDY SAYS SHE'S A PAIN IN THE NECK?
I DUNNO, EDUARDO. WHAT DOES *YOUR DAD* TELL YOU?
I GOT A QUESTION!
LUNELLA SAYS TO *TELL YOUR DADDY* THIS SCHOOL ALREADY HAS THE SMARTEST PERSON IN THE WORLD...
HER!
LUNELLA!
EDUARDO?!

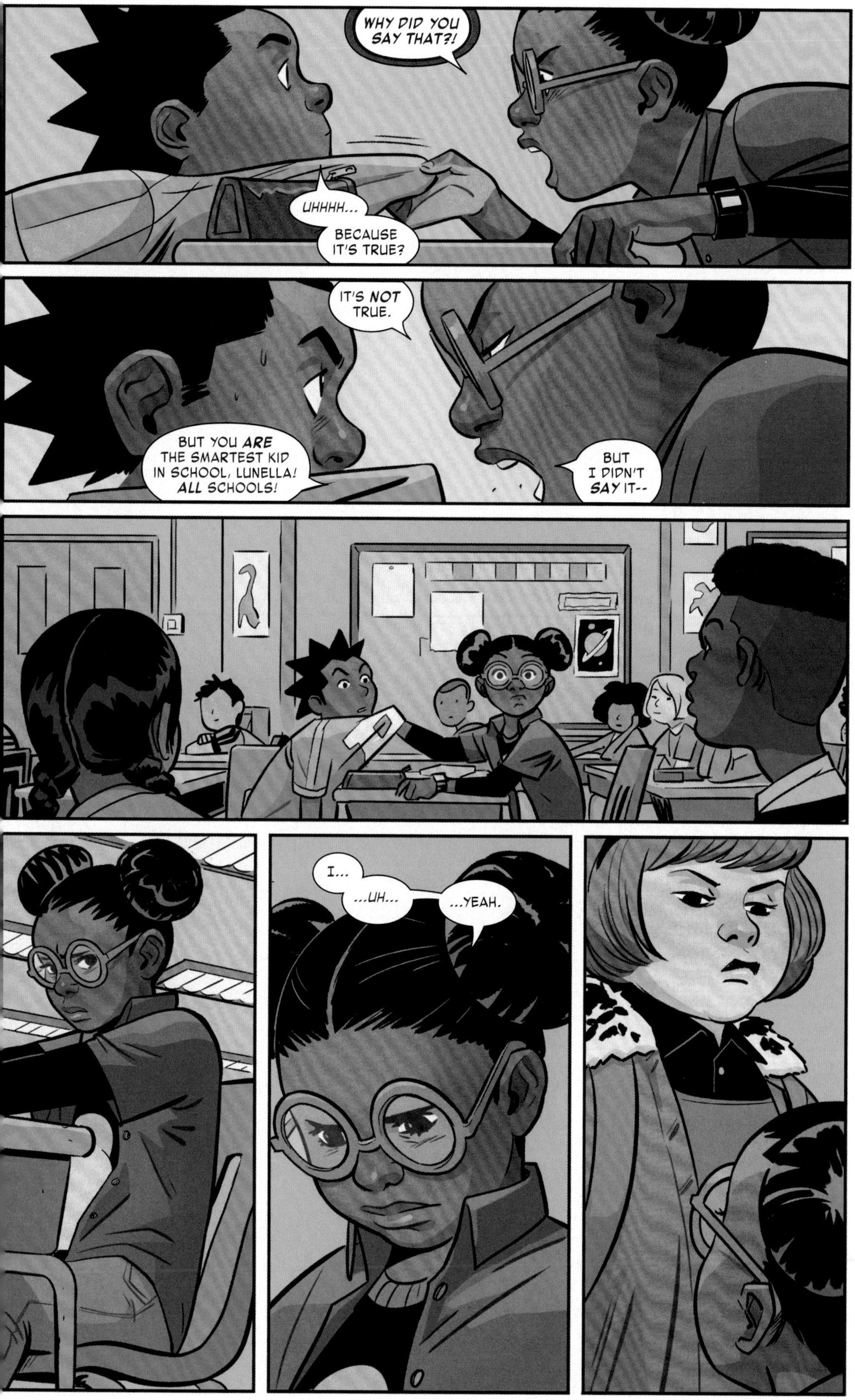
WHY DID YOU SAY THAT?!
UHHHH...
BECAUSE IT'S TRUE?
IT'S NOT TRUE.
BUT YOU ARE THE SMARTEST KID IN SCHOOL, LUNELLA! ALL SCHOOLS!
BUT I DIDN'T SAY IT--
I...
...UH...
...YEAH.

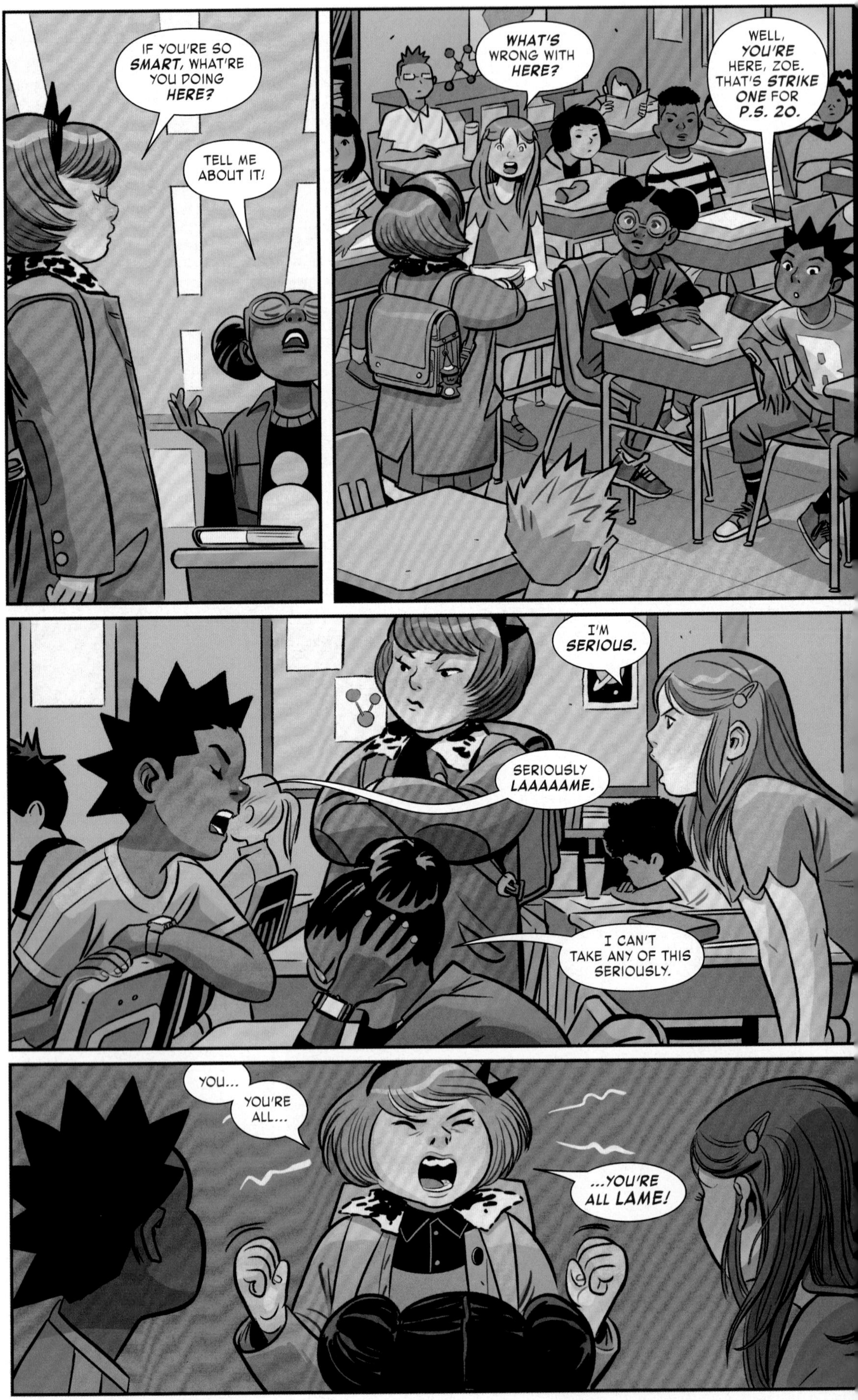
IF YOU'RE SO SMART, WHAT'RE YOU DOING HERE?
TELL ME ABOUT IT!
WHAT'S WRONG WITH HERE?
WELL, YOU'RE HERE, ZOE. THAT'S STRIKE ONE FOR P.S. 20.
I'M SERIOUS.
SERIOUSLY LAAAAAME.
I CAN'T TAKE ANY OF THIS SERIOUSLY.
YOU...
YOU'RE ALL...
...YOU'RE ALL LAME!

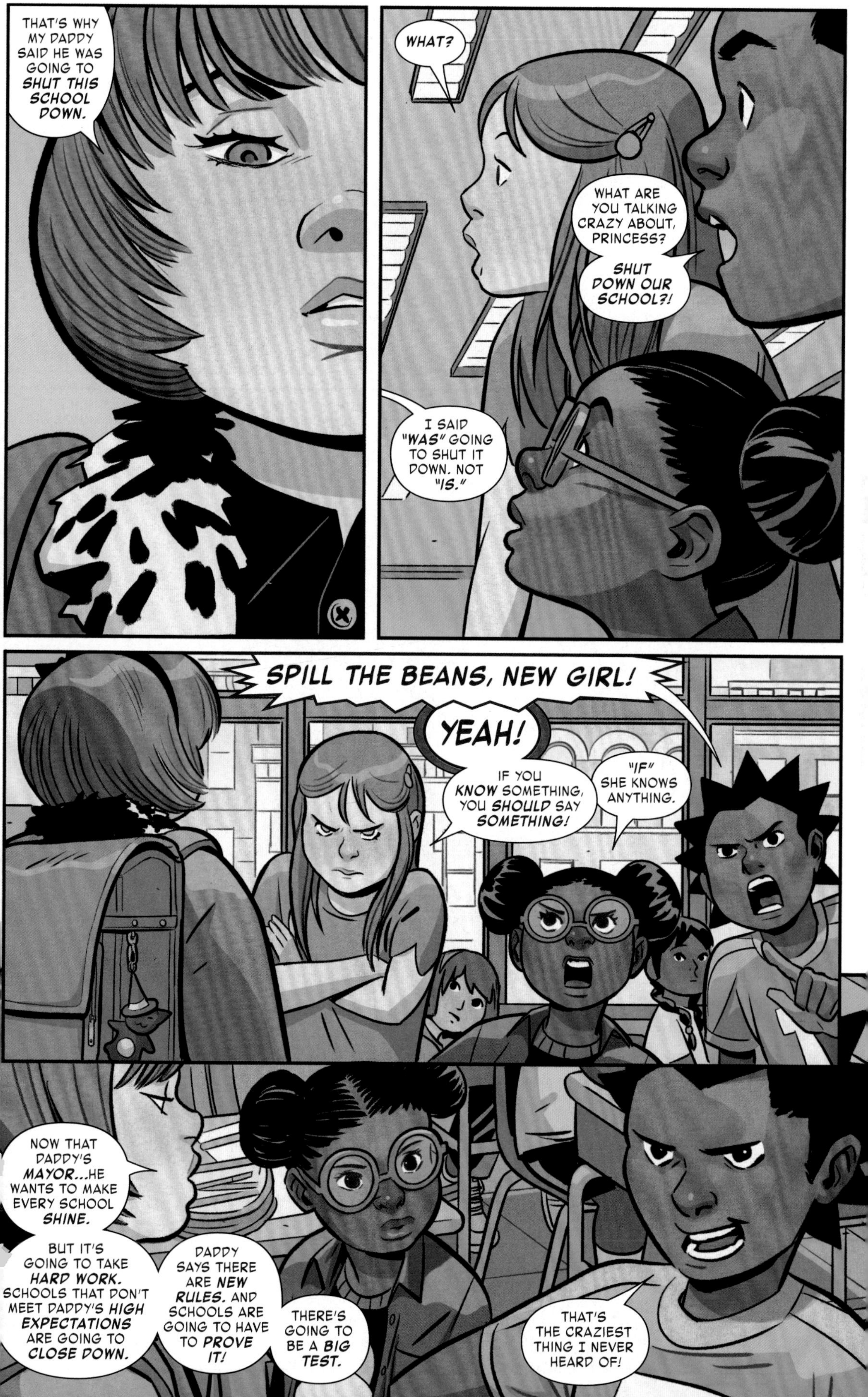
THAT'S WHY MY DADDY SAID HE WAS GOING TO SHUT THIS SCHOOL DOWN.
WHAT?
WHAT ARE YOU TALKING CRAZY ABOUT, PRINCESS?
SHUT DOWN OUR SCHOOL?!
I SAID "WAS" GOING TO SHUT IT DOWN. NOT "IS."
SPILL THE BEANS, NEW GIRL!
YEAH!
IF YOU KNOW SOMETHING, YOU SHOULD SAY SOMETHING!
"IF" SHE KNOWS ANYTHING.
NOW THAT DADDY'S MAYOR...HE WANTS TO MAKE EVERY SCHOOL SHINE.
BUT IT'S GOING TO TAKE HARD WORK. SCHOOLS THAT DON'T MEET DADDY'S HIGH EXPECTATIONS ARE GOING TO CLOSE DOWN.
DADDY SAYS THERE ARE NEW RULES. AND SCHOOLS ARE GOING TO HAVE TO PROVE IT!
THERE'S GOING TO BE A BIG TEST.
THAT'S THE CRAZIEST THING I NEVER HEARD OF!

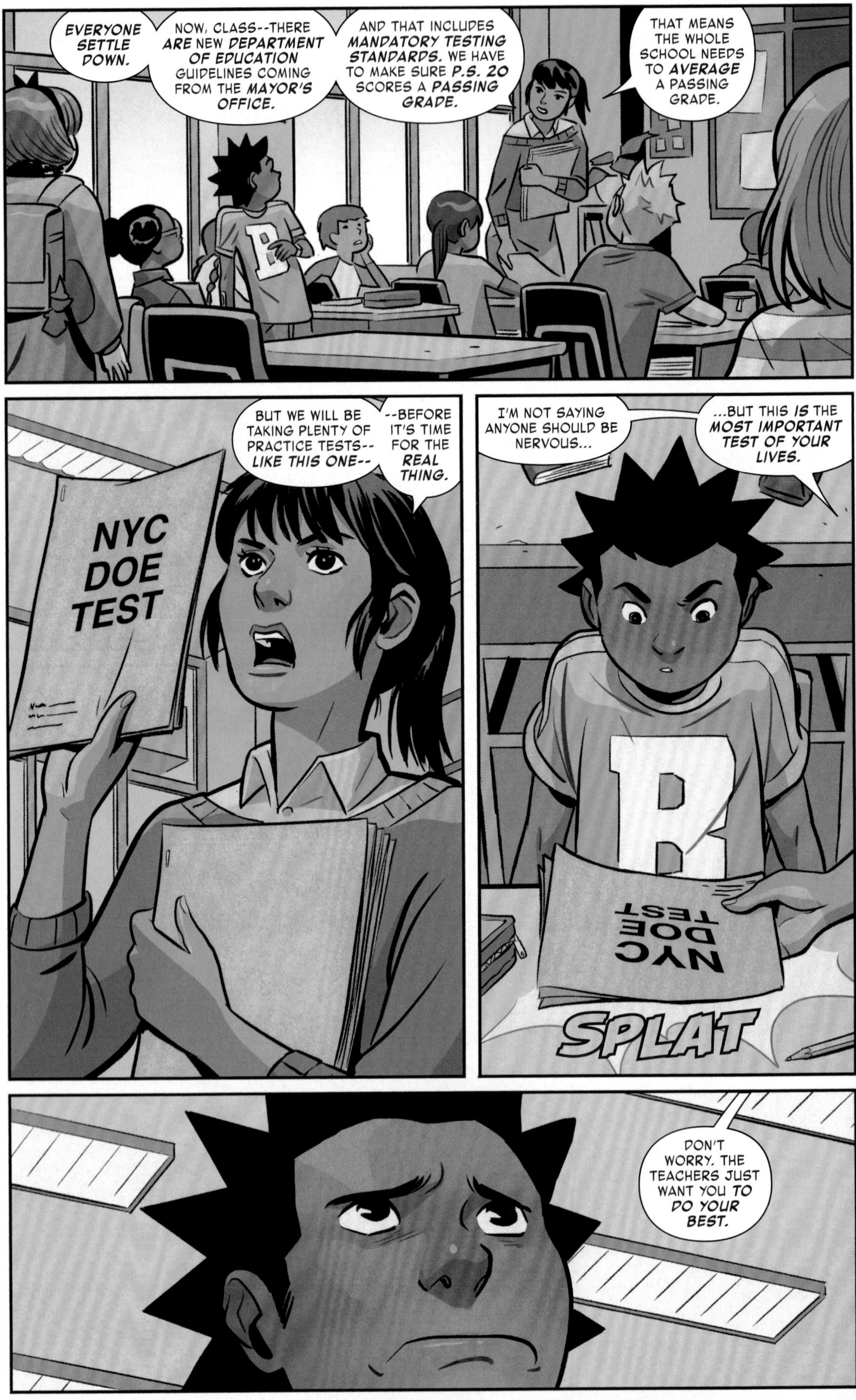
EVERYONE SETTLE DOWN.
NOW, CLASS--THERE ARE NEW DEPARTMENT OF EDUCATION GUIDELINES COMING FROM THE MAYOR'S OFFICE.
AND THAT INCLUDES MANDATORY TESTING STANDARDS. WE HAVE TO MAKE SURE P.S. 20 SCORES A PASSING GRADE.
THAT MEANS THE WHOLE SCHOOL NEEDS TO AVERAGE A PASSING GRADE.
BUT WE WILL BE TAKING PLENTY OF PRACTICE TESTS-- LIKE THIS ONE--
--BEFORE IT'S TIME FOR THE REAL THING.
NYC DOE TEST
I'M NOT SAYING ANYONE SHOULD BE NERVOUS...
...BUT THIS IS THE MOST IMPORTANT TEST OF YOUR LIVES.
NYC DOE TEST
SPLAT
DON'T WORRY. THE TEACHERS JUST WANT YOU TO DO YOUR BEST.

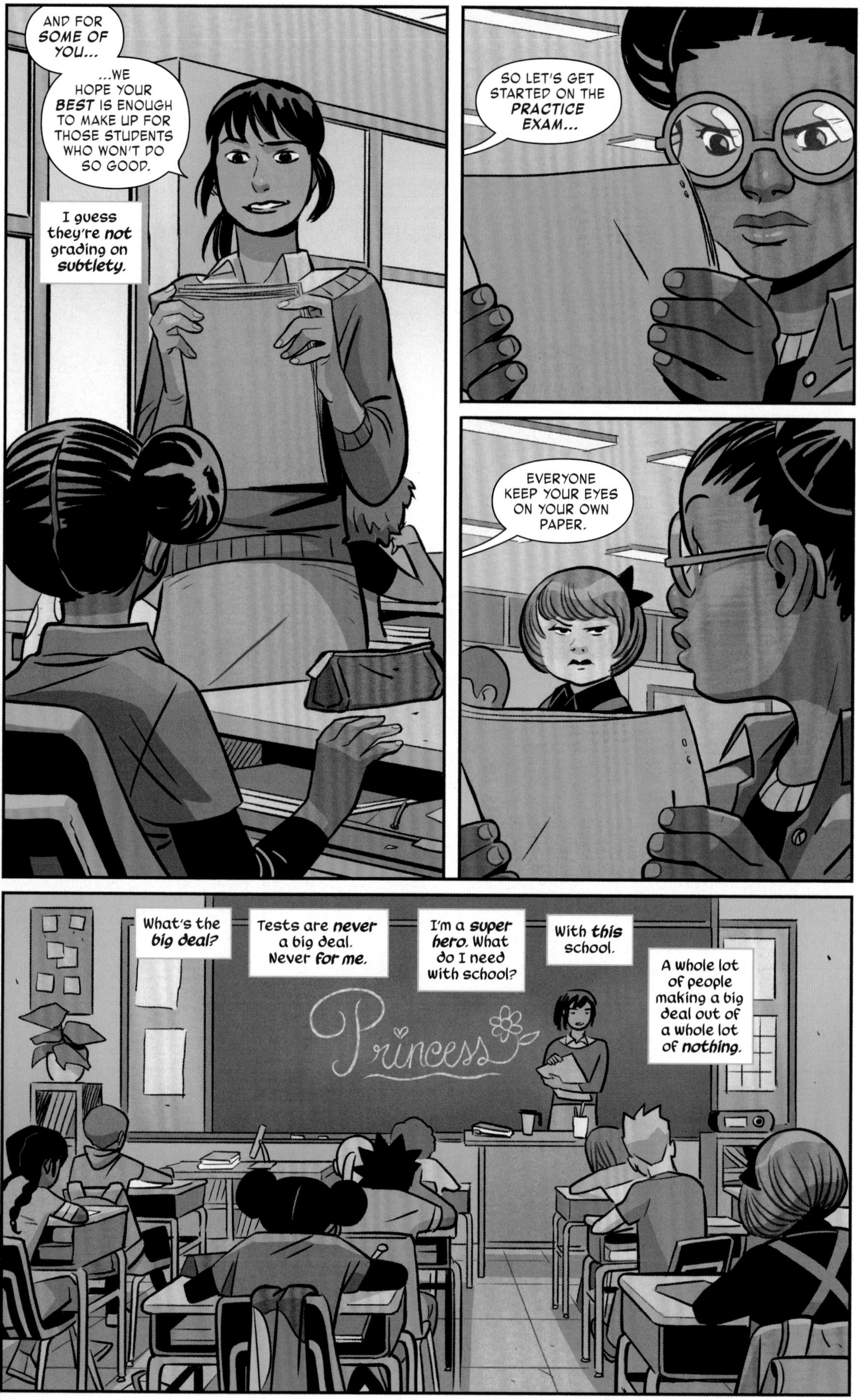
AND FOR SOME OF YOU...
...WE HOPE YOUR BEST IS ENOUGH TO MAKE UP FOR THOSE STUDENTS WHO WON'T DO SO GOOD.
I guess they're not grading on subtlety.
SO LET'S GET STARTED ON THE PRACTICE EXAM...
EVERYONE KEEP YOUR EYES ON YOUR OWN PAPER.
What's the big deal?
Tests are never a big deal. Never for me.
I'm a super hero. What do I need with school?
With this school.
A whole lot of people making a big deal out of a whole lot of nothing.
Princess

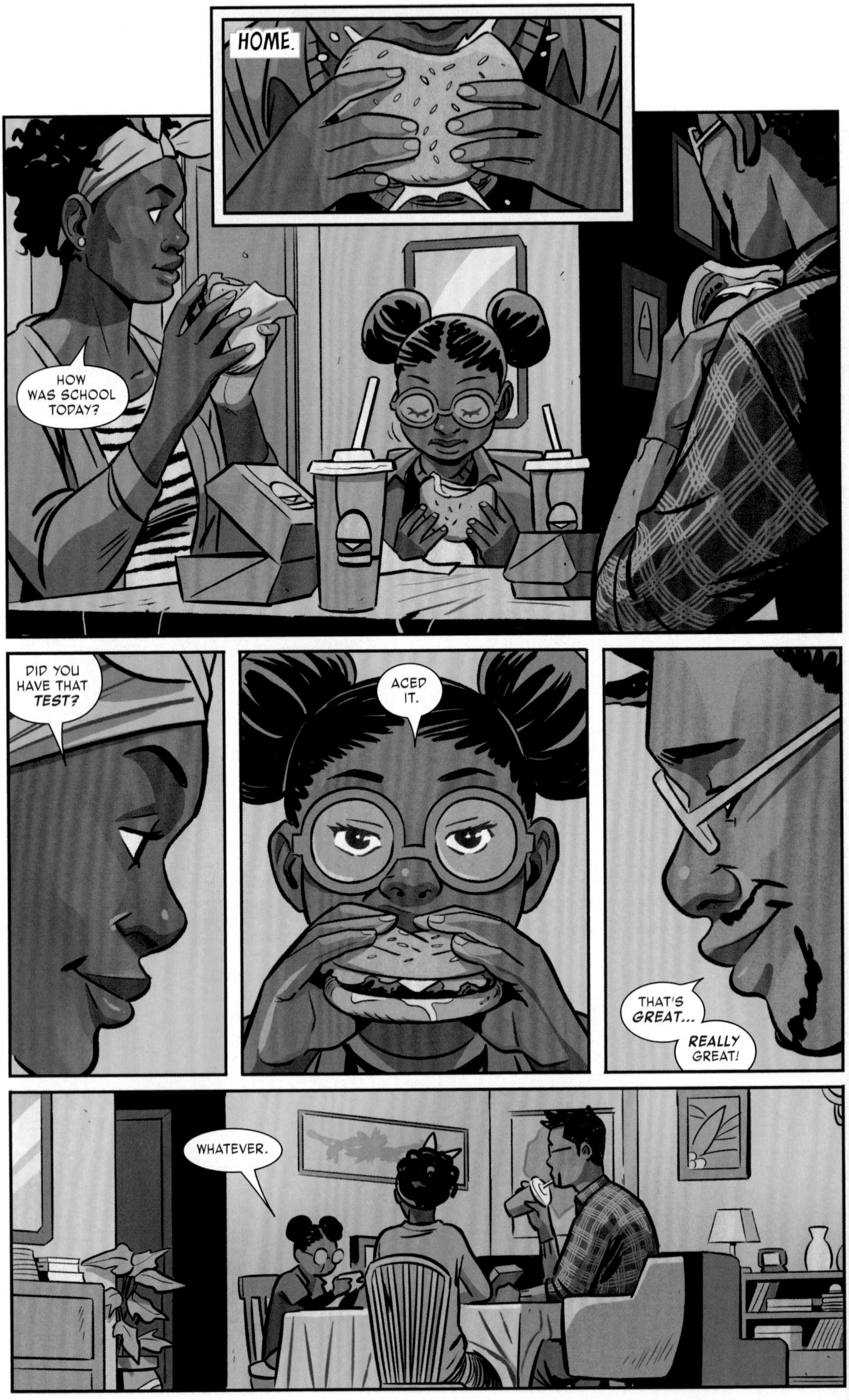
HOME.
HOW WAS SCHOOL TODAY?
DID YOU HAVE THAT *TEST?*
ACED IT.
THAT'S *GREAT...*
REALLY GREAT!
WHATEVER.

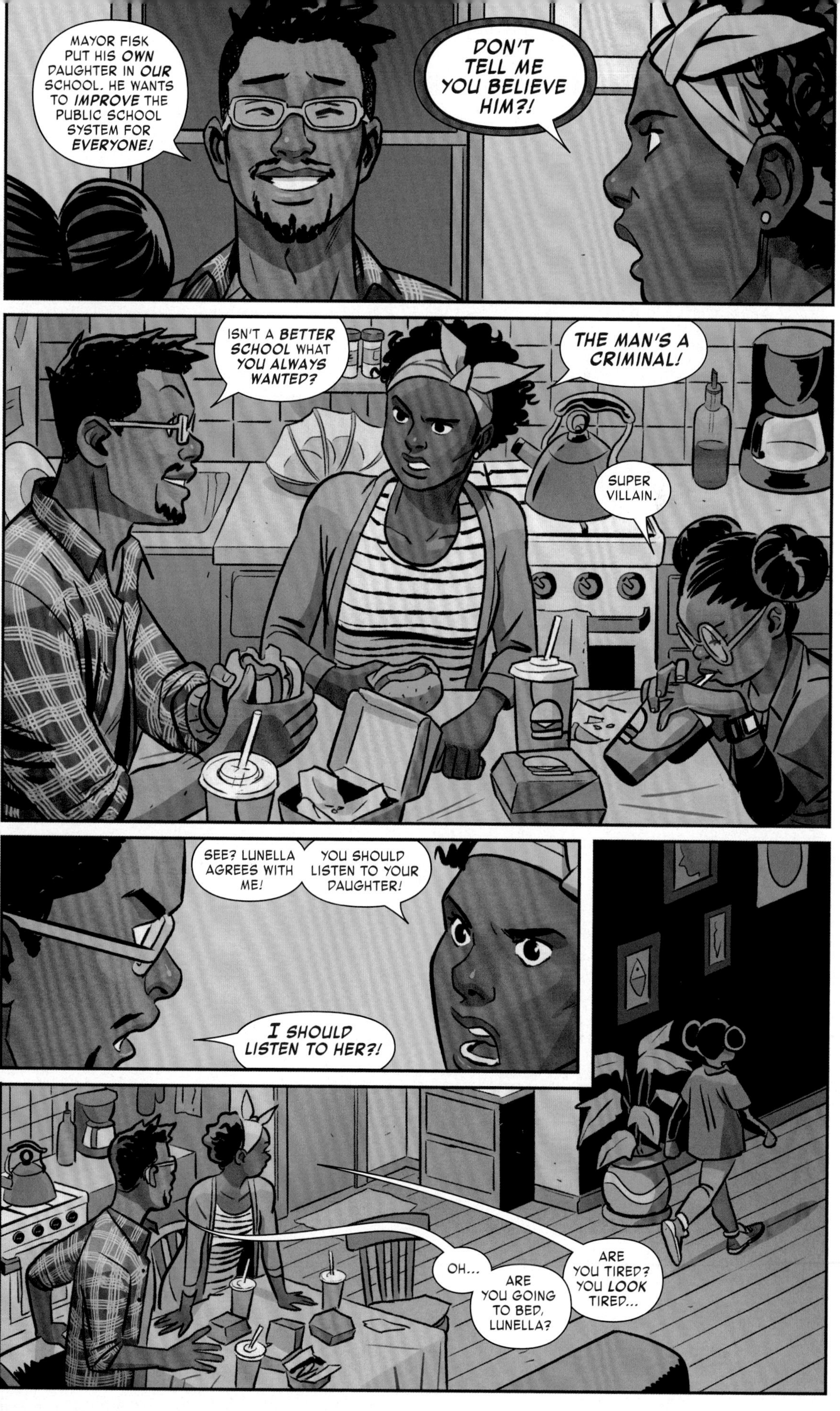
MAYOR FISK PUT HIS OWN DAUGHTER IN OUR SCHOOL. HE WANTS TO IMPROVE THE PUBLIC SCHOOL SYSTEM FOR EVERYONE!
DON'T TELL ME YOU BELIEVE HIM?!
ISN'T A BETTER SCHOOL WHAT YOU ALWAYS WANTED?
THE MAN'S A CRIMINAL!
SUPER VILLAIN.
SEE? LUNELLA AGREES WITH ME!
YOU SHOULD LISTEN TO YOUR DAUGHTER!
I SHOULD LISTEN TO HER?!
OH...
ARE YOU GOING TO BED, LUNELLA?
ARE YOU TIRED? YOU LOOK TIRED...

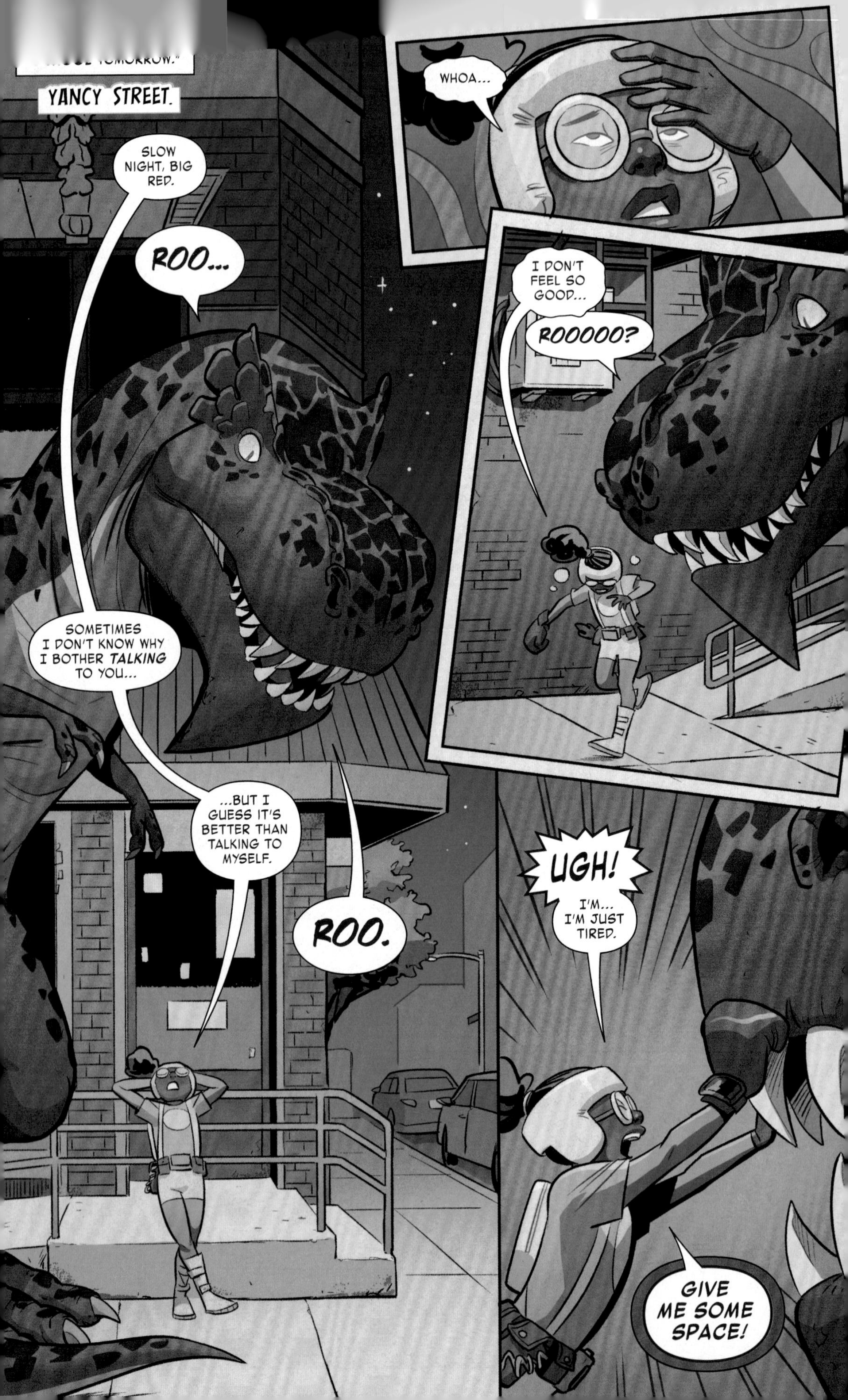
YANCY STREET.
SLOW NIGHT, BIG RED.
ROO...
SOMETIMES I DON'T KNOW WHY I BOTHER TALKING TO YOU...
...BUT I GUESS IT'S BETTER THAN TALKING TO MYSELF.
ROO.
WHOA...
I DON'T FEEL SO GOOD...
ROOOOO?
UGH!
I'M... I'M JUST TIRED.
GIVE ME SOME SPACE!

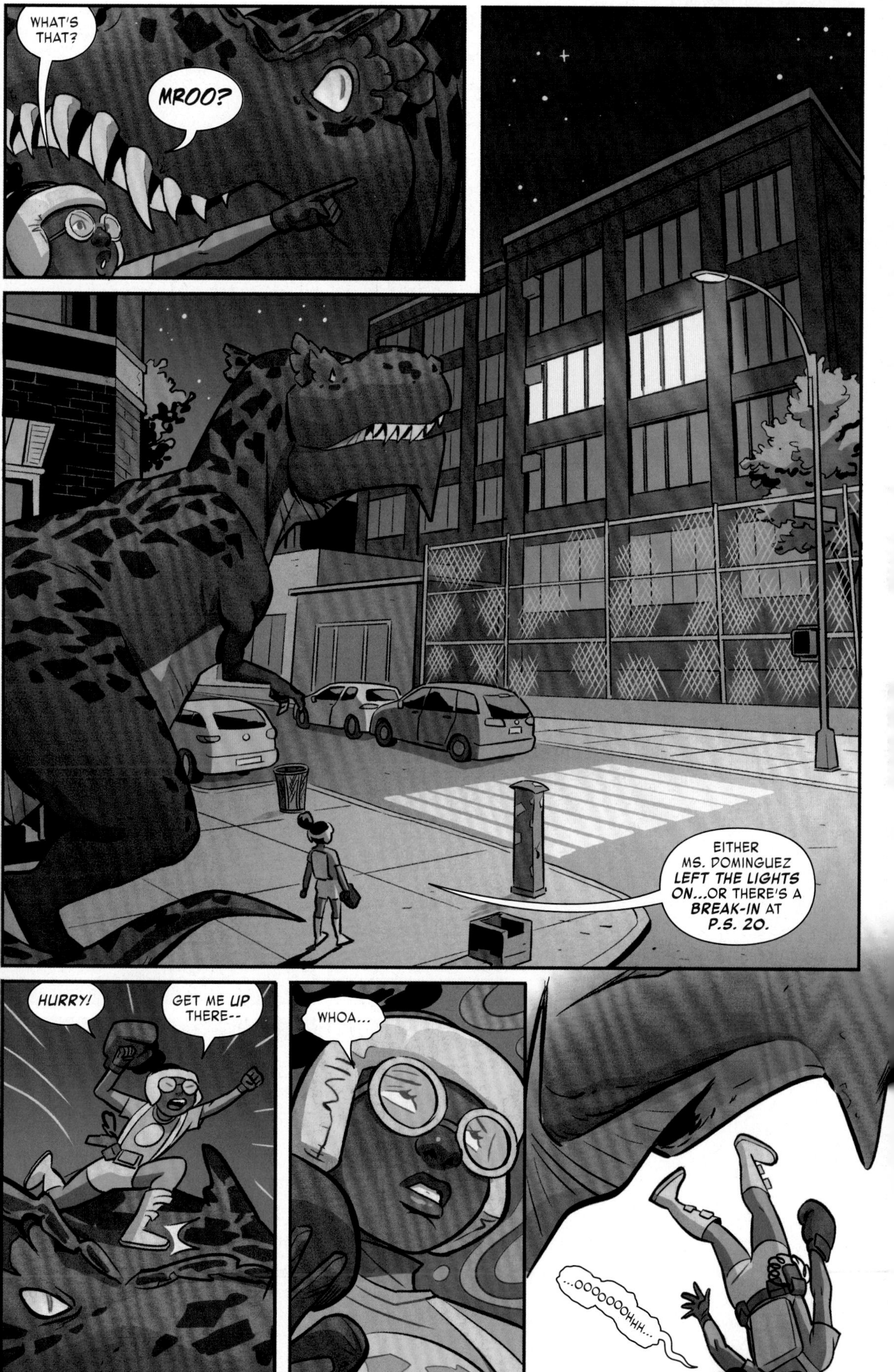

WHAT'S THAT?
MROO?
EITHER MS. DOMINGUEZ LEFT THE LIGHTS ON...OR THERE'S A BREAK-IN AT P.S. 20.
HURRY!
GET ME UP THERE--
WHOA...
...OOOOOOOOHHH...

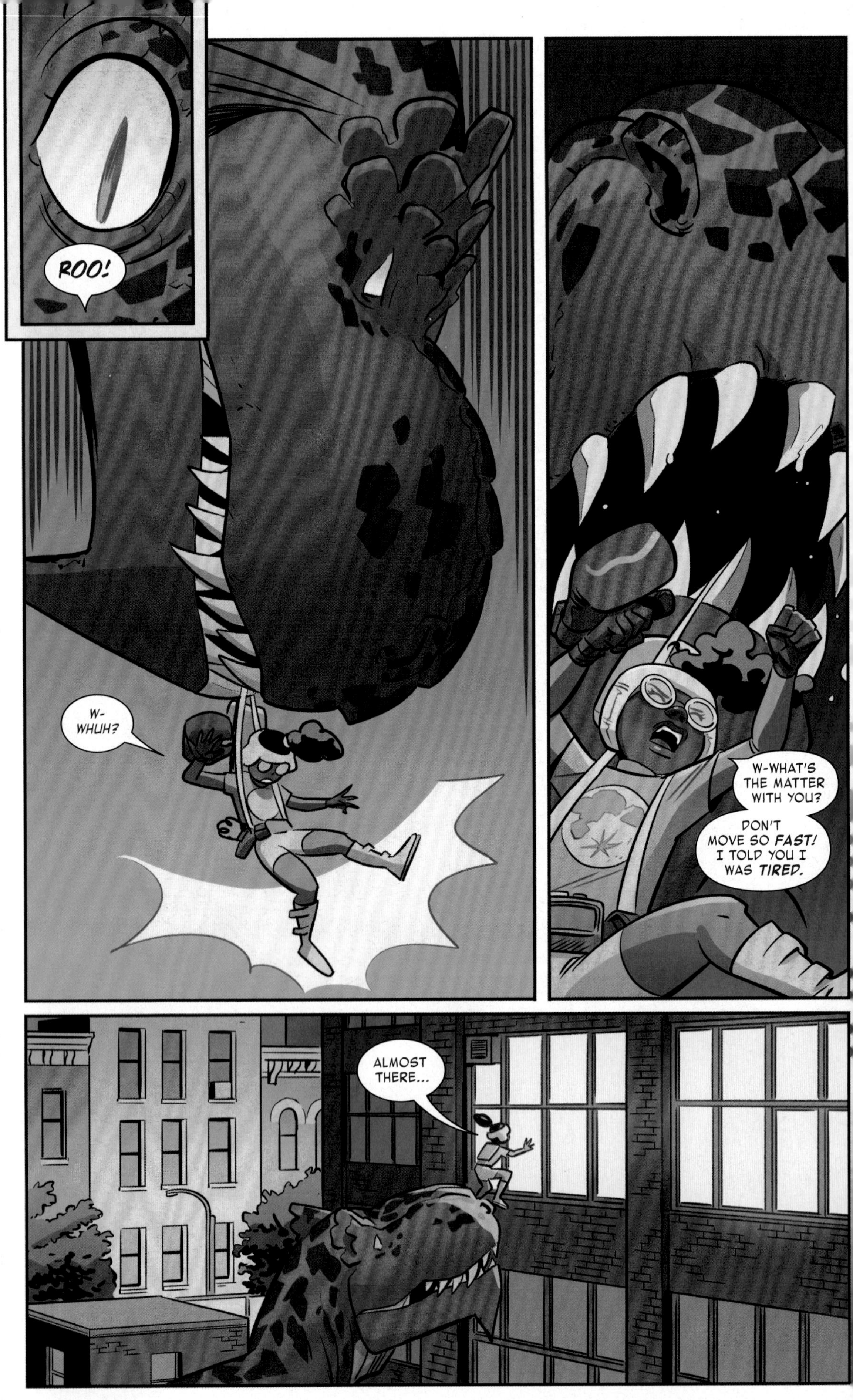
ROO!
W-WHUH?
W-WHAT'S THE MATTER WITH YOU?
DON'T MOVE SO FAST! I TOLD YOU I WAS TIRED.
ALMOST THERE...

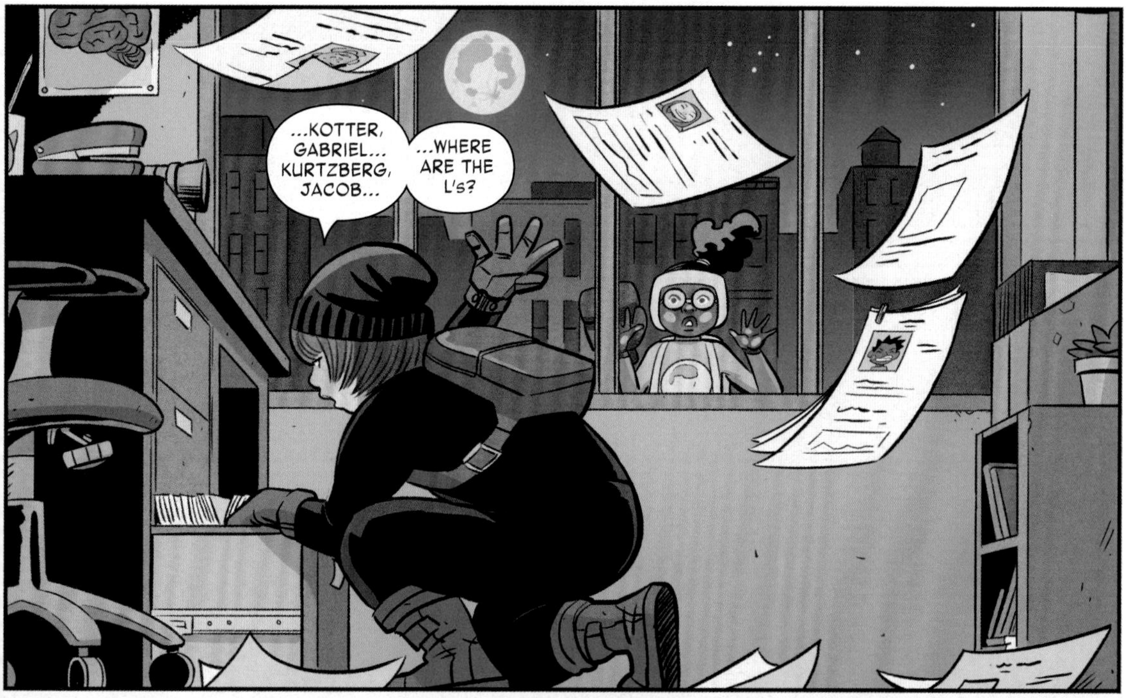
...KOTTER, GABRIEL... KURTZBERG, JACOB...
...WHERE ARE THE L's?

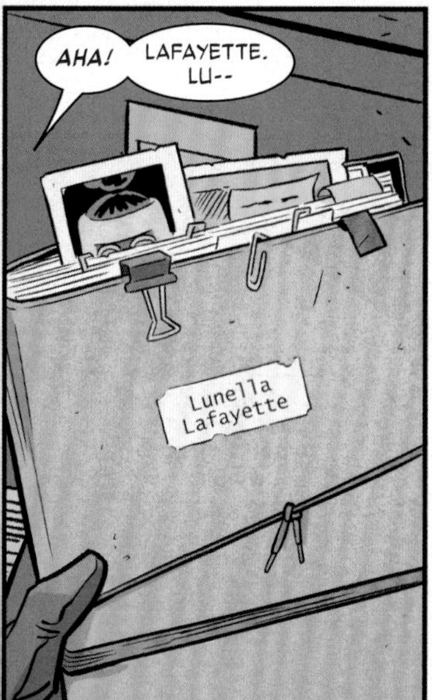
AHA!
LAFAYETTE. LU--
Lunella Lafayette

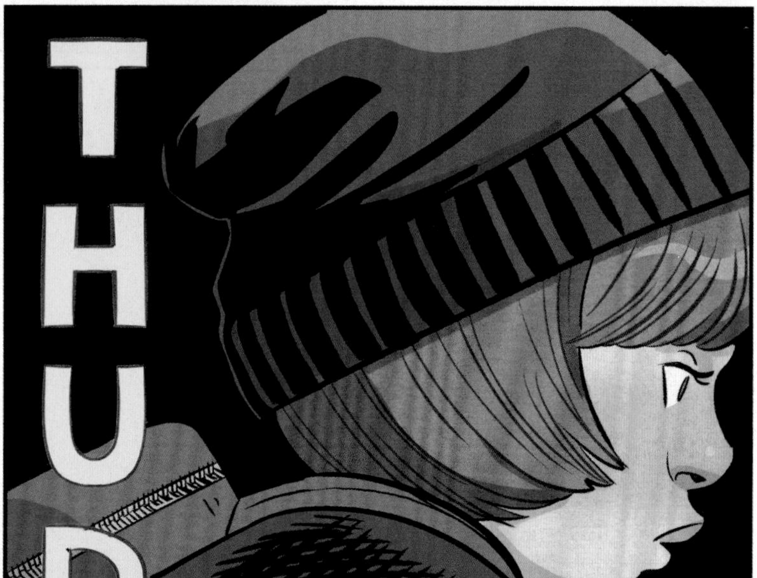
THUD

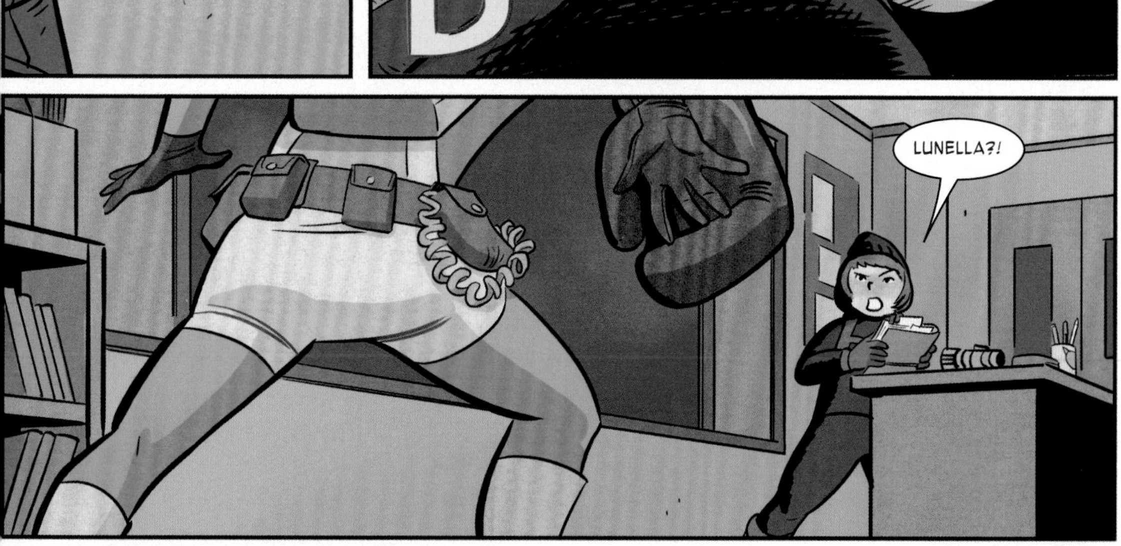
LUNELLA?!

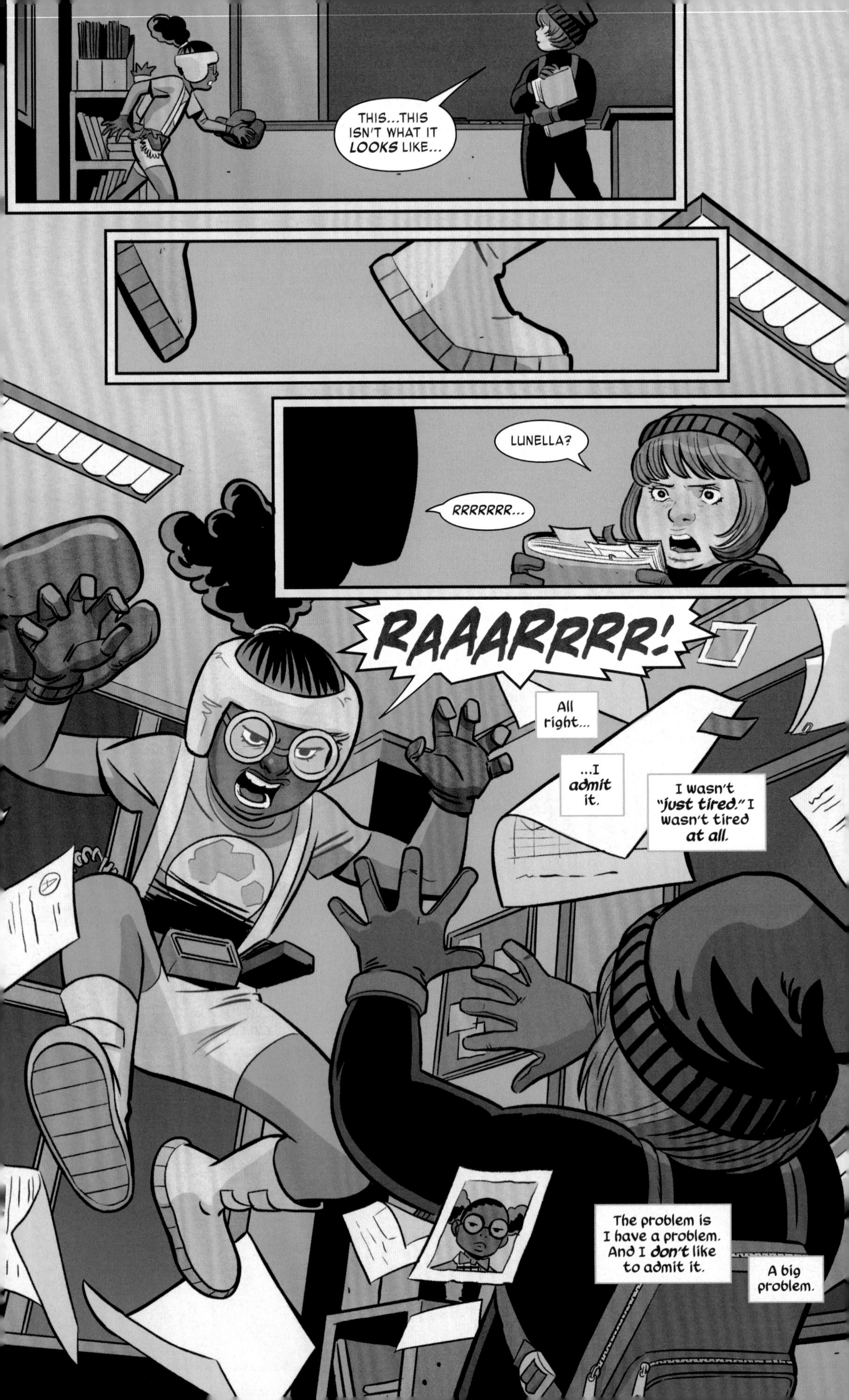
THIS...THIS ISN'T WHAT IT *LOOKS* LIKE...
LUNELLA?
RRRRRRR...
RAAARRRR!
All right...
...I *admit* it.
I wasn't *"just tired."* I wasn't tired *at all.*
The problem is I have a problem. And I *don't* like to admit it.
A big problem.

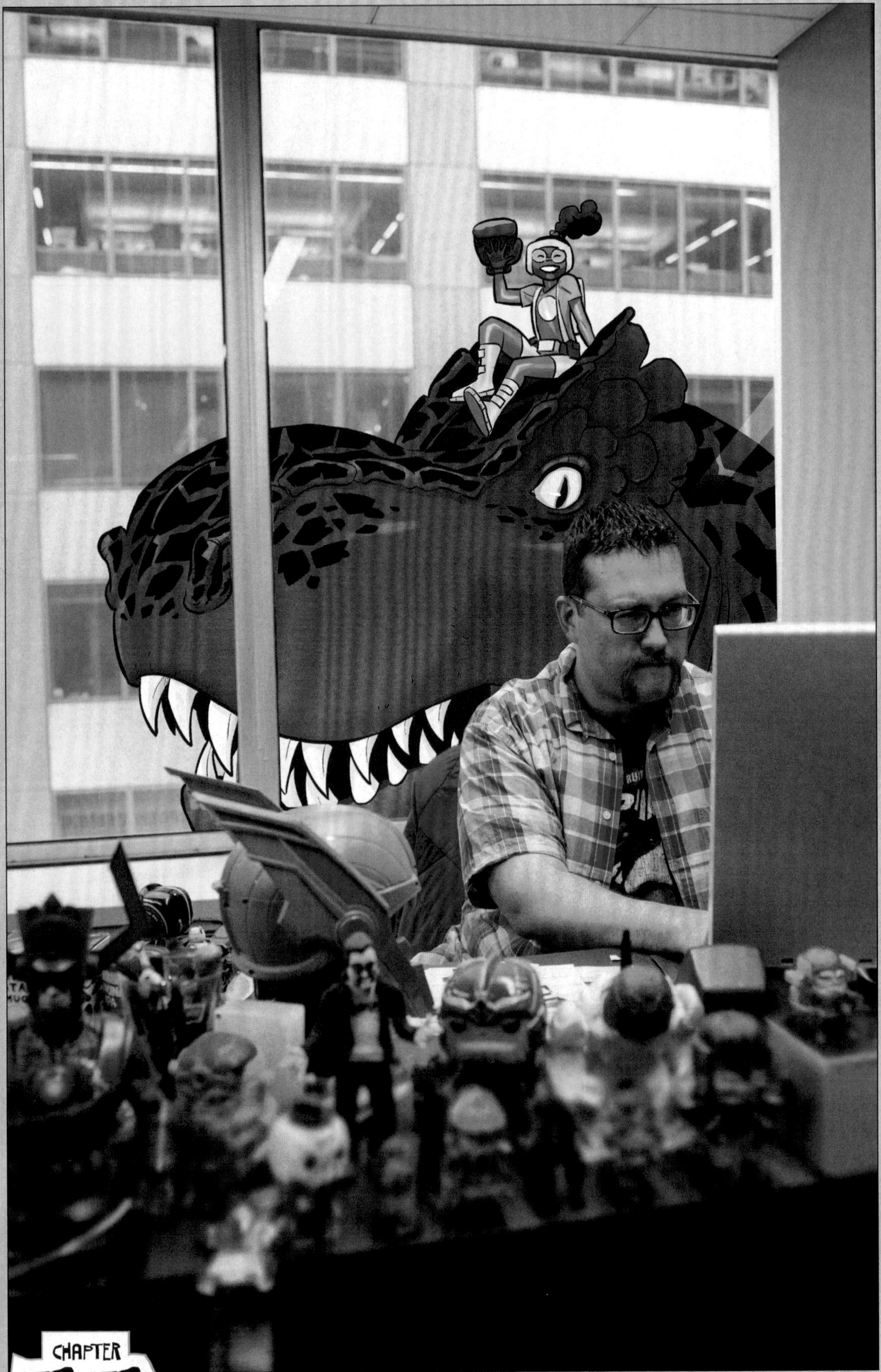

CHAPTER

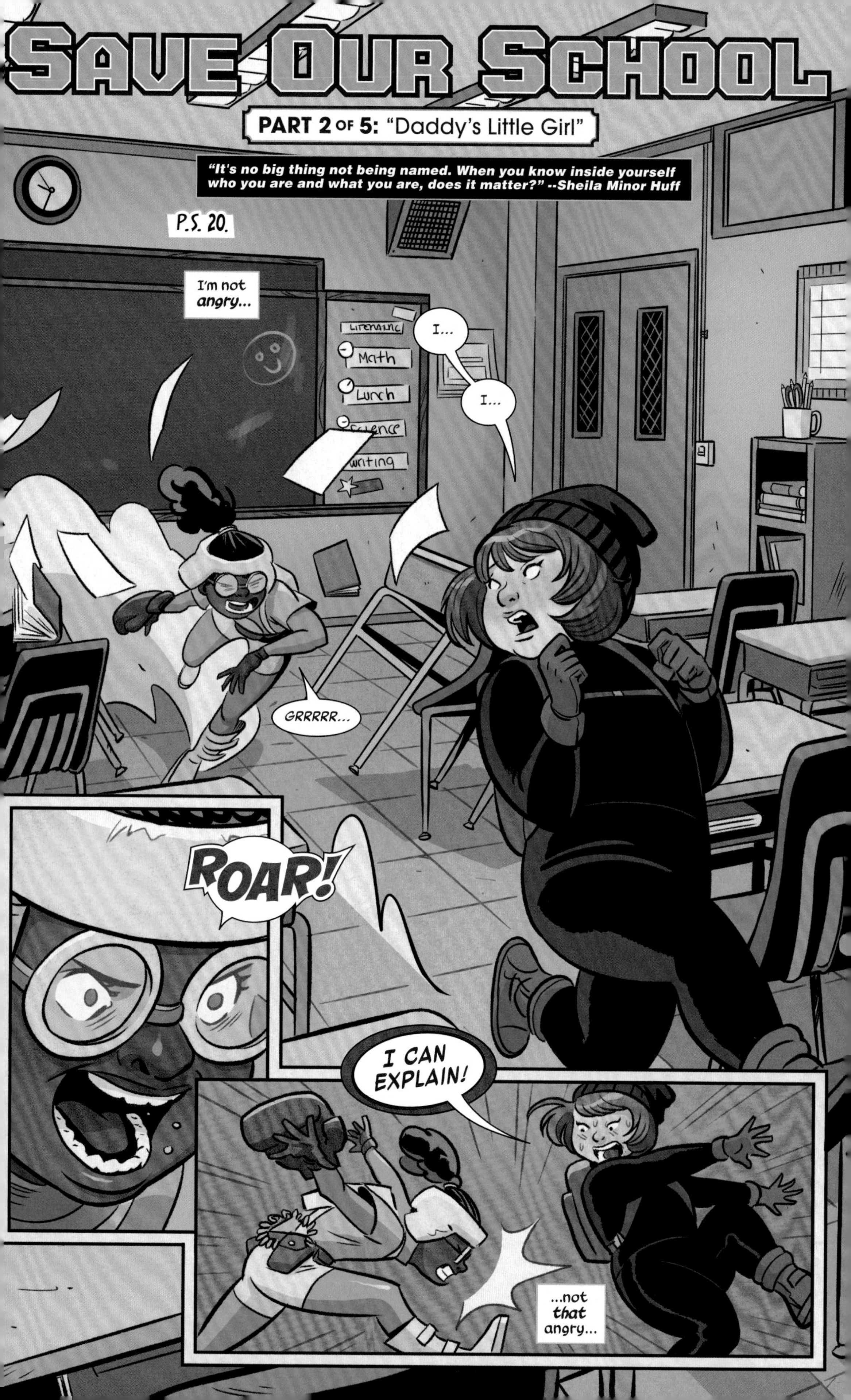
SAVE OUR SCHOOL
PART 2 OF 5: "Daddy's Little Girl"
"It's no big thing not being named. When you know inside yourself who you are and what you are, does it matter?" --Sheila Minor Huff
P.S. 20.
I'm not angry...
Math
Lunch
Writing
I...
I...
GRRRRR...
ROAR!
I CAN EXPLAIN!
...not that angry...

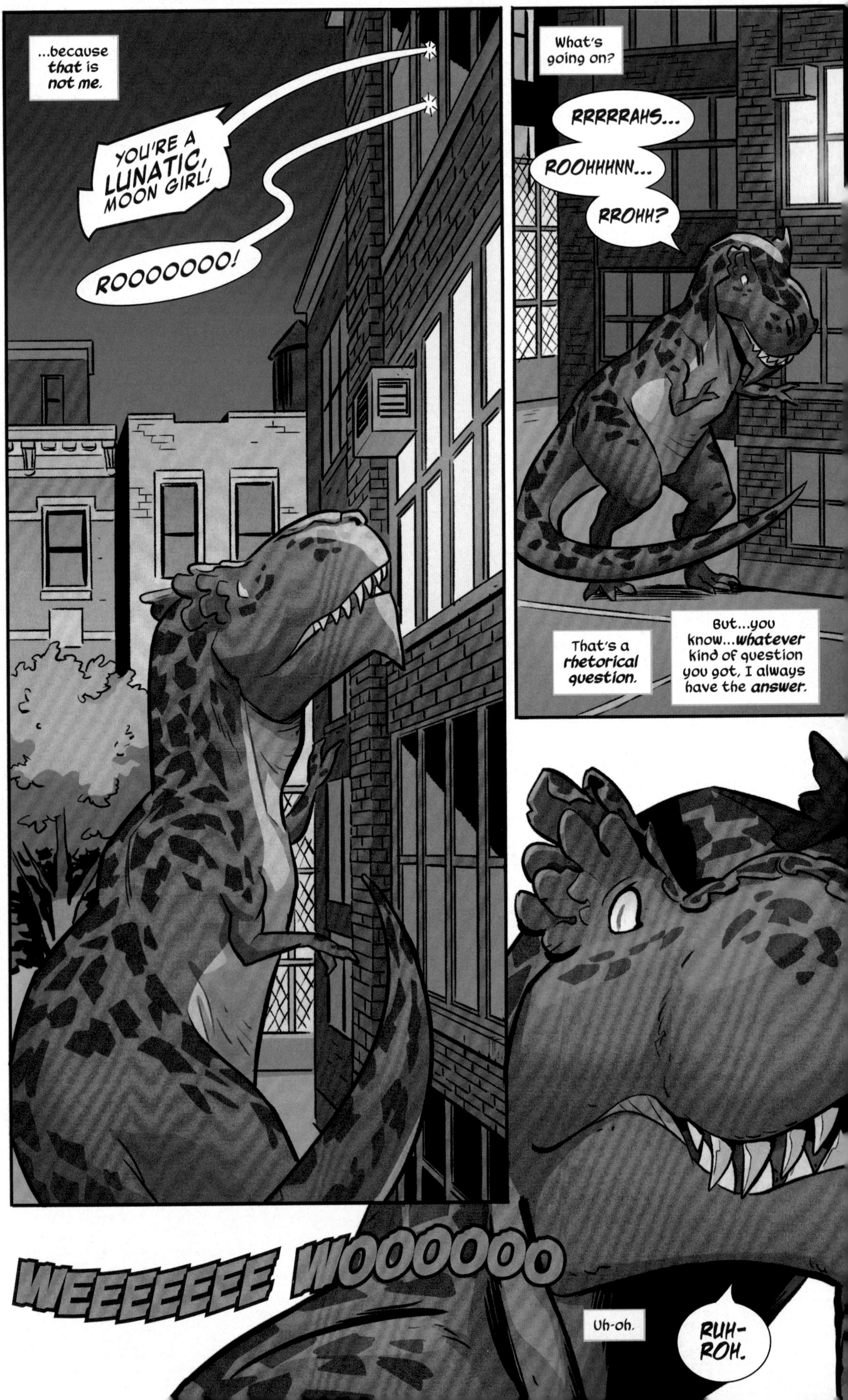
...because that is not me.
YOU'RE A LUNATIC, MOON GIRL!
ROOOOOOO!
What's going on?
RRRRRAHS...
ROOHHHNN...
RROHH?
That's a rhetorical question.
But...you know...whatever kind of question you got, I always have the answer.
WEEEEEEE WOOOOOO
Uh-oh.
RUH-ROH.

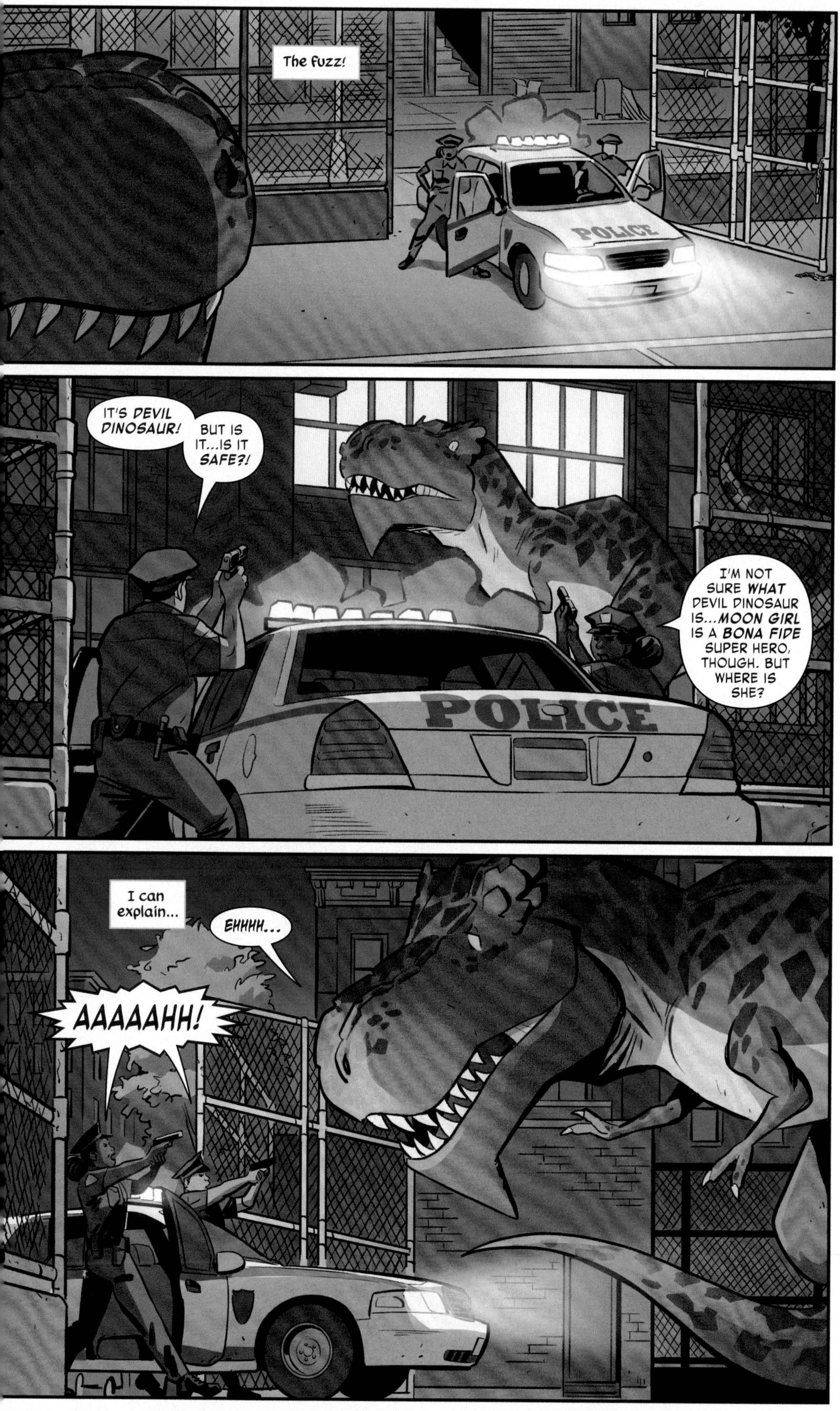

The fuzz!
IT'S DEVIL DINOSAUR!
BUT IS IT...IS IT SAFE?!
I'M NOT SURE WHAT DEVIL DINOSAUR IS...MOON GIRL IS A BONA FIDE SUPER HERO, THOUGH. BUT WHERE IS SHE?
I can explain...
EHHHH...
AAAAAHH!

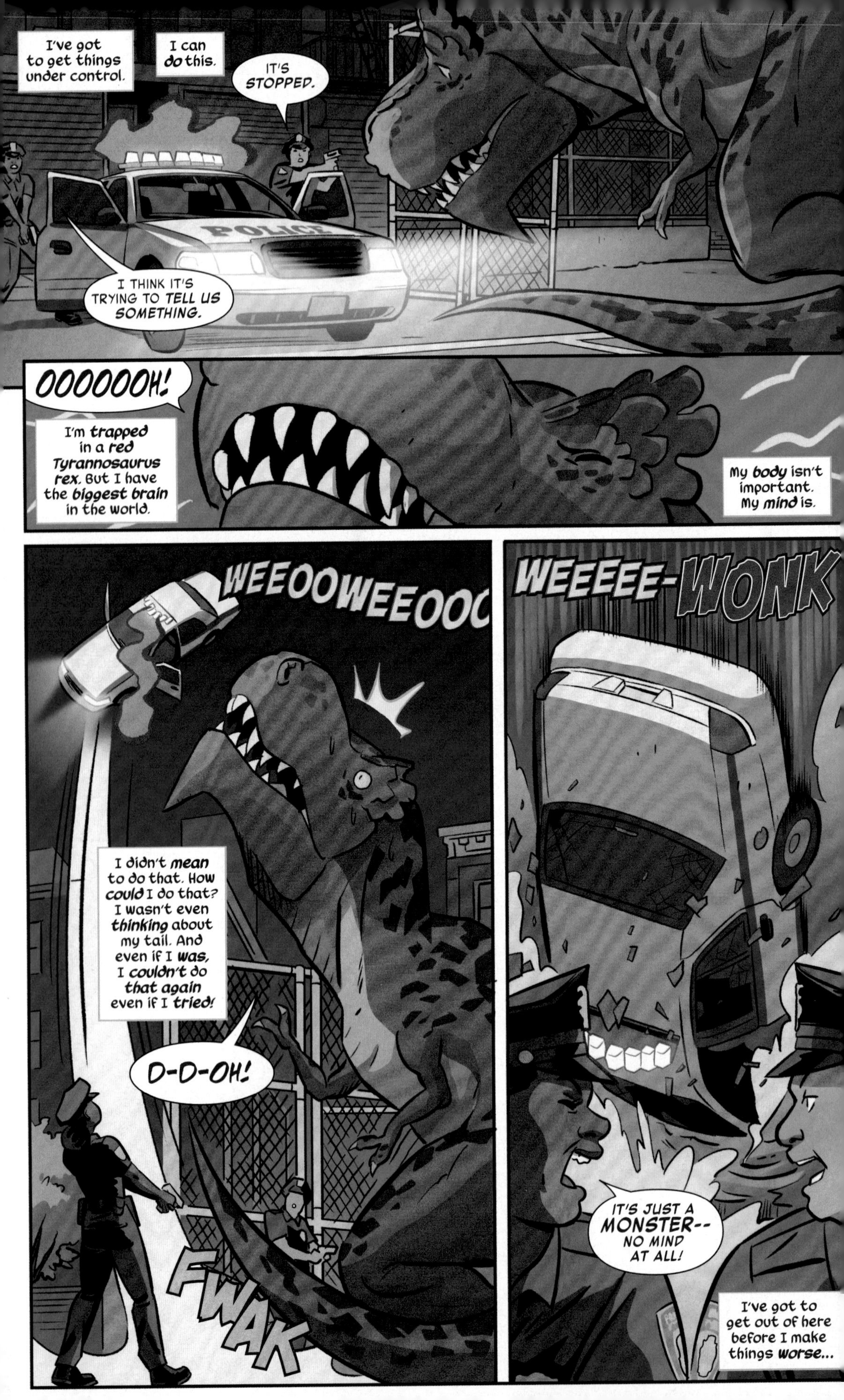
I've got to get things under control.
I can do this.
IT'S STOPPED.
I THINK IT'S TRYING TO TELL US SOMETHING.
OOOOOOH!
I'm trapped in a red Tyrannosaurus rex. But I have the biggest brain in the world.
My body isn't important. My mind is.
WEEOOWEEOOO
I didn't mean to do that. How could I do that? I wasn't even thinking about my tail. And even if I was, I couldn't do that again even if I tried!
D-D-OH!
FWAK
WEEEEE-WONK
IT'S JUST A MONSTER-- NO MIND AT ALL!
I've got to get out of here before I make things worse...

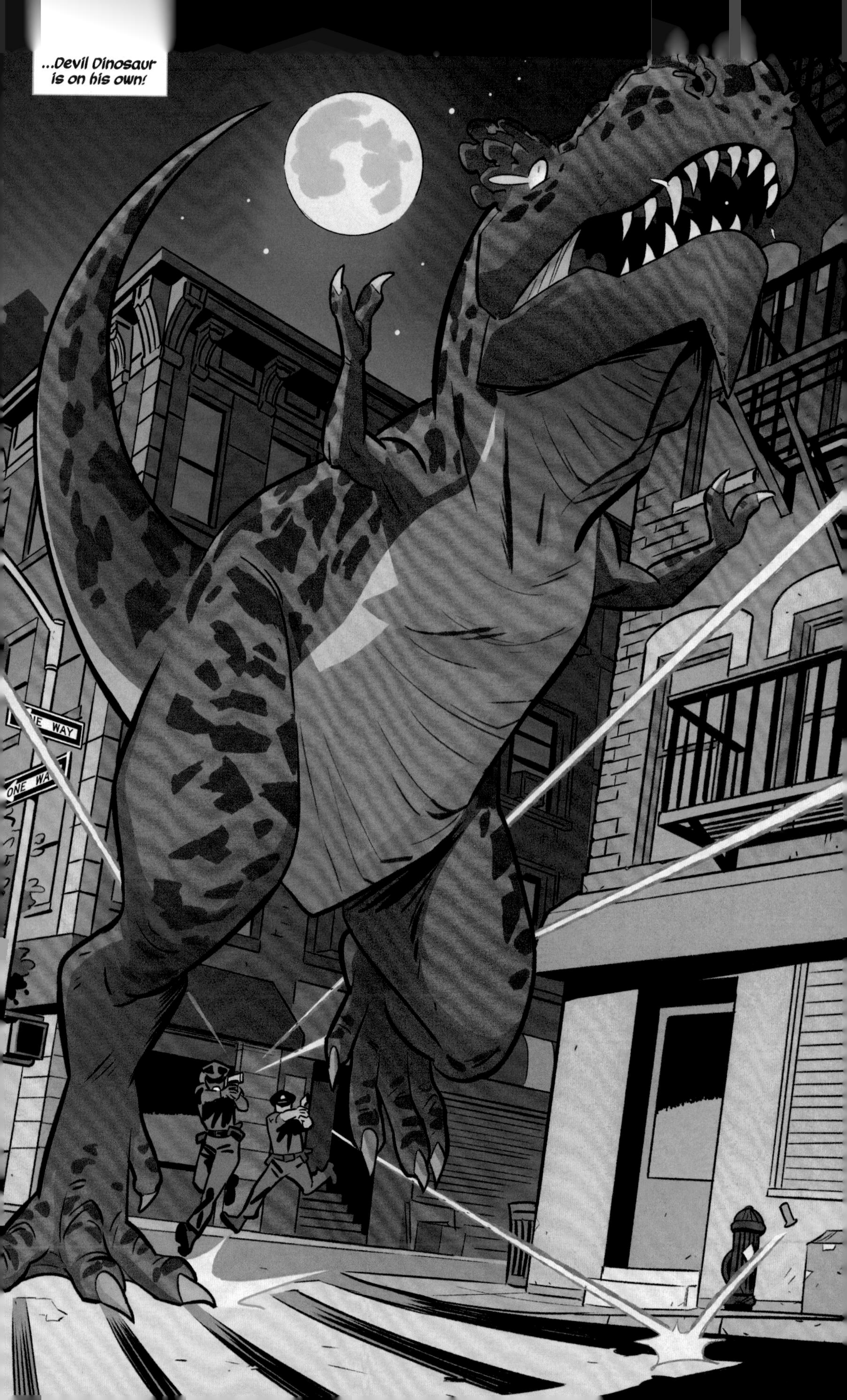
...Devil Dinosaur is on his own!

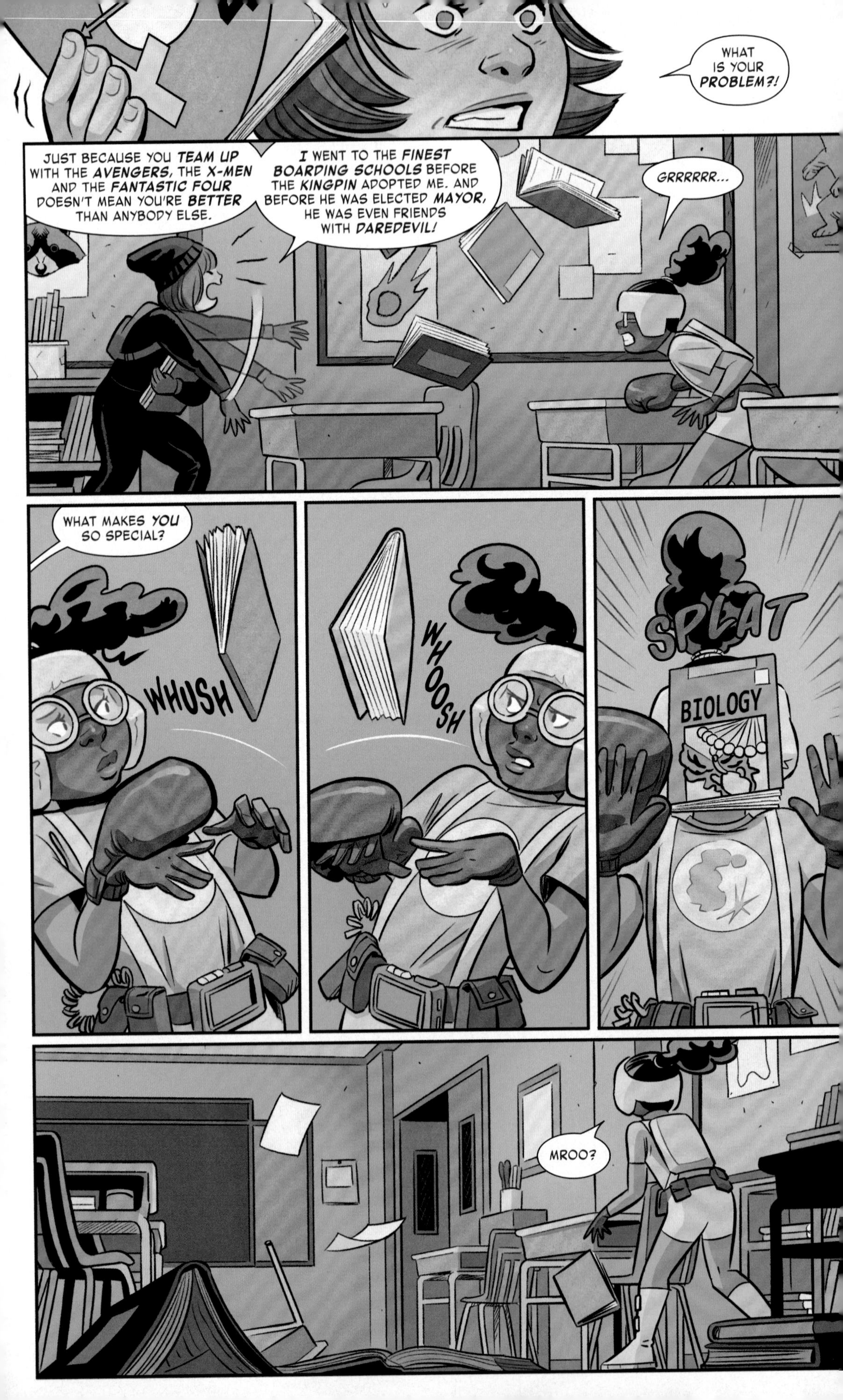
WHAT IS YOUR PROBLEM?!
JUST BECAUSE YOU TEAM UP WITH THE AVENGERS, THE X-MEN AND THE FANTASTIC FOUR DOESN'T MEAN YOU'RE BETTER THAN ANYBODY ELSE.
I WENT TO THE FINEST BOARDING SCHOOLS BEFORE THE KINGPIN ADOPTED ME. AND BEFORE HE WAS ELECTED MAYOR, HE WAS EVEN FRIENDS WITH DAREDEVIL!
GRRRRRR...
WHAT MAKES YOU SO SPECIAL?
WHUSH
WHOOSH
SPLAT
BIOLOGY
MROO?

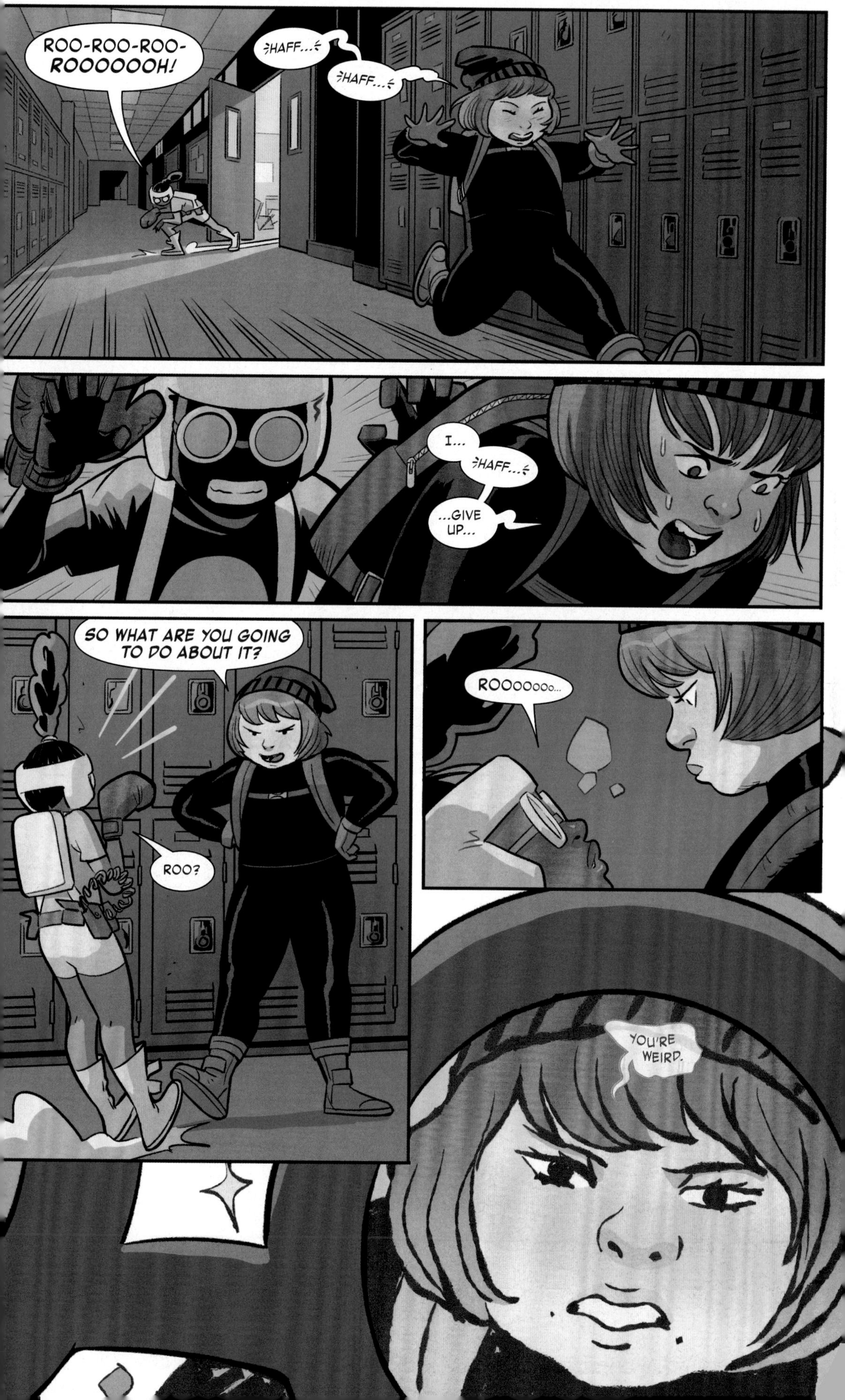
ROO-ROO-ROO-ROOOOOOH!
HAFF...
HAFF...
I...
HAFF...
...GIVE UP...
SO WHAT ARE YOU GOING TO DO ABOUT IT?
ROO?
ROOooooo...
YOU'RE WEIRD.

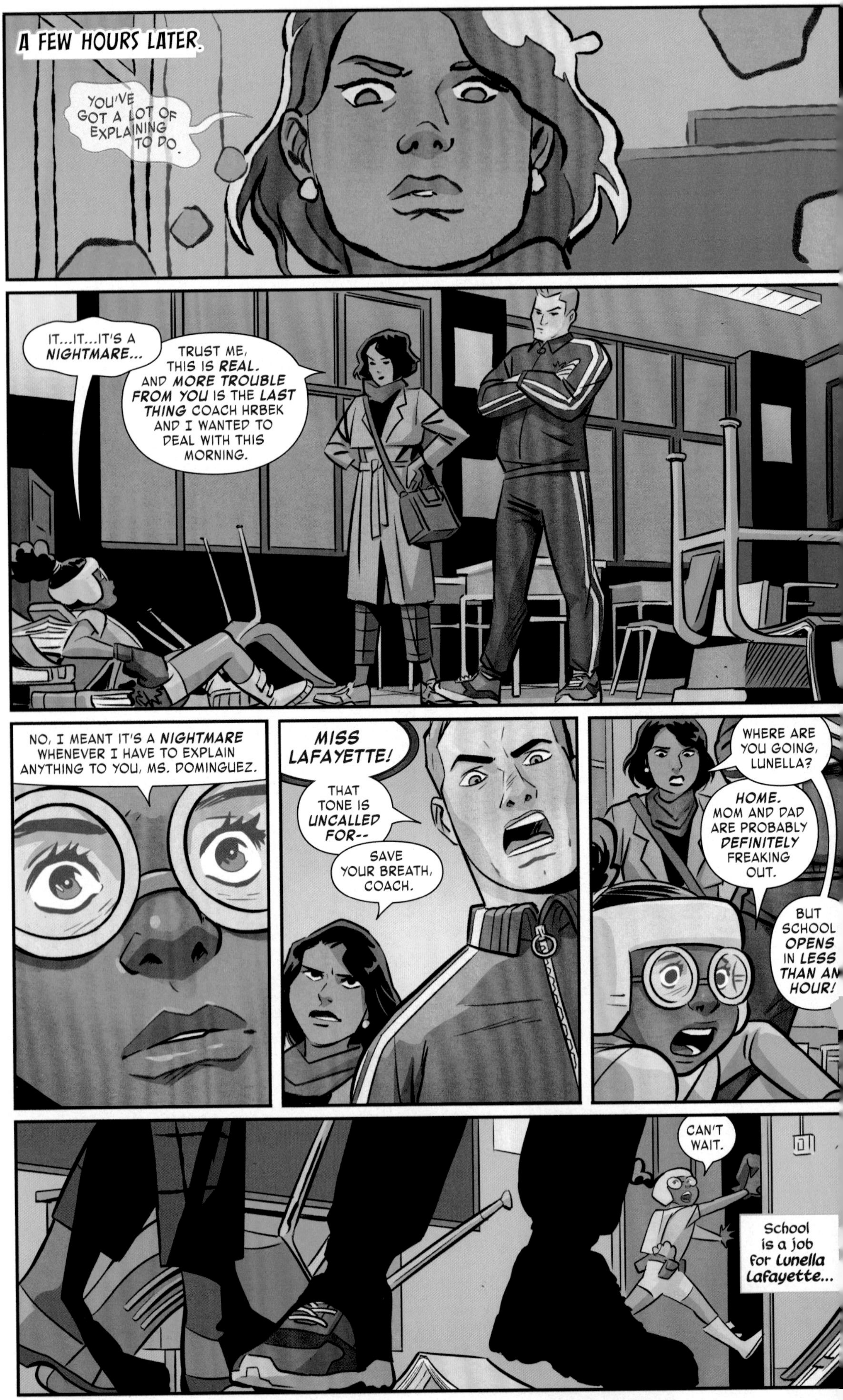
A FEW HOURS LATER.
YOU'VE GOT A LOT OF EXPLAINING TO DO.
IT...IT...IT'S A NIGHTMARE...
TRUST ME, THIS IS REAL. AND MORE TROUBLE FROM YOU IS THE LAST THING COACH HRBEK AND I WANTED TO DEAL WITH THIS MORNING.
NO, I MEANT IT'S A NIGHTMARE WHENEVER I HAVE TO EXPLAIN ANYTHING TO YOU, MS. DOMINGUEZ.
MISS LAFAYETTE!
THAT TONE IS UNCALLED FOR--
SAVE YOUR BREATH, COACH.
WHERE ARE YOU GOING, LUNELLA?
HOME. MOM AND DAD ARE PROBABLY DEFINITELY FREAKING OUT.
BUT SCHOOL OPENS IN LESS THAN AN HOUR!
CAN'T WAIT.
School is a job for Lunella Lafayette...

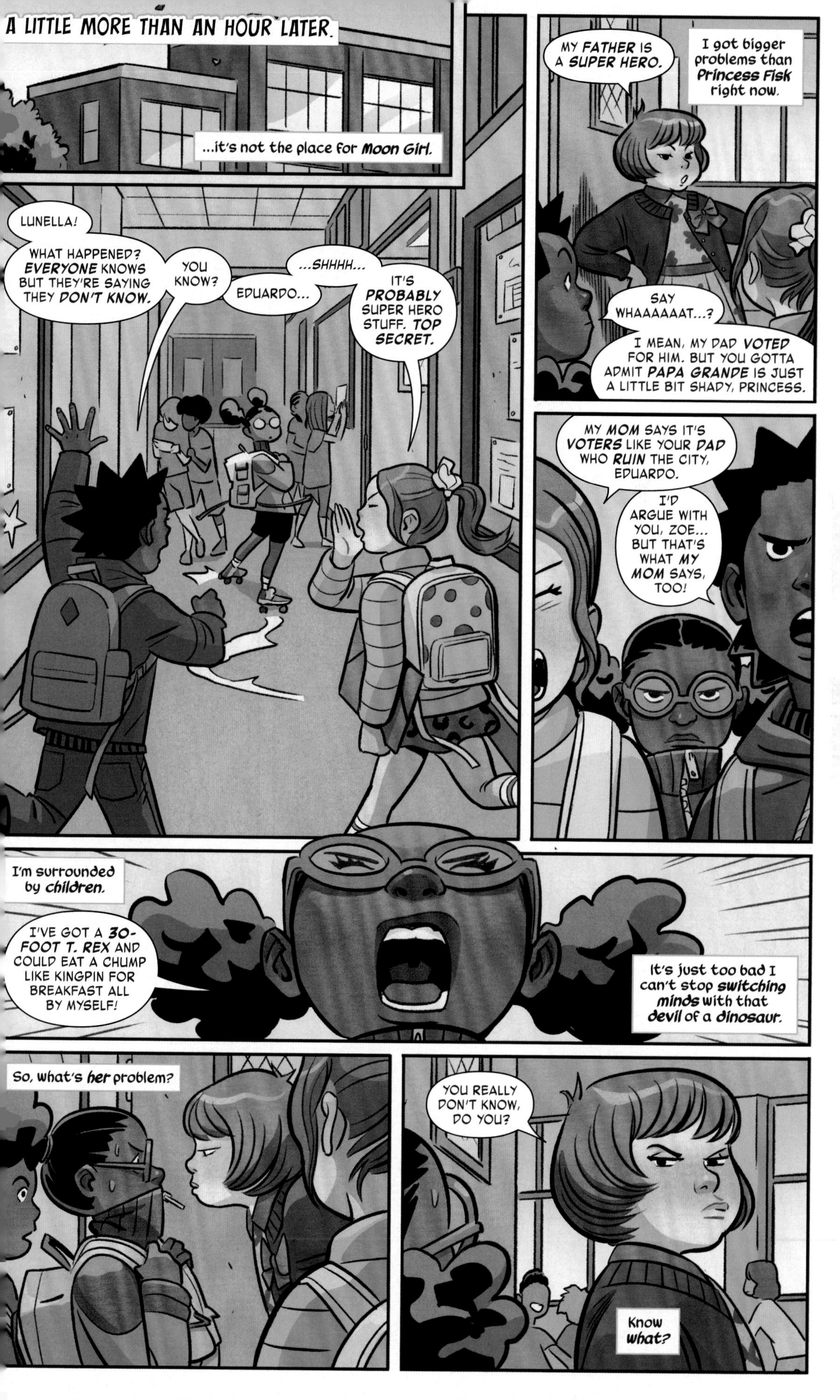

A LITTLE MORE THAN AN HOUR LATER.
...it's not the place for Moon Girl.
MY FATHER IS A SUPER HERO.
I got bigger problems than Princess Fisk right now.
SAY WHAAAAAAT...?
I MEAN, MY DAD VOTED FOR HIM. BUT YOU GOTTA ADMIT PAPA GRANDE IS JUST A LITTLE BIT SHADY, PRINCESS.
LUNELLA!
WHAT HAPPENED? EVERYONE KNOWS BUT THEY'RE SAYING THEY DON'T KNOW.
YOU KNOW?
EDUARDO...
...SHHHH...
IT'S PROBABLY SUPER HERO STUFF. TOP SECRET.
MY MOM SAYS IT'S VOTERS LIKE YOUR DAD WHO RUIN THE CITY, EDUARDO.
I'D ARGUE WITH YOU, ZOE... BUT THAT'S WHAT MY MOM SAYS, TOO!
I'm surrounded by children.
I'VE GOT A 30-FOOT T. REX AND COULD EAT A CHUMP LIKE KINGPIN FOR BREAKFAST ALL BY MYSELF!
It's just too bad I can't stop switching minds with that devil of a dinosaur.
So, what's her problem?
YOU REALLY DON'T KNOW, DO YOU?
Know what?

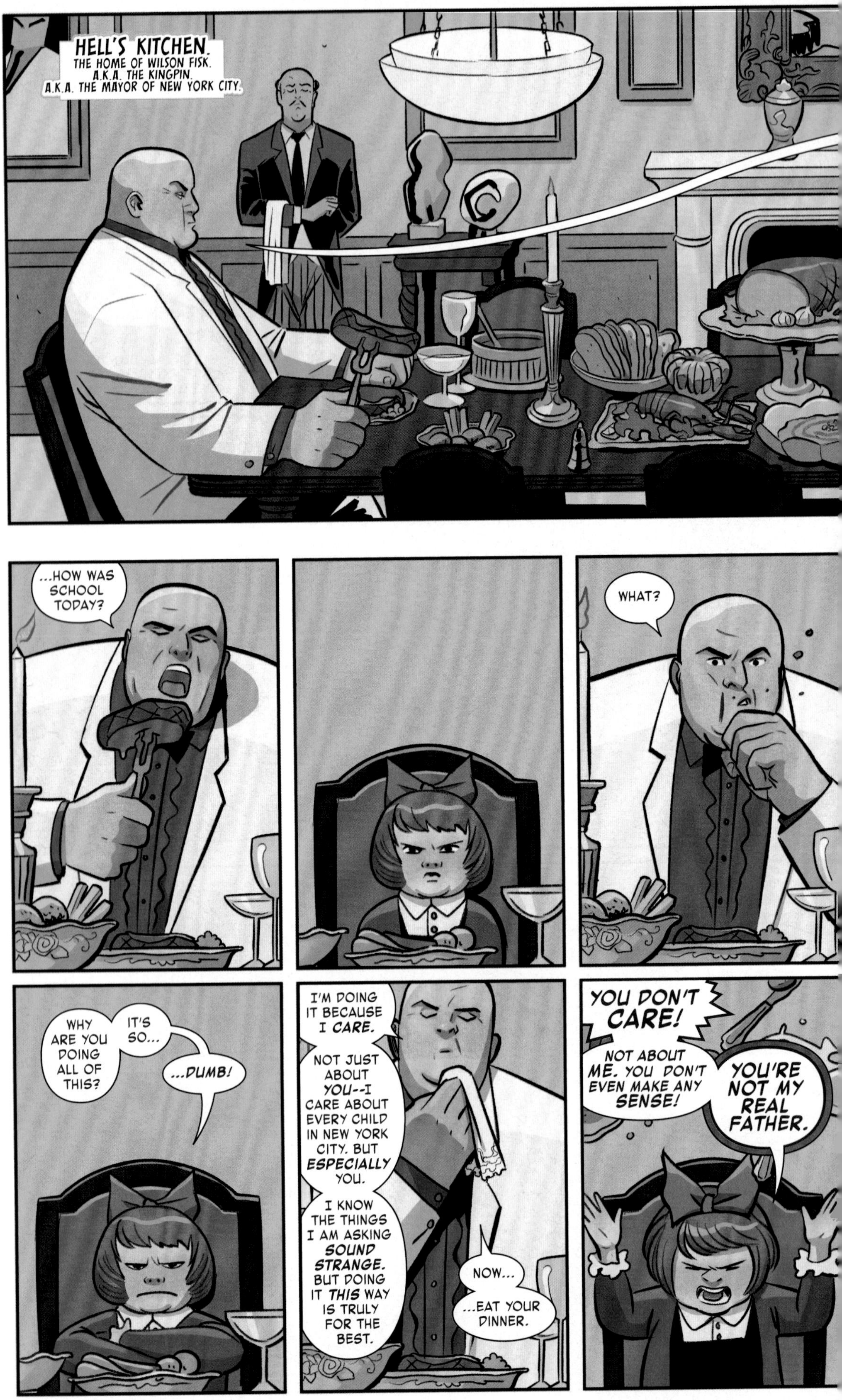
HELL'S KITCHEN.
THE HOME OF WILSON FISK.
A.K.A. THE KINGPIN.
A.K.A. THE MAYOR OF NEW YORK CITY.
...HOW WAS SCHOOL TODAY?
WHAT?
WHY ARE YOU DOING ALL OF THIS?
IT'S SO...
...DUMB!
I'M DOING IT BECAUSE I CARE.
NOT JUST ABOUT YOU--I CARE ABOUT EVERY CHILD IN NEW YORK CITY. BUT ESPECIALLY YOU.
I KNOW THE THINGS I AM ASKING SOUND STRANGE. BUT DOING IT THIS WAY IS TRULY FOR THE BEST.
NOW...
...EAT YOUR DINNER.
YOU DON'T CARE!
NOT ABOUT ME. YOU DON'T EVEN MAKE ANY SENSE!
YOU'RE NOT MY REAL FATHER.

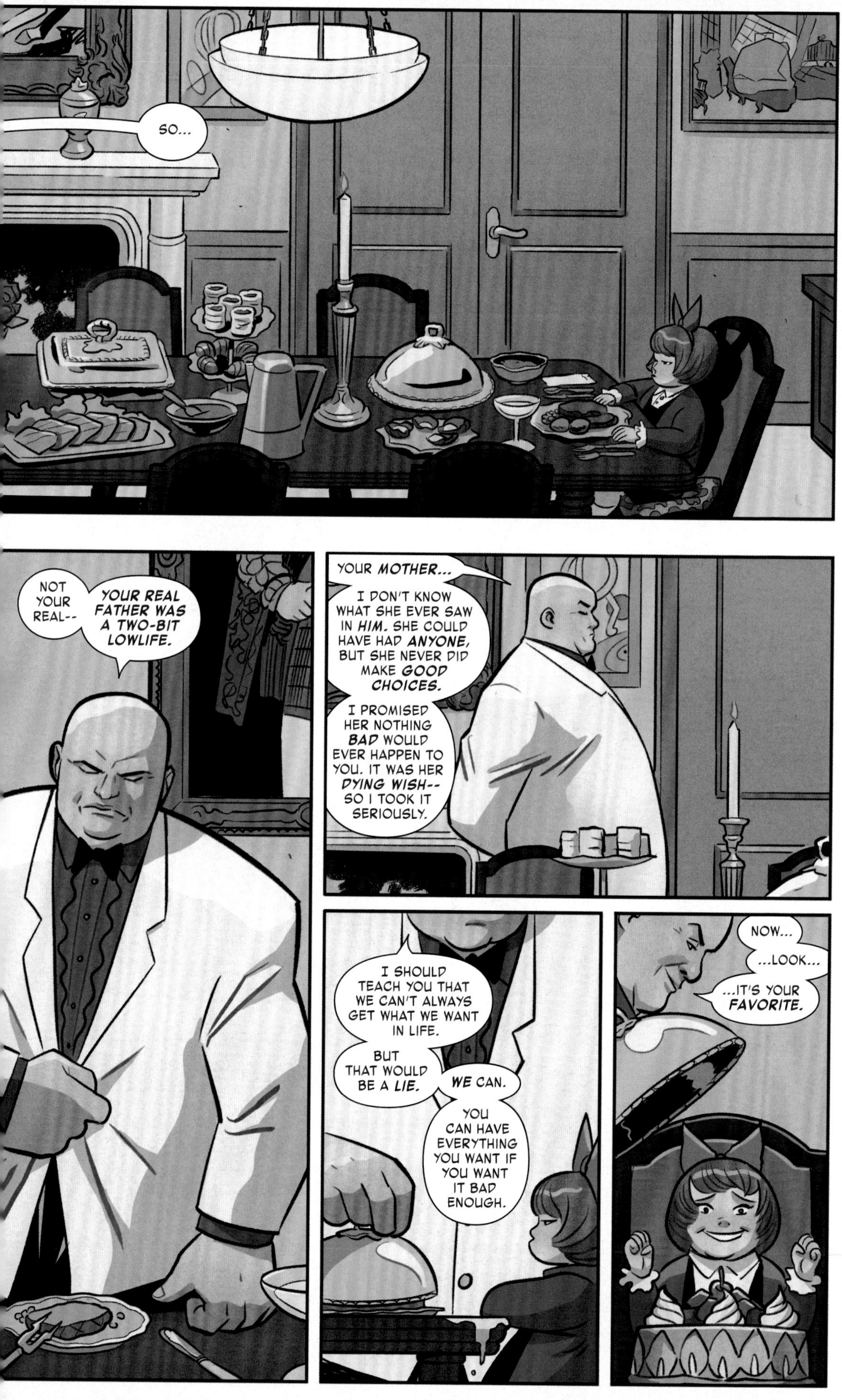
SO...
NOT YOUR REAL--
YOUR REAL FATHER WAS A TWO-BIT LOWLIFE.
YOUR MOTHER...
I DON'T KNOW WHAT SHE EVER SAW IN HIM. SHE COULD HAVE HAD ANYONE, BUT SHE NEVER DID MAKE GOOD CHOICES.
I PROMISED HER NOTHING BAD WOULD EVER HAPPEN TO YOU. IT WAS HER DYING WISH-- SO I TOOK IT SERIOUSLY.
I SHOULD TEACH YOU THAT WE CAN'T ALWAYS GET WHAT WE WANT IN LIFE.
BUT THAT WOULD BE A LIE.
WE CAN.
YOU CAN HAVE EVERYTHING YOU WANT IF YOU WANT IT BAD ENOUGH.
NOW...
...LOOK...
...IT'S YOUR FAVORITE.

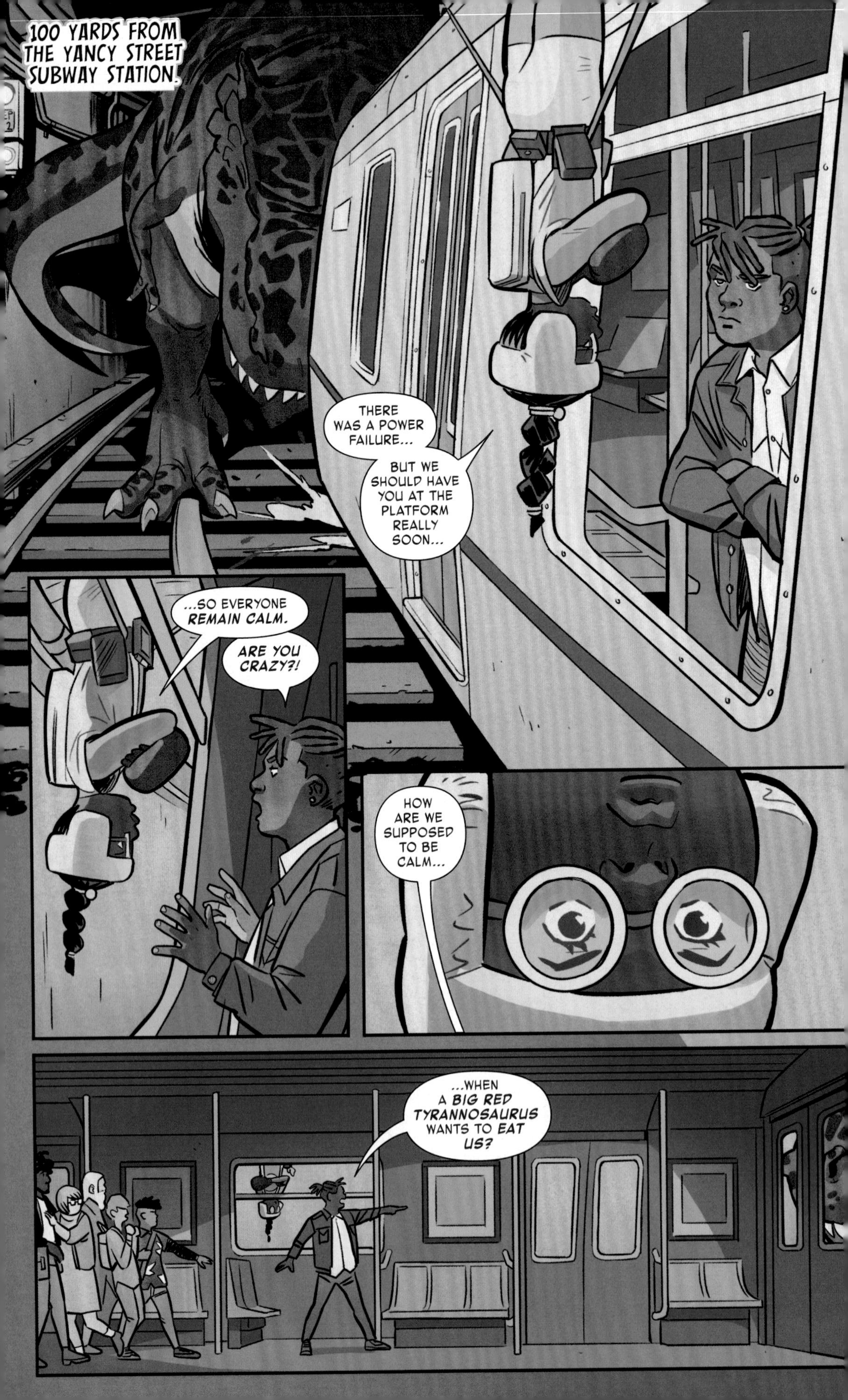
100 YARDS FROM THE YANCY STREET SUBWAY STATION.
THERE WAS A POWER FAILURE...
BUT WE SHOULD HAVE YOU AT THE PLATFORM REALLY SOON...
...SO EVERYONE REMAIN CALM.
ARE YOU CRAZY?!
HOW ARE WE SUPPOSED TO BE CALM...
...WHEN A BIG RED TYRANNOSAURUS WANTS TO EAT US?

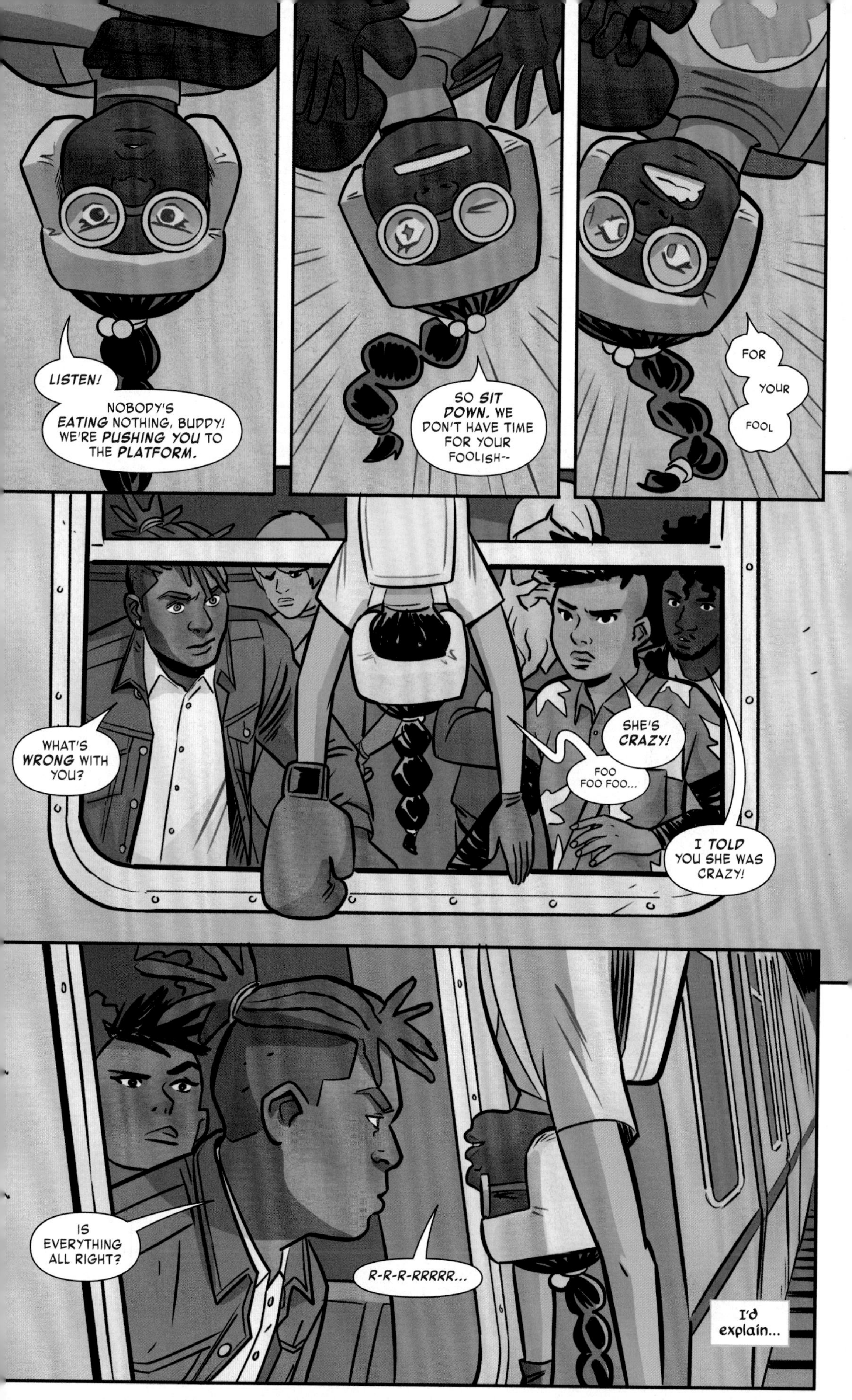

LISTEN!
NOBODY'S EATING NOTHING, BUDDY! WE'RE PUSHING YOU TO THE PLATFORM.
SO SIT DOWN. WE DON'T HAVE TIME FOR YOUR FOOLISH--
FOR
YOUR
FOOL
WHAT'S WRONG WITH YOU?
SHE'S CRAZY!
FOO FOO FOO...
I TOLD YOU SHE WAS CRAZY!
IS EVERYTHING ALL RIGHT?
R-R-R-RRRRR...
I'd explain...

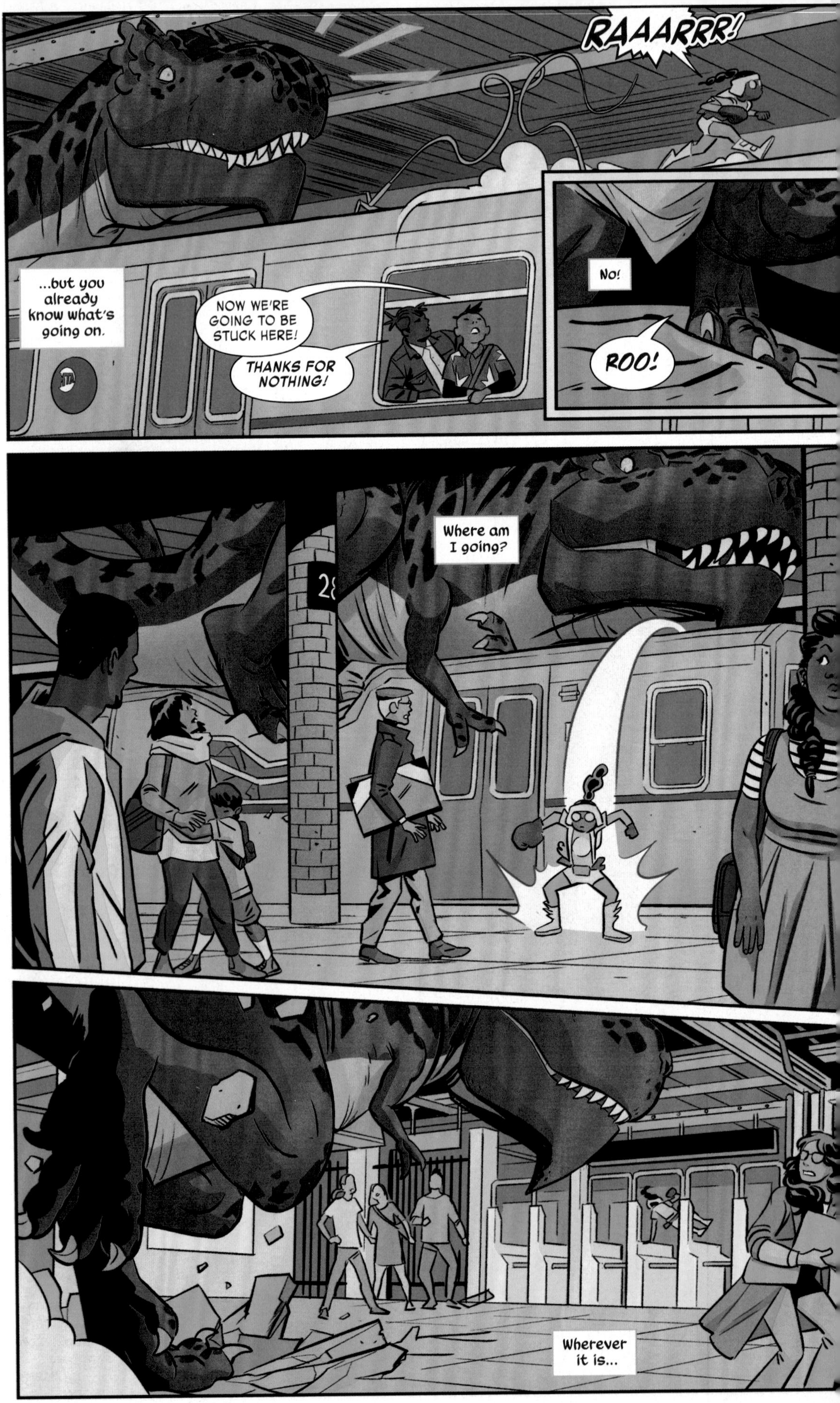
RAAARRR!
...but you already know what's going on.
NOW WE'RE GOING TO BE STUCK HERE!
THANKS FOR NOTHING!
No!
ROO!
Where am I going?
Wherever it is...

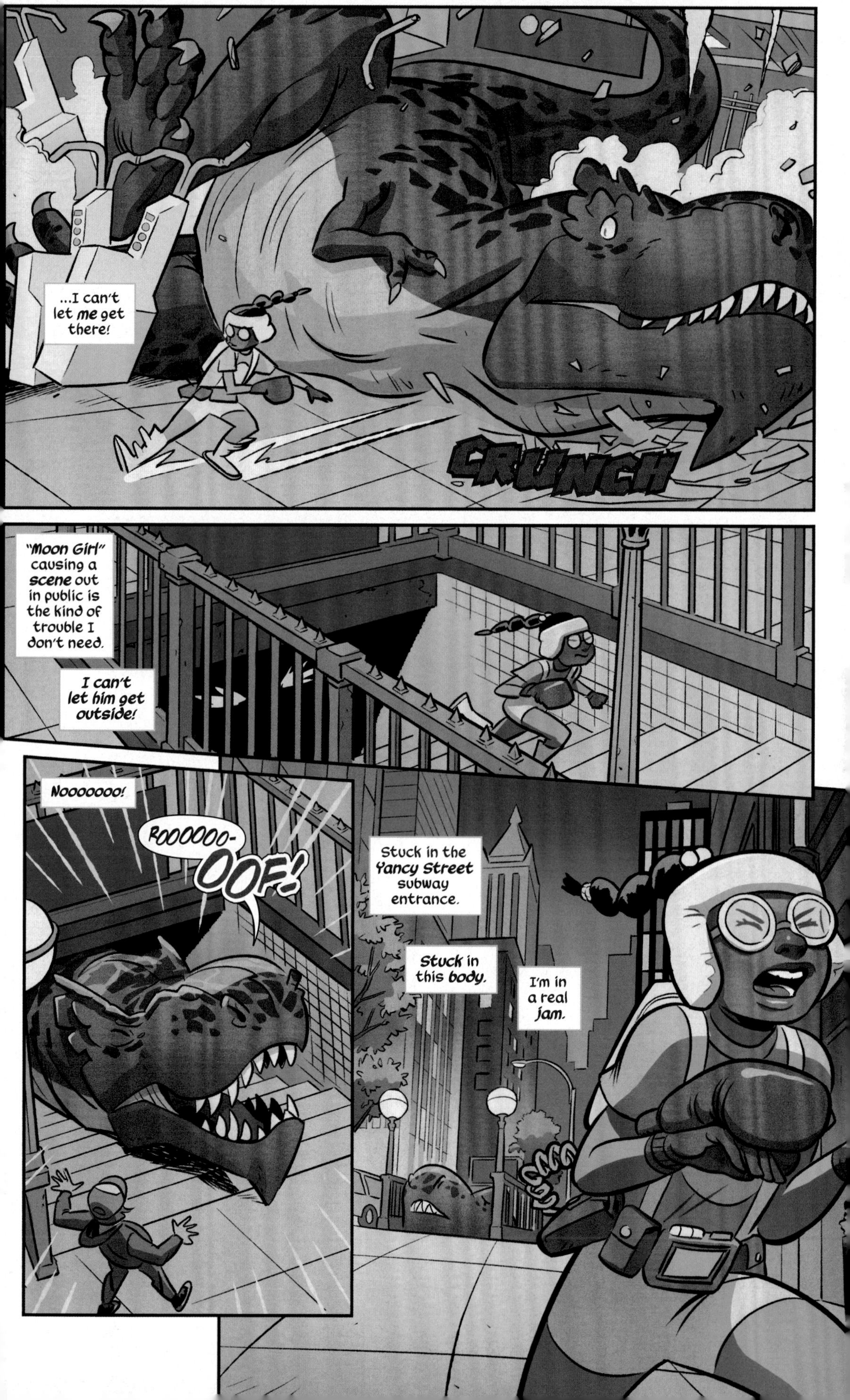

...I can't let *me* get there!
CRUNCH
"Moon Girl" causing a *scene* out in public is the kind of trouble I don't need.
I can't let him get outside!
Noooooo!
ROOOOOO-OOF!
Stuck in the *Yancy Street* subway entrance.
Stuck in this *body*.
I'm in a real *jam*.

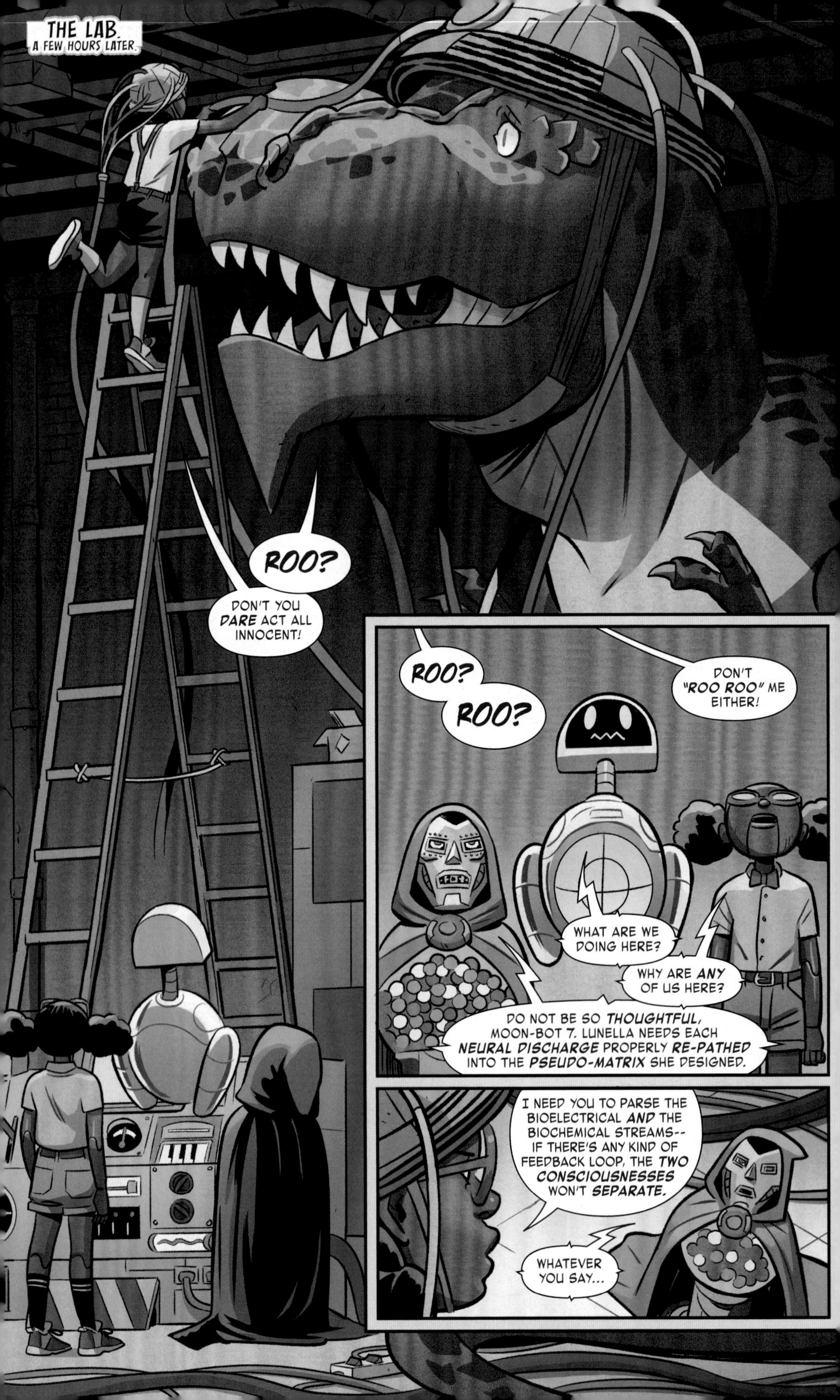
THE LAB.
A FEW HOURS LATER.
ROO?
DON'T YOU DARE ACT ALL INNOCENT!
ROO?
ROO?
DON'T "ROO ROO" ME EITHER!
WHAT ARE WE DOING HERE?
WHY ARE ANY OF US HERE?
DO NOT BE SO THOUGHTFUL, MOON-BOT 7. LUNELLA NEEDS EACH NEURAL DISCHARGE PROPERLY RE-PATHED INTO THE PSEUDO-MATRIX SHE DESIGNED.
I NEED YOU TO PARSE THE BIOELECTRICAL AND THE BIOCHEMICAL STREAMS-- IF THERE'S ANY KIND OF FEEDBACK LOOP, THE TWO CONSCIOUSNESSES WON'T SEPARATE.
WHATEVER YOU SAY...

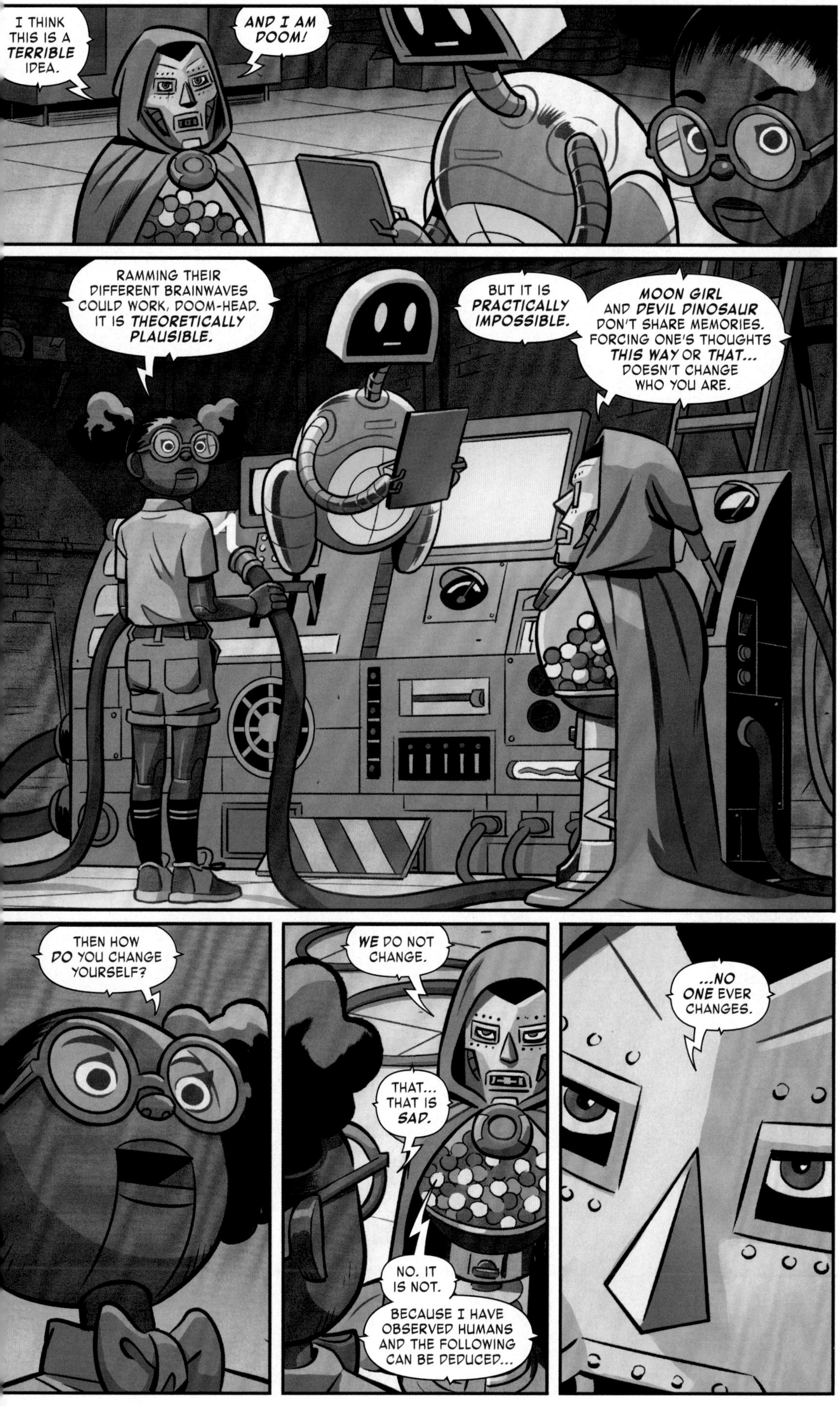

I THINK THIS IS A TERRIBLE IDEA.
AND I AM DOOM!
RAMMING THEIR DIFFERENT BRAINWAVES COULD WORK, DOOM-HEAD. IT IS THEORETICALLY PLAUSIBLE.
BUT IT IS PRACTICALLY IMPOSSIBLE.
MOON GIRL AND DEVIL DINOSAUR DON'T SHARE MEMORIES. FORCING ONE'S THOUGHTS THIS WAY OR THAT... DOESN'T CHANGE WHO YOU ARE.
THEN HOW DO YOU CHANGE YOURSELF?
WE DO NOT CHANGE.
THAT... THAT IS SAD.
NO. IT IS NOT.
BECAUSE I HAVE OBSERVED HUMANS AND THE FOLLOWING CAN BE DEDUCED...
...NO ONE EVER CHANGES.

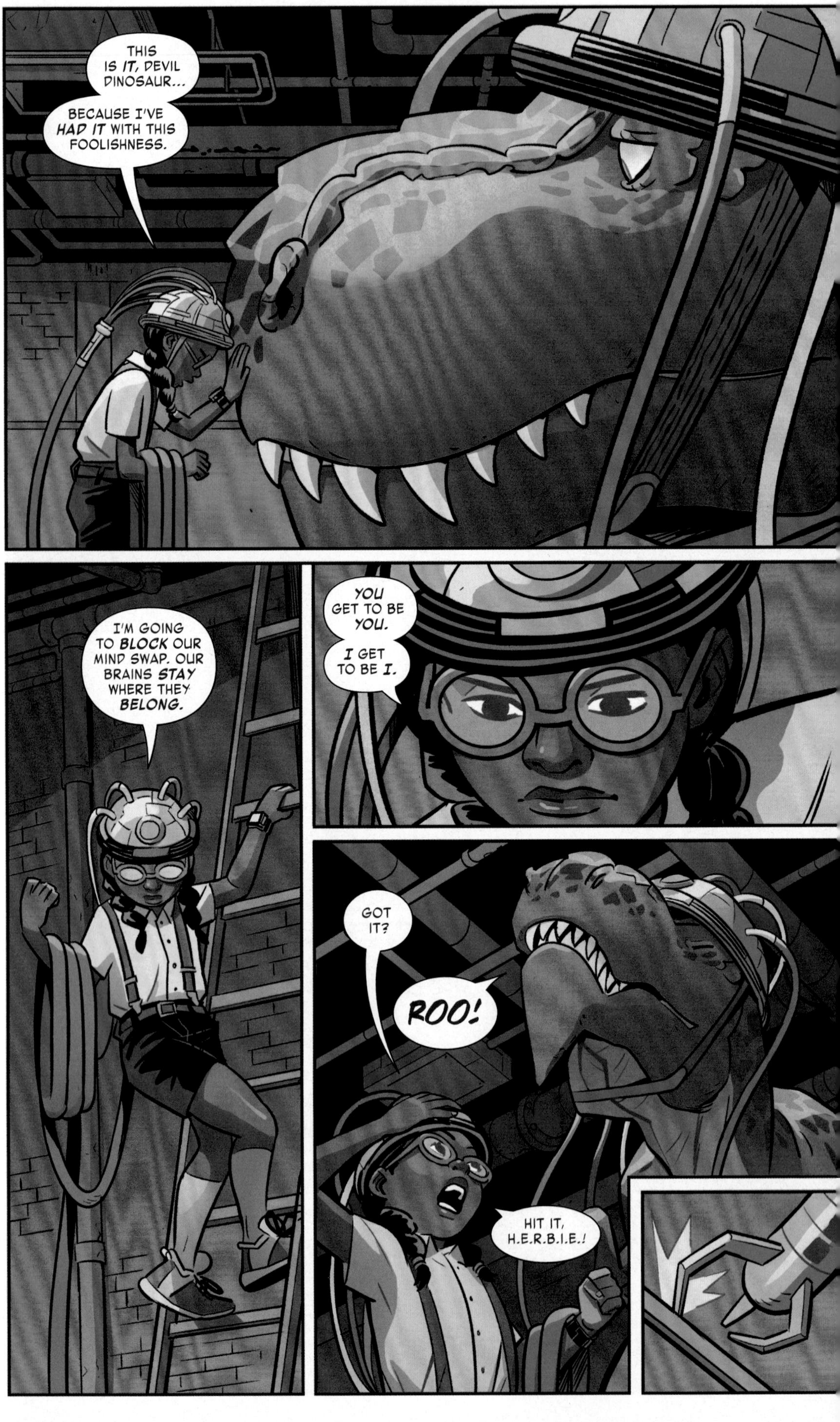
THIS IS IT, DEVIL DINOSAUR...
BECAUSE I'VE HAD IT WITH THIS FOOLISHNESS.
I'M GOING TO BLOCK OUR MIND SWAP. OUR BRAINS STAY WHERE THEY BELONG.
YOU GET TO BE YOU.
I GET TO BE I.
GOT IT?
ROO!
HIT IT, H.E.R.B.I.E.!

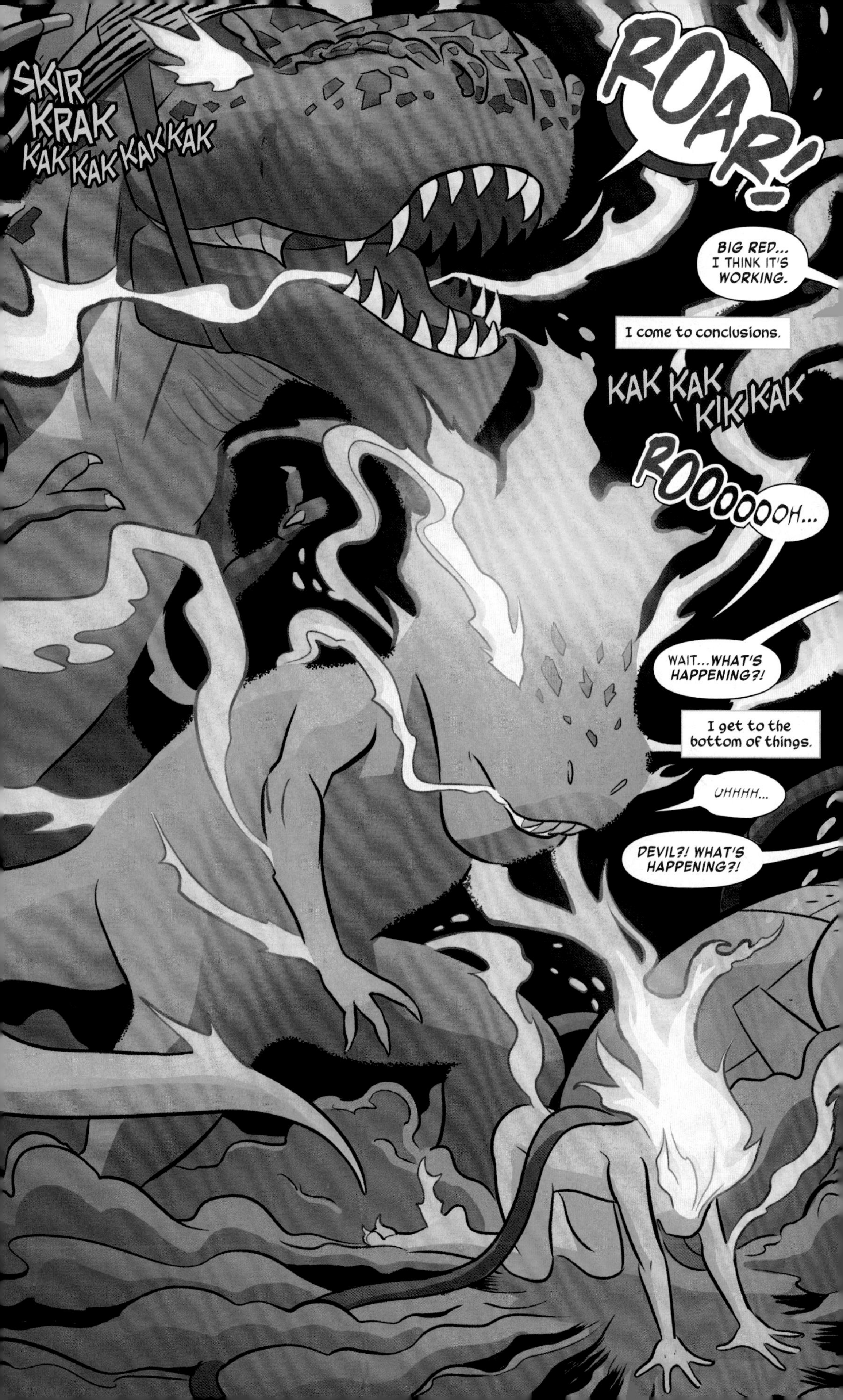
SKIR KRAK KAK KAK KAK KAK
ROAR!
BIG RED... I THINK IT'S WORKING.
I come to conclusions.
KAK KAK KIK KAK
ROOOOOOOH...
WAIT...WHAT'S HAPPENING?!
I get to the bottom of things.
UHHHH...
DEVIL?! WHAT'S HAPPENING?!

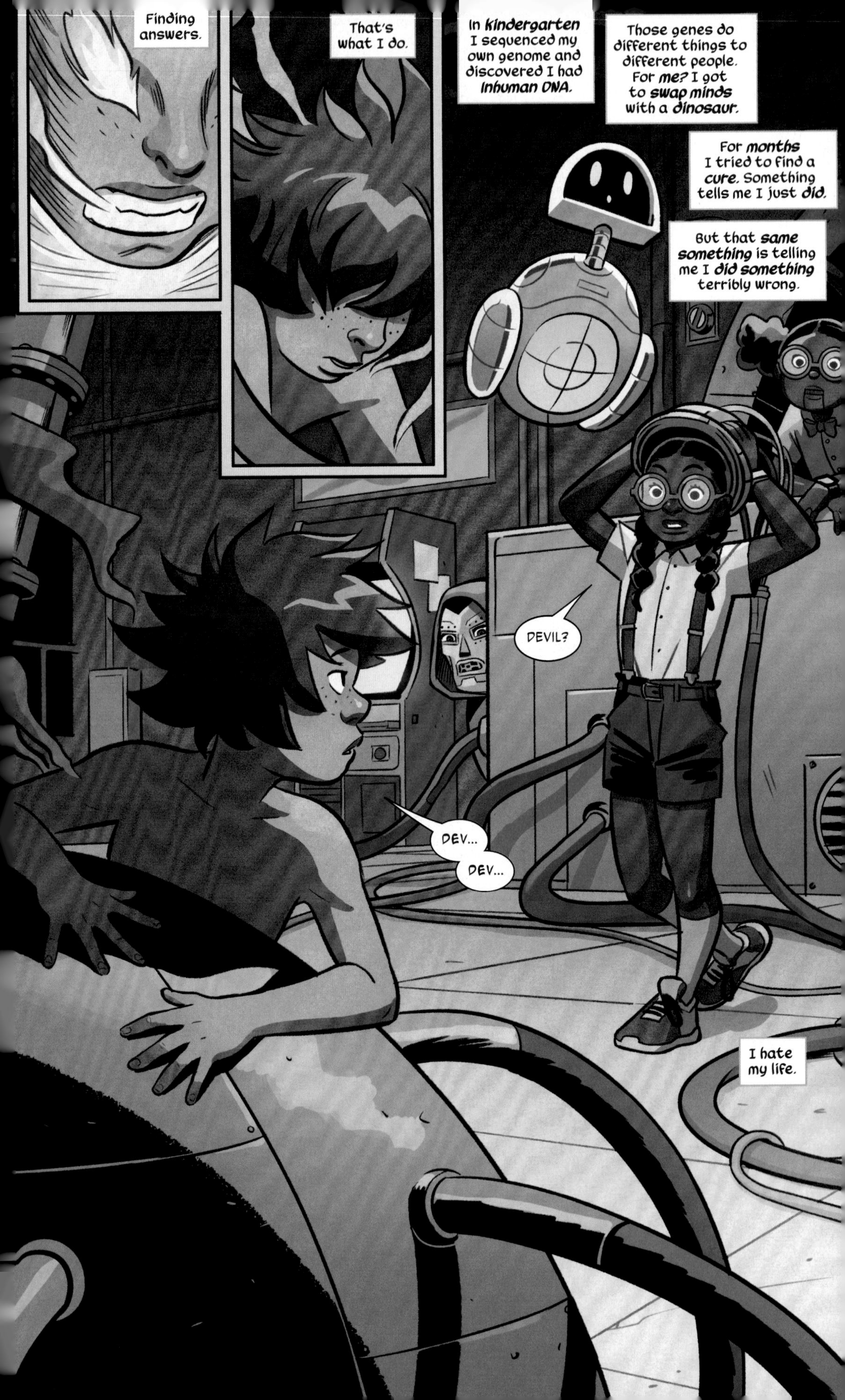
Finding answers.
That's what I do.
In kindergarten I sequenced my own genome and discovered I had Inhuman DNA.
Those genes do different things to different people. For me? I got to swap minds with a dinosaur.
For months I tried to find a cure. Something tells me I just did.
But that same something is telling me I did something terribly wrong.
DEVIL?
DEV...
DEV...
I hate my life.

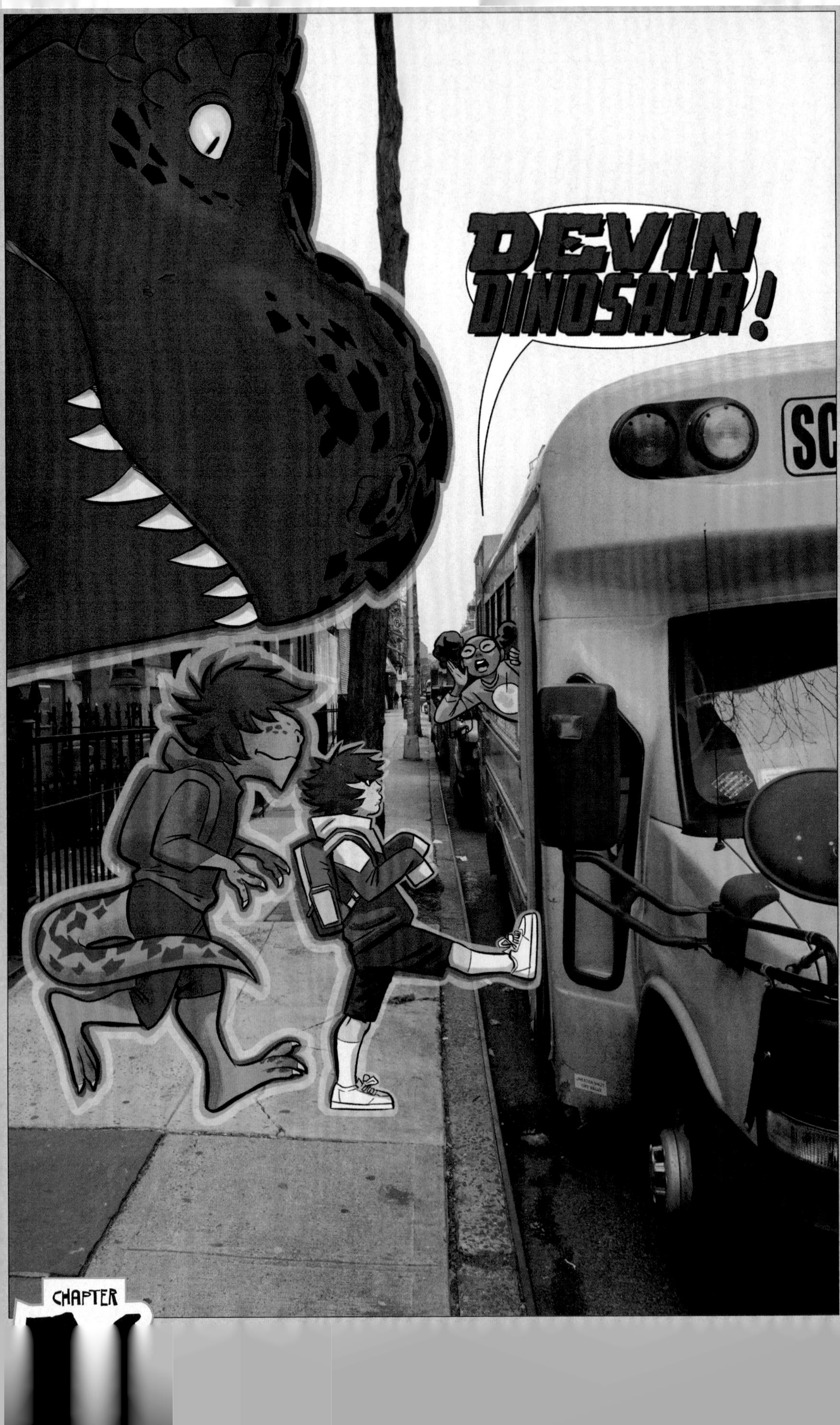
DEVIN DINOSAUR!
CHAPTER

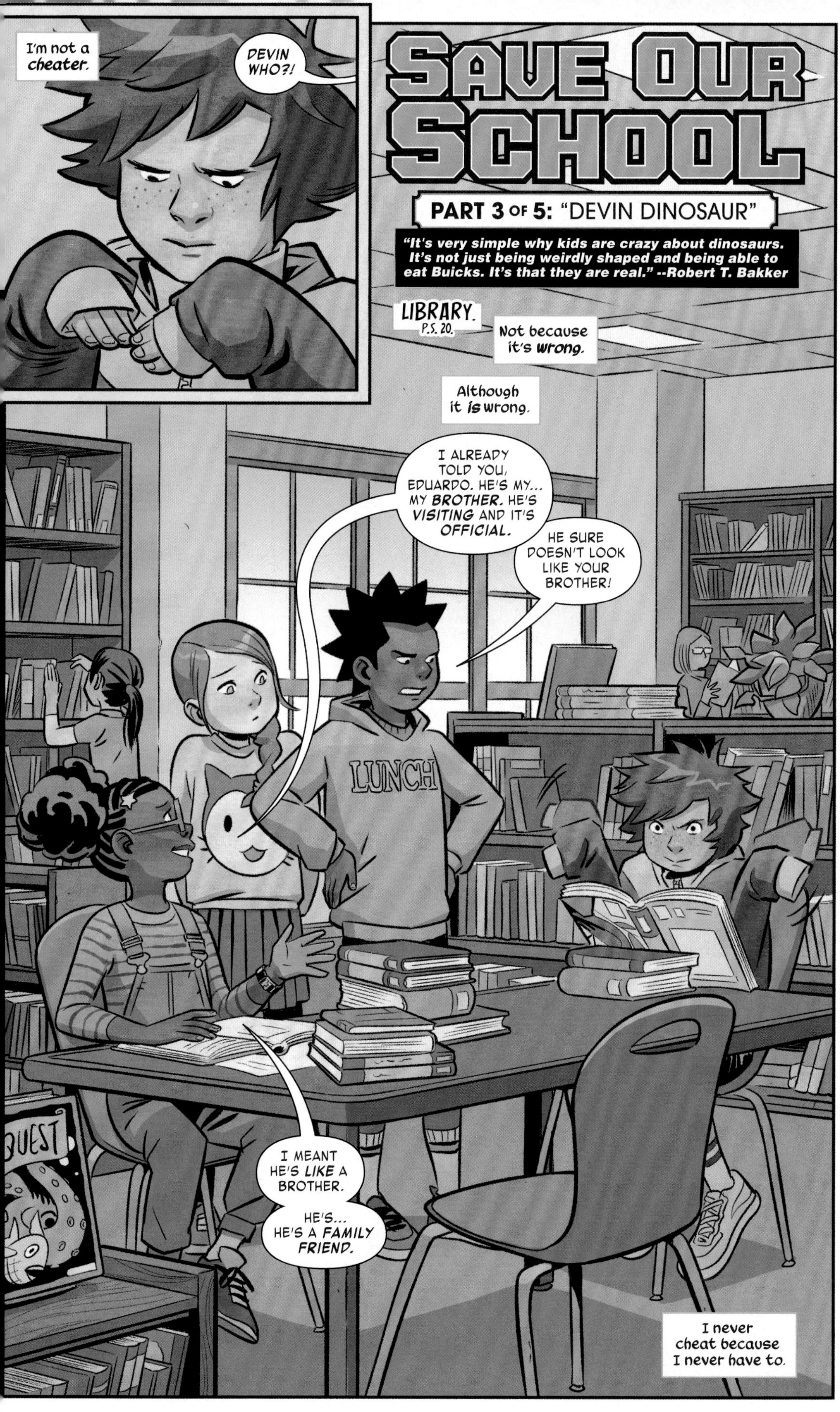

I'm not a cheater.
DEVIN WHO?!
SAVE OUR SCHOOL
PART 3 OF 5: "DEVIN DINOSAUR"
"It's very simple why kids are crazy about dinosaurs. It's not just being weirdly shaped and being able to eat Buicks. It's that they are real." --Robert T. Bakker
LIBRARY. P.S. 20.
Not because it's wrong.
Although it is wrong.
I ALREADY TOLD YOU, EDUARDO. HE'S MY... MY BROTHER. HE'S VISITING AND IT'S OFFICIAL.
HE SURE DOESN'T LOOK LIKE YOUR BROTHER!
LUNCH
I MEANT HE'S LIKE A BROTHER.
HE'S... HE'S A FAMILY FRIEND.
QUEST
I never cheat because I never have to.

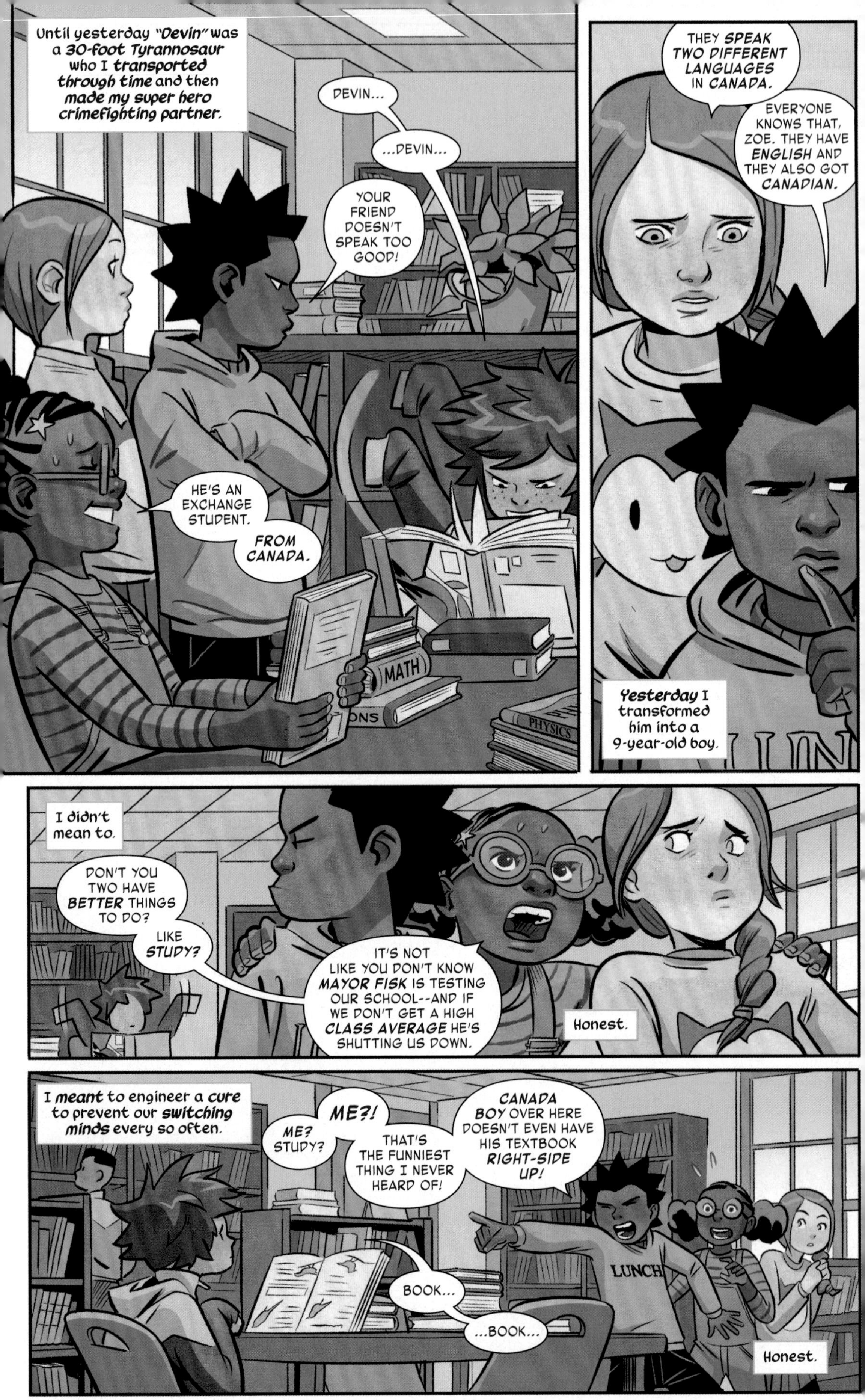

Until yesterday "Devin" was a 30-foot Tyrannosaur who I transported through time and then made my super hero crimefighting partner.
DEVIN...
...DEVIN...
YOUR FRIEND DOESN'T SPEAK TOO GOOD!
HE'S AN EXCHANGE STUDENT.
FROM CANADA.
MATH
ONS
PHYSICS
THEY SPEAK TWO DIFFERENT LANGUAGES IN CANADA.
EVERYONE KNOWS THAT, ZOE. THEY HAVE ENGLISH AND THEY ALSO GOT CANADIAN.
Yesterday I transformed him into a 9-year-old boy.
I didn't mean to.
DON'T YOU TWO HAVE BETTER THINGS TO DO?
LIKE STUDY?
IT'S NOT LIKE YOU DON'T KNOW MAYOR FISK IS TESTING OUR SCHOOL--AND IF WE DON'T GET A HIGH CLASS AVERAGE HE'S SHUTTING US DOWN.
Honest.
I meant to engineer a cure to prevent our switching minds every so often.
ME? STUDY?
ME?!
THAT'S THE FUNNIEST THING I NEVER HEARD OF!
CANADA BOY OVER HERE DOESN'T EVEN HAVE HIS TEXTBOOK RIGHT-SIDE UP!
LUNCH
BOOK...
...BOOK...
Honest.

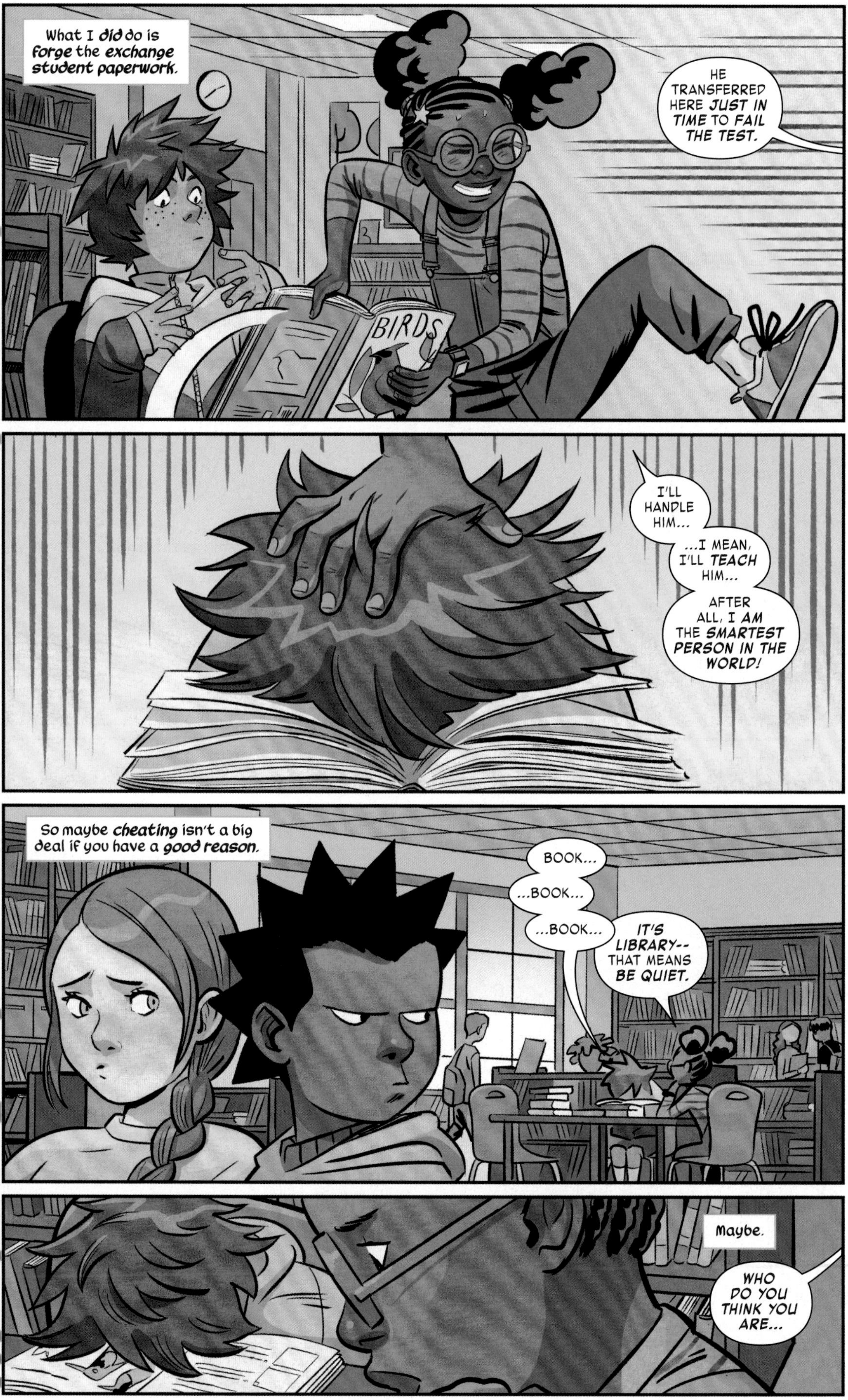
What I did do is forge the exchange student paperwork.
HE TRANSFERRED HERE JUST IN TIME TO FAIL THE TEST.
BIRDS
I'LL HANDLE HIM...
...I MEAN, I'LL TEACH HIM...
AFTER ALL, I AM THE SMARTEST PERSON IN THE WORLD!
So maybe cheating isn't a big deal if you have a good reason.
BOOK...
...BOOK...
...BOOK...
IT'S LIBRARY-- THAT MEANS BE QUIET.
Maybe.
WHO DO YOU THINK YOU ARE...

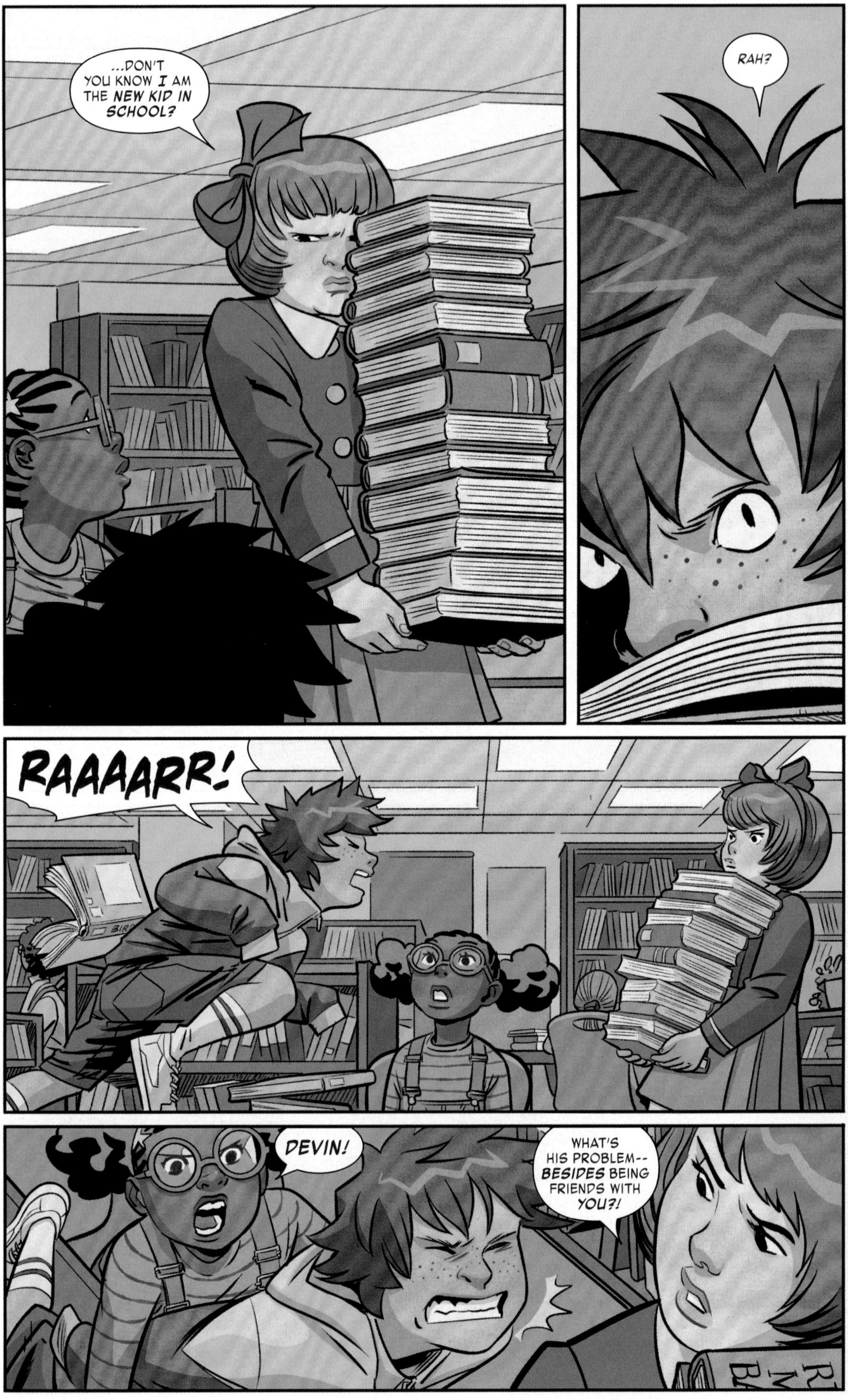
...DON'T YOU KNOW I AM THE NEW KID IN SCHOOL?
RAH?
RAAAARR!
BIRD
DEVIN!
WHAT'S HIS PROBLEM-- BESIDES BEING FRIENDS WITH YOU?!

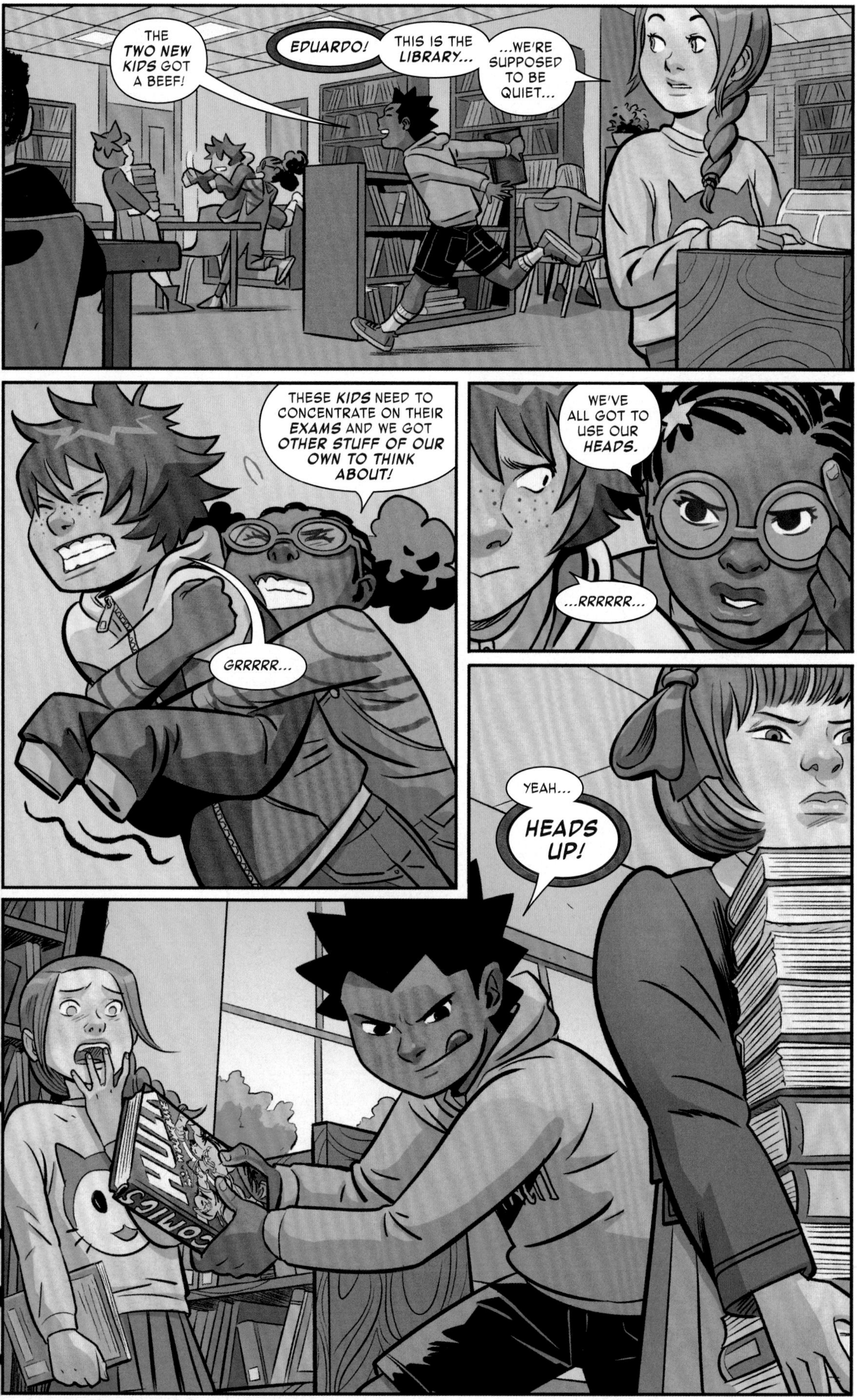
THE TWO NEW KIDS GOT A BEEF!
EDUARDO!
THIS IS THE LIBRARY...
...WE'RE SUPPOSED TO BE QUIET...
THESE KIDS NEED TO CONCENTRATE ON THEIR EXAMS AND WE GOT OTHER STUFF OF OUR OWN TO THINK ABOUT!
GRRRRR...
WE'VE ALL GOT TO USE OUR HEADS.
...RRRRRR...
YEAH...
HEADS UP!
HULK
COMICS

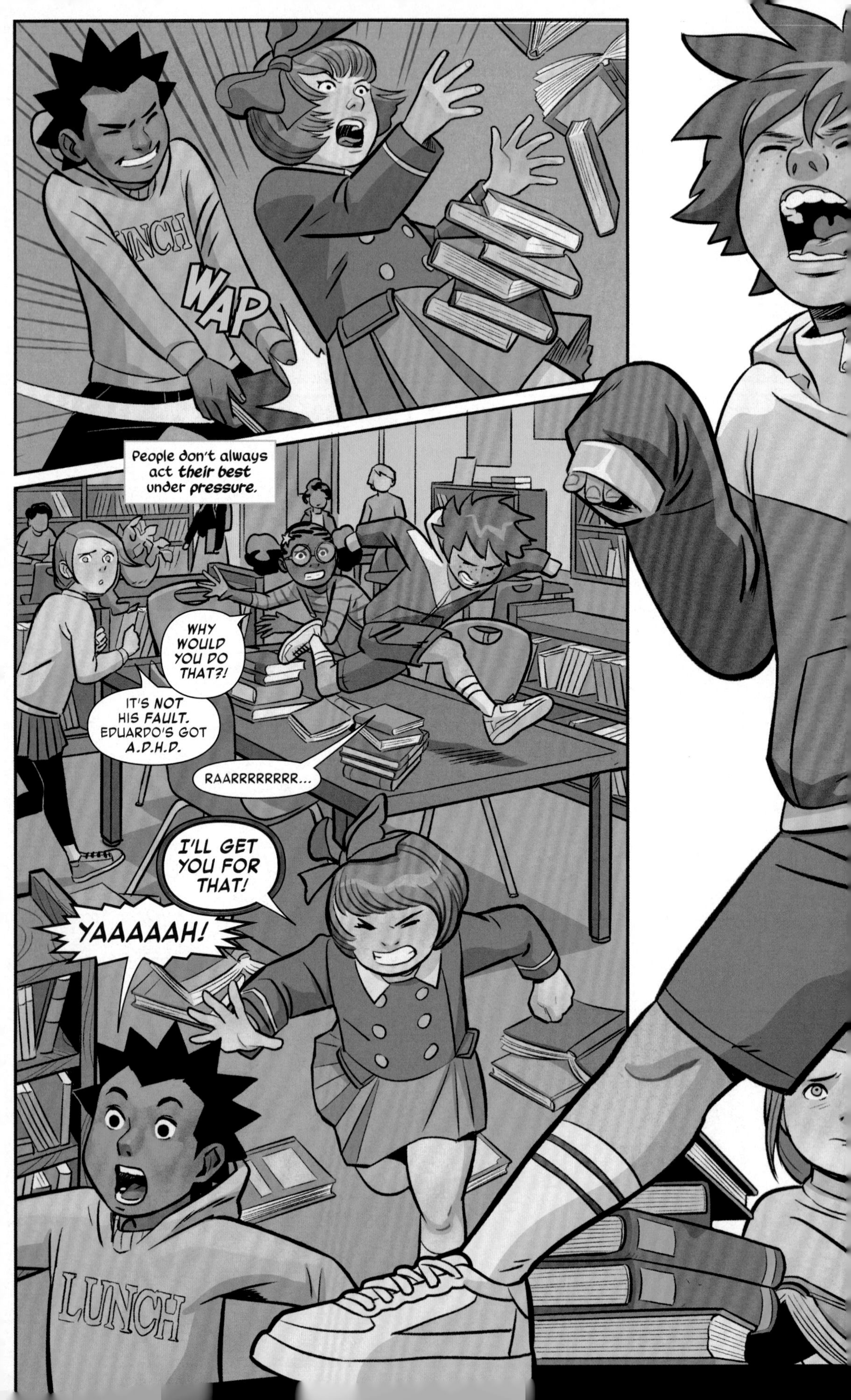
LUNCH
WAP
People don't always act *their best* under *pressure.*
WHY WOULD YOU DO THAT?!
IT'S NOT HIS FAULT. EDUARDO'S GOT A.D.H.D.
RAARRRRRRRR...
I'LL GET YOU FOR THAT!
YAAAAAH!
LUNCH

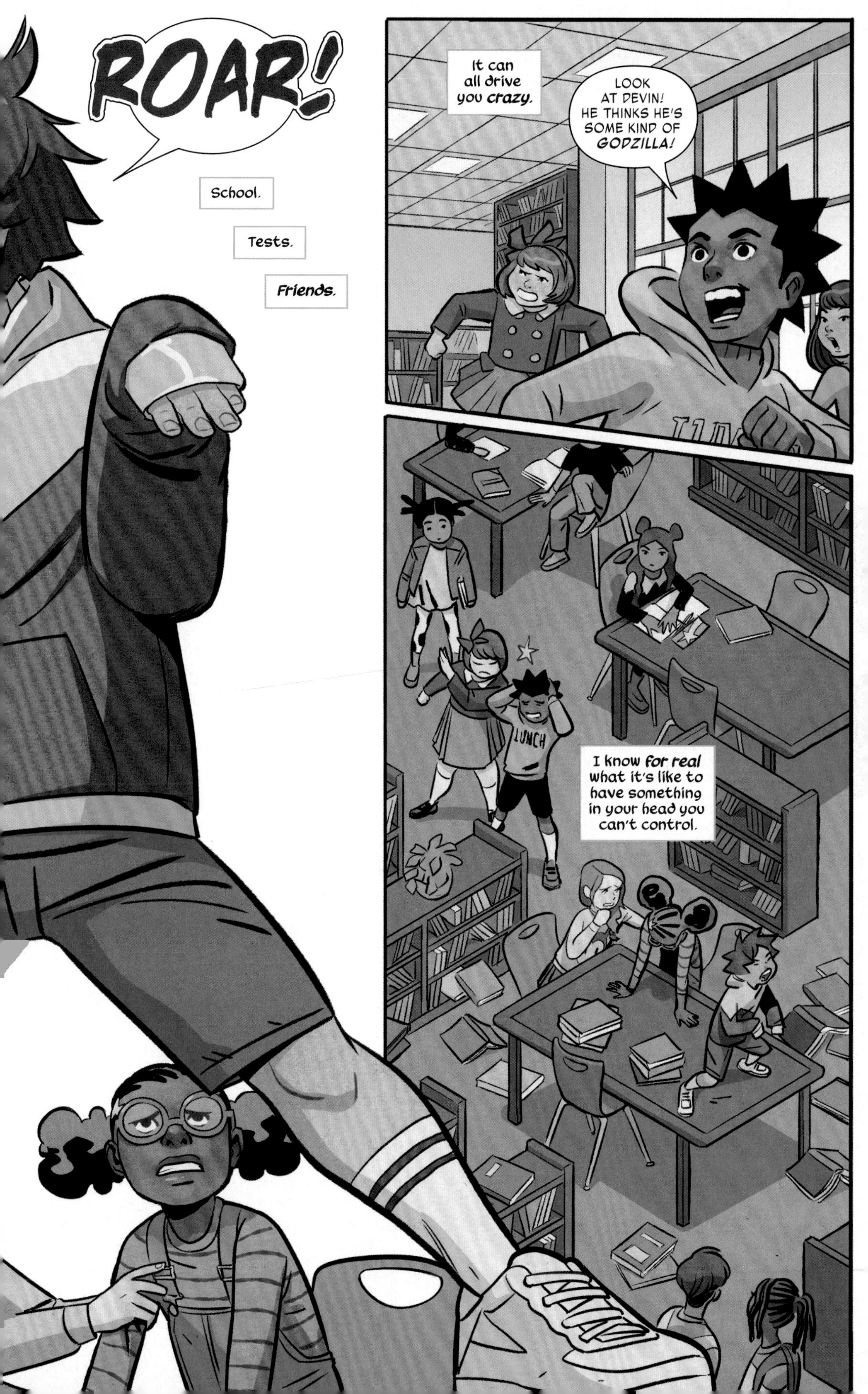
ROAR!
School.
Tests.
Friends.
It can all drive you crazy.
LOOK AT DEVIN! HE THINKS HE'S SOME KIND OF GODZILLA!
I know for real what it's like to have something in your head you can't control.
LUNCH

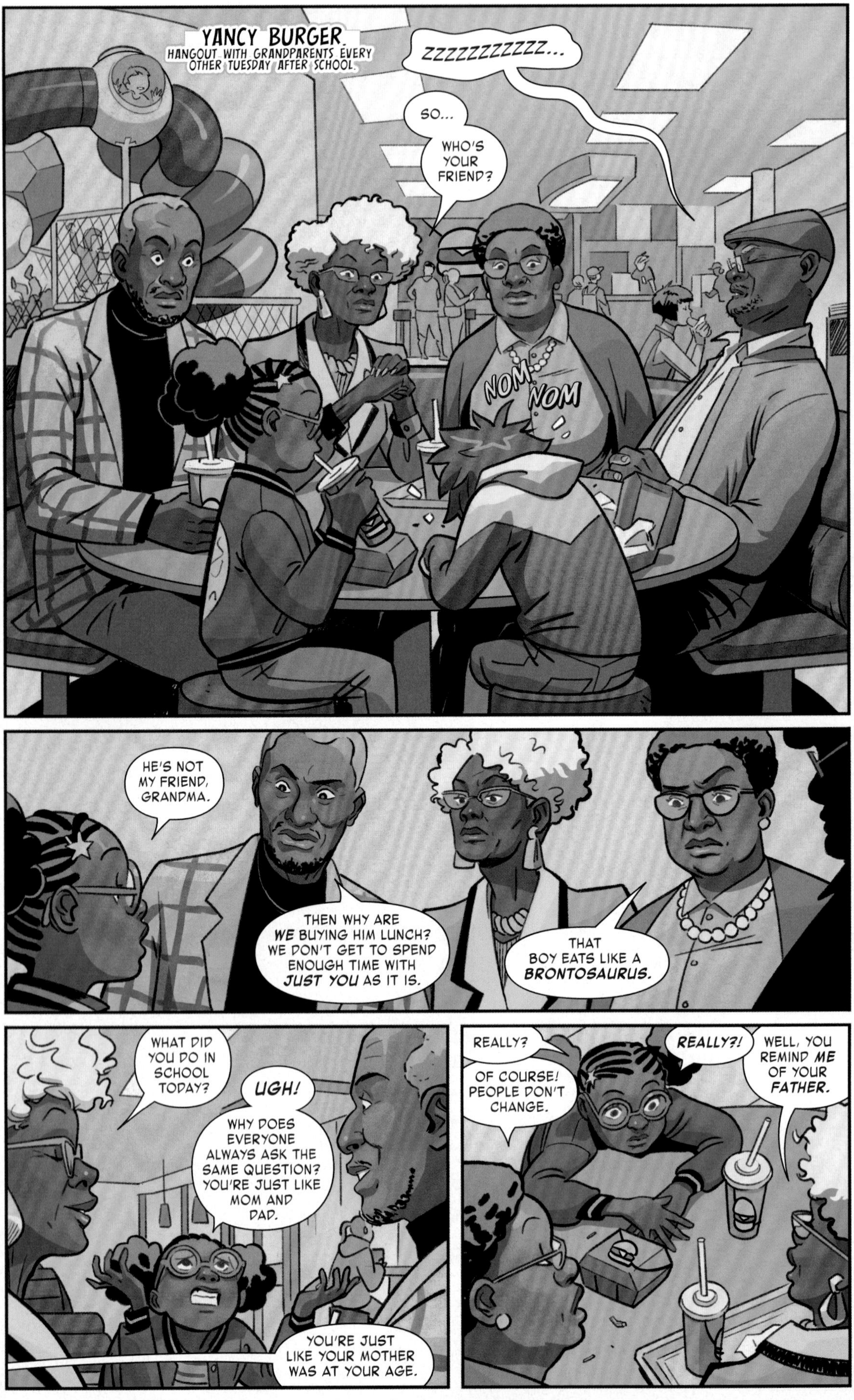

YANCY BURGER.
HANGOUT WITH GRANDPARENTS EVERY OTHER TUESDAY AFTER SCHOOL.
ZZZZZZZZZZZ...
SO...
WHO'S YOUR FRIEND?
NOM NOM
HE'S NOT MY FRIEND, GRANDMA.
THEN WHY ARE WE BUYING HIM LUNCH? WE DON'T GET TO SPEND ENOUGH TIME WITH JUST YOU AS IT IS.
THAT BOY EATS LIKE A BRONTOSAURUS.
WHAT DID YOU DO IN SCHOOL TODAY?
UGH!
WHY DOES EVERYONE ALWAYS ASK THE SAME QUESTION? YOU'RE JUST LIKE MOM AND DAD.
YOU'RE JUST LIKE YOUR MOTHER WAS AT YOUR AGE.
REALLY?
OF COURSE! PEOPLE DON'T CHANGE.
REALLY?!
WELL, YOU REMIND ME OF YOUR FATHER.

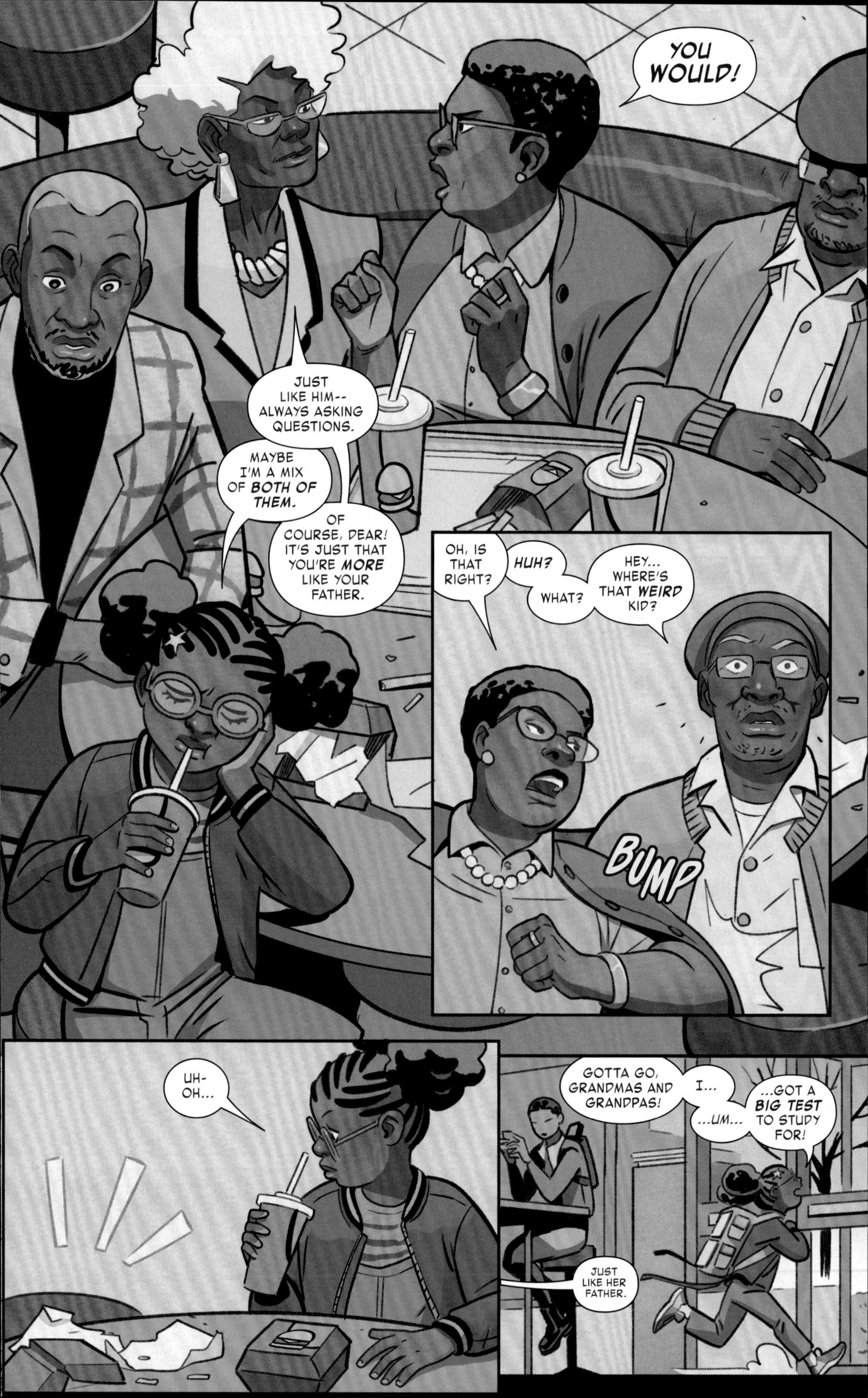
YOU WOULD!
JUST LIKE HIM-- ALWAYS ASKING QUESTIONS.
MAYBE I'M A MIX OF BOTH OF THEM.
OF COURSE, DEAR! IT'S JUST THAT YOU'RE MORE LIKE YOUR FATHER.
OH, IS THAT RIGHT?
HUH?
WHAT?
HEY... WHERE'S THAT WEIRD KID?
BUMP
UH-OH...
GOTTA GO, GRANDMAS AND GRANDPAS!
I...
...UM...
...GOT A BIG TEST TO STUDY FOR!
JUST LIKE HER FATHER.

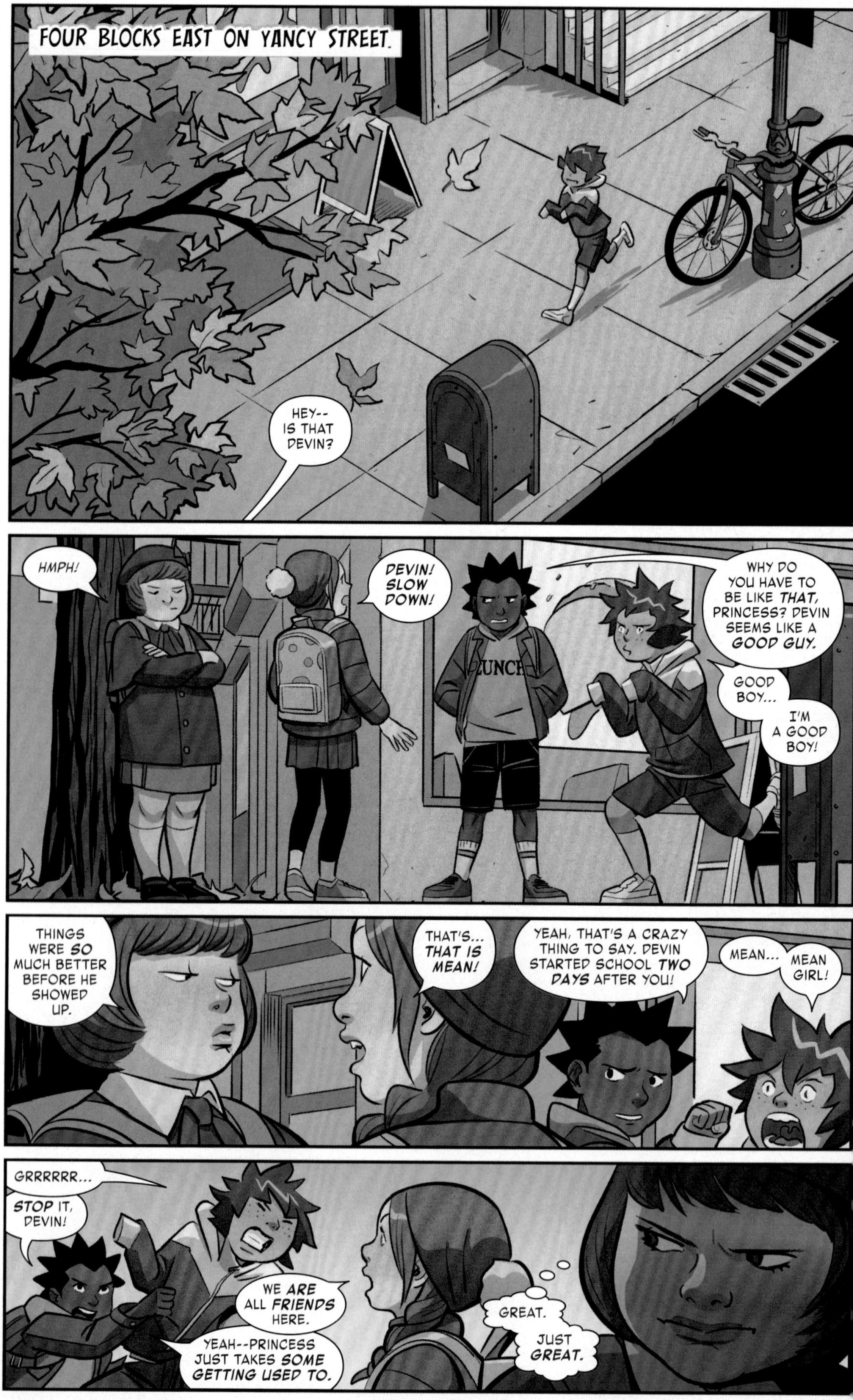
FOUR BLOCKS EAST ON YANCY STREET.
HEY-- IS THAT DEVIN?
HMPH!
DEVIN! SLOW DOWN!
WHY DO YOU HAVE TO BE LIKE THAT, PRINCESS? DEVIN SEEMS LIKE A GOOD GUY.
GOOD BOY...
I'M A GOOD BOY!
THINGS WERE SO MUCH BETTER BEFORE HE SHOWED UP.
THAT'S... THAT IS MEAN!
YEAH, THAT'S A CRAZY THING TO SAY. DEVIN STARTED SCHOOL TWO DAYS AFTER YOU!
MEAN...
MEAN GIRL!
GRRRRRR...
STOP IT, DEVIN!
WE ARE ALL FRIENDS HERE.
YEAH--PRINCESS JUST TAKES SOME GETTING USED TO.
GREAT.
JUST GREAT.

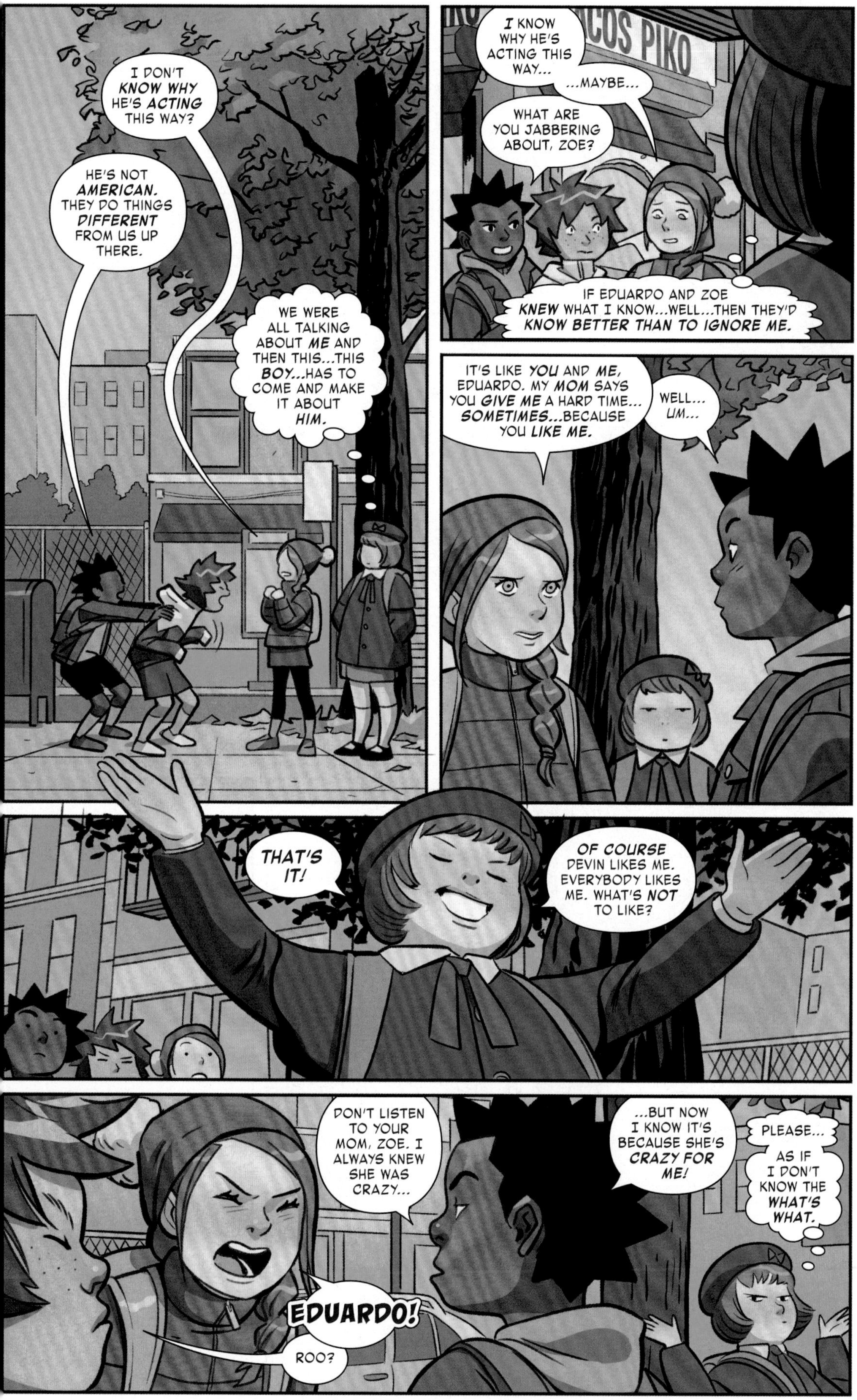
I DON'T KNOW WHY HE'S ACTING THIS WAY?
HE'S NOT AMERICAN. THEY DO THINGS DIFFERENT FROM US UP THERE.
WE WERE ALL TALKING ABOUT ME AND THEN THIS...THIS BOY...HAS TO COME AND MAKE IT ABOUT HIM.
ACOS PIKO
I KNOW WHY HE'S ACTING THIS WAY...
...MAYBE...
WHAT ARE YOU JABBERING ABOUT, ZOE?
IF EDUARDO AND ZOE KNEW WHAT I KNOW...WELL...THEN THEY'D KNOW BETTER THAN TO IGNORE ME.
IT'S LIKE YOU AND ME, EDUARDO. MY MOM SAYS YOU GIVE ME A HARD TIME... SOMETIMES...BECAUSE YOU LIKE ME.
WELL... UM...
THAT'S IT!
OF COURSE DEVIN LIKES ME. EVERYBODY LIKES ME. WHAT'S NOT TO LIKE?
DON'T LISTEN TO YOUR MOM, ZOE. I ALWAYS KNEW SHE WAS CRAZY...
...BUT NOW I KNOW IT'S BECAUSE SHE'S CRAZY FOR ME!
PLEASE...
AS IF I DON'T KNOW THE WHAT'S WHAT.
EDUARDO!
ROO?

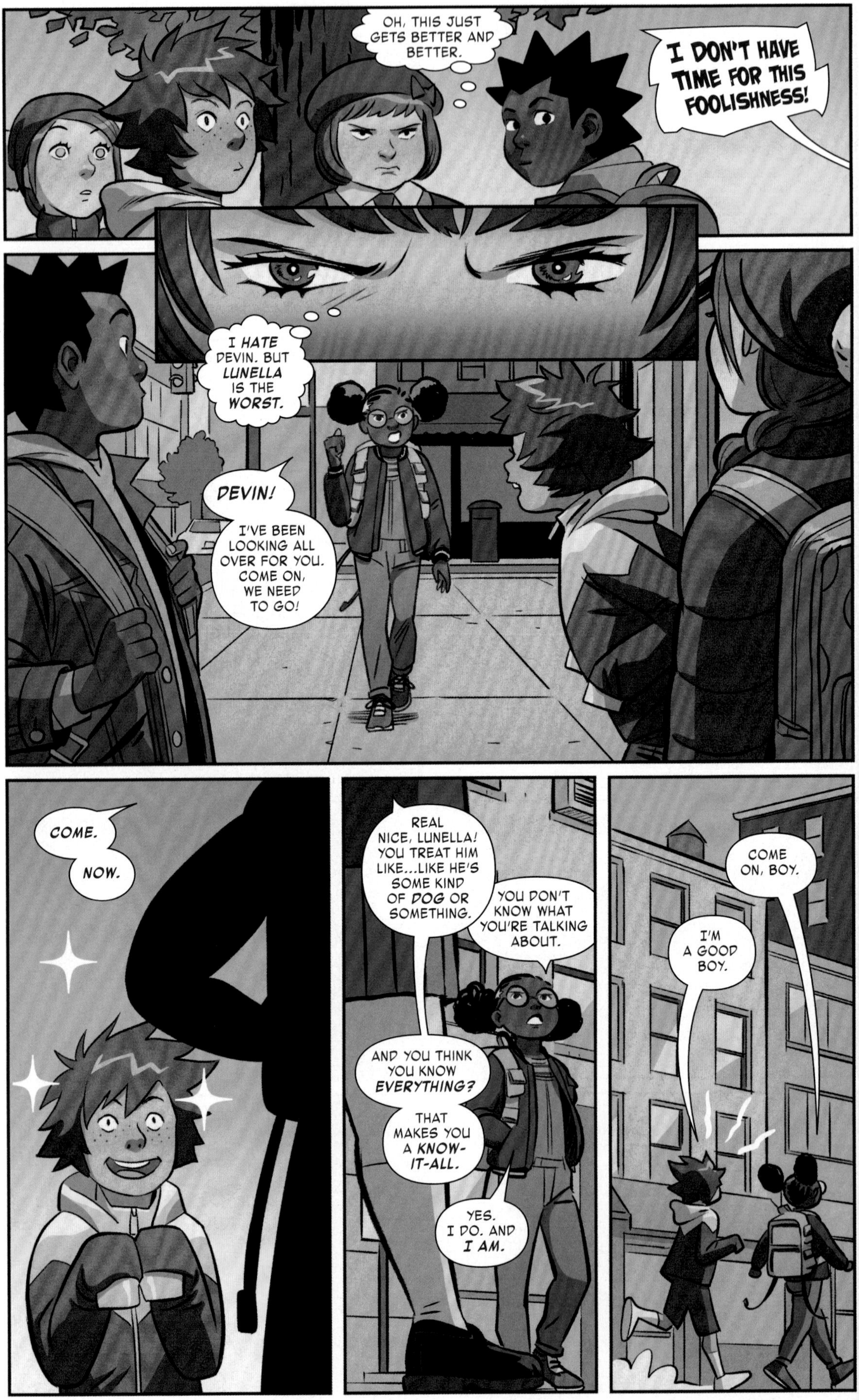
OH, THIS JUST GETS BETTER AND BETTER.
I DON'T HAVE TIME FOR THIS FOOLISHNESS!
I HATE DEVIN. BUT LUNELLA IS THE WORST.
DEVIN!
I'VE BEEN LOOKING ALL OVER FOR YOU. COME ON, WE NEED TO GO!
COME.
NOW.
REAL NICE, LUNELLA! YOU TREAT HIM LIKE...LIKE HE'S SOME KIND OF DOG OR SOMETHING.
YOU DON'T KNOW WHAT YOU'RE TALKING ABOUT.
AND YOU THINK YOU KNOW EVERYTHING?
THAT MAKES YOU A KNOW-IT-ALL.
YES. I DO. AND I AM.
COME ON, BOY.
I'M A GOOD BOY.

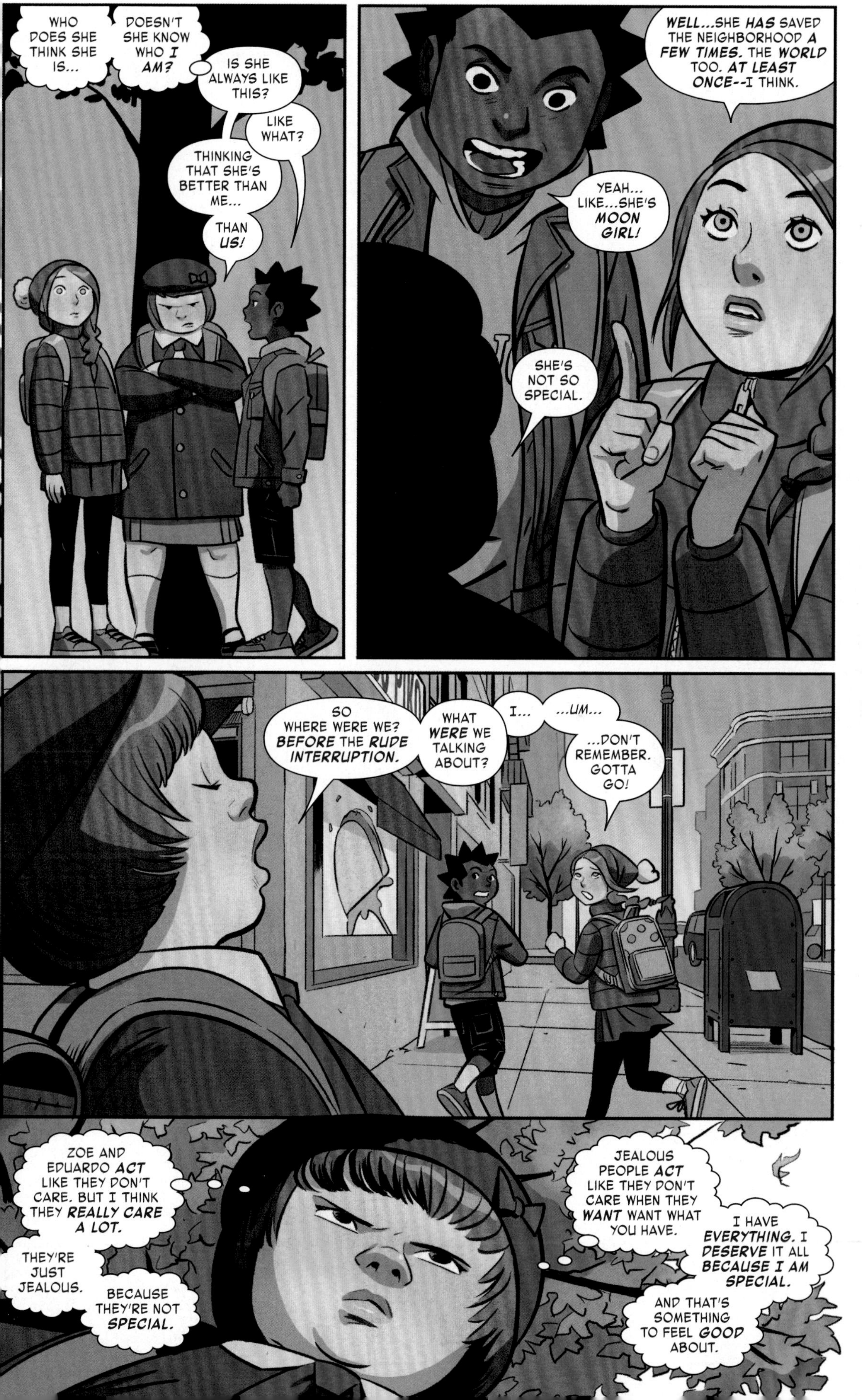
WHO DOES SHE THINK SHE IS...
DOESN'T SHE KNOW WHO *I AM?*
IS SHE ALWAYS LIKE THIS?
LIKE WHAT?
THINKING THAT SHE'S BETTER THAN ME...
THAN *US!*
*WELL...*SHE *HAS* SAVED THE NEIGHBORHOOD *A FEW TIMES.* THE *WORLD* TOO. *AT LEAST ONCE*--I THINK.
YEAH... LIKE...SHE'S *MOON GIRL!*
SHE'S NOT SO SPECIAL.
SO WHERE WERE WE? *BEFORE* THE *RUDE INTERRUPTION.*
WHAT *WERE* WE TALKING ABOUT?
I...
...UM...
...DON'T REMEMBER. GOTTA GO!
ZOE AND EDUARDO *ACT* LIKE THEY DON'T CARE. BUT I THINK THEY *REALLY CARE A LOT.*
THEY'RE JUST JEALOUS.
BECAUSE THEY'RE NOT *SPECIAL.*
JEALOUS PEOPLE *ACT* LIKE THEY DON'T CARE WHEN THEY *WANT* WANT WHAT YOU HAVE.
I HAVE *EVERYTHING.* I *DESERVE* IT ALL *BECAUSE I AM SPECIAL.*
AND THAT'S SOMETHING TO FEEL *GOOD* ABOUT.

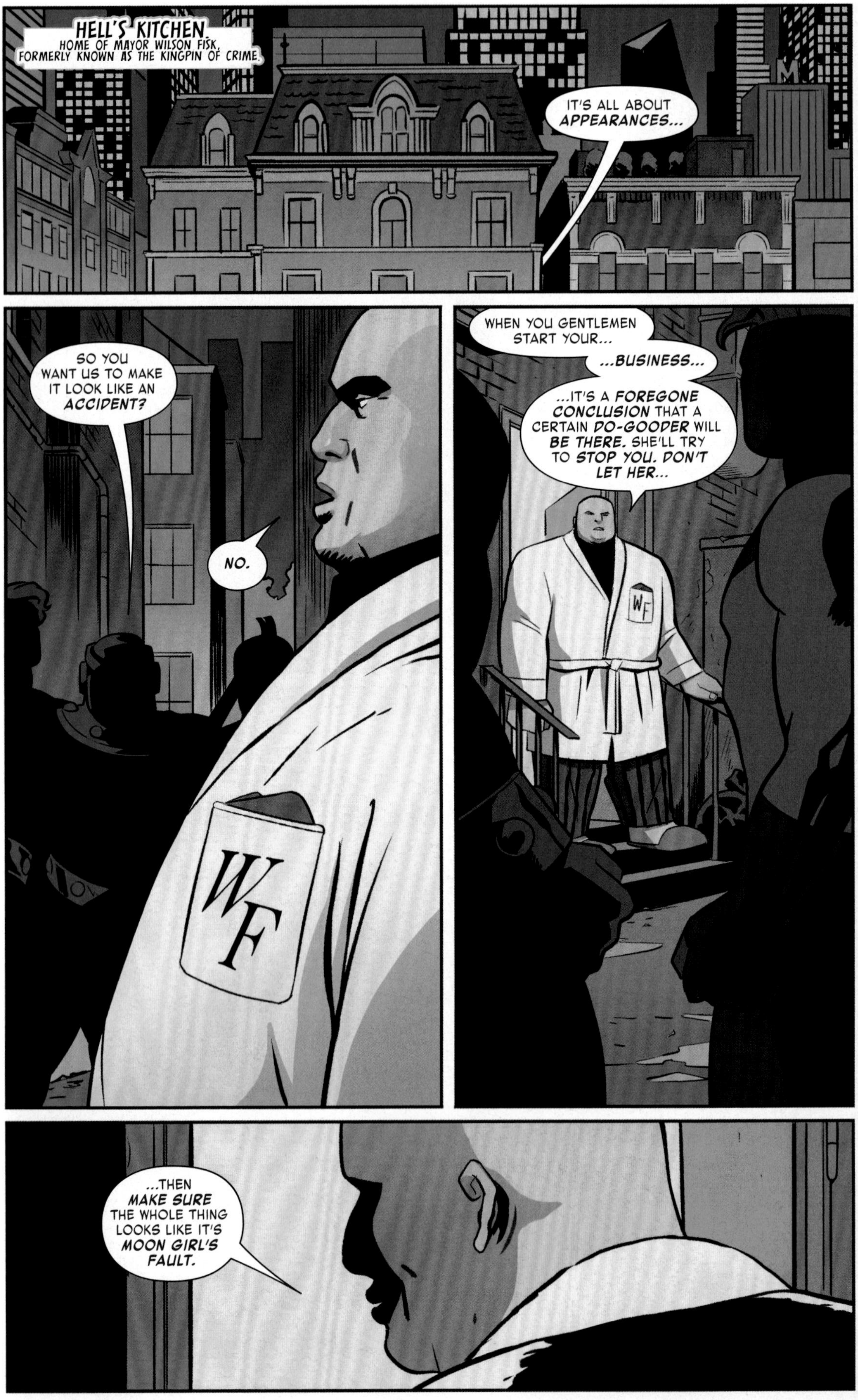
HELL'S KITCHEN.
HOME OF MAYOR WILSON FISK, FORMERLY KNOWN AS THE KINGPIN OF CRIME.
IT'S ALL ABOUT APPEARANCES...
SO YOU WANT US TO MAKE IT LOOK LIKE AN ACCIDENT?
NO.
WF
WHEN YOU GENTLEMEN START YOUR...
...BUSINESS...
...IT'S A FOREGONE CONCLUSION THAT A CERTAIN DO-GOODER WILL BE THERE. SHE'LL TRY TO STOP YOU. DON'T LET HER...
WF
...THEN MAKE SURE THE WHOLE THING LOOKS LIKE IT'S MOON GIRL'S FAULT.

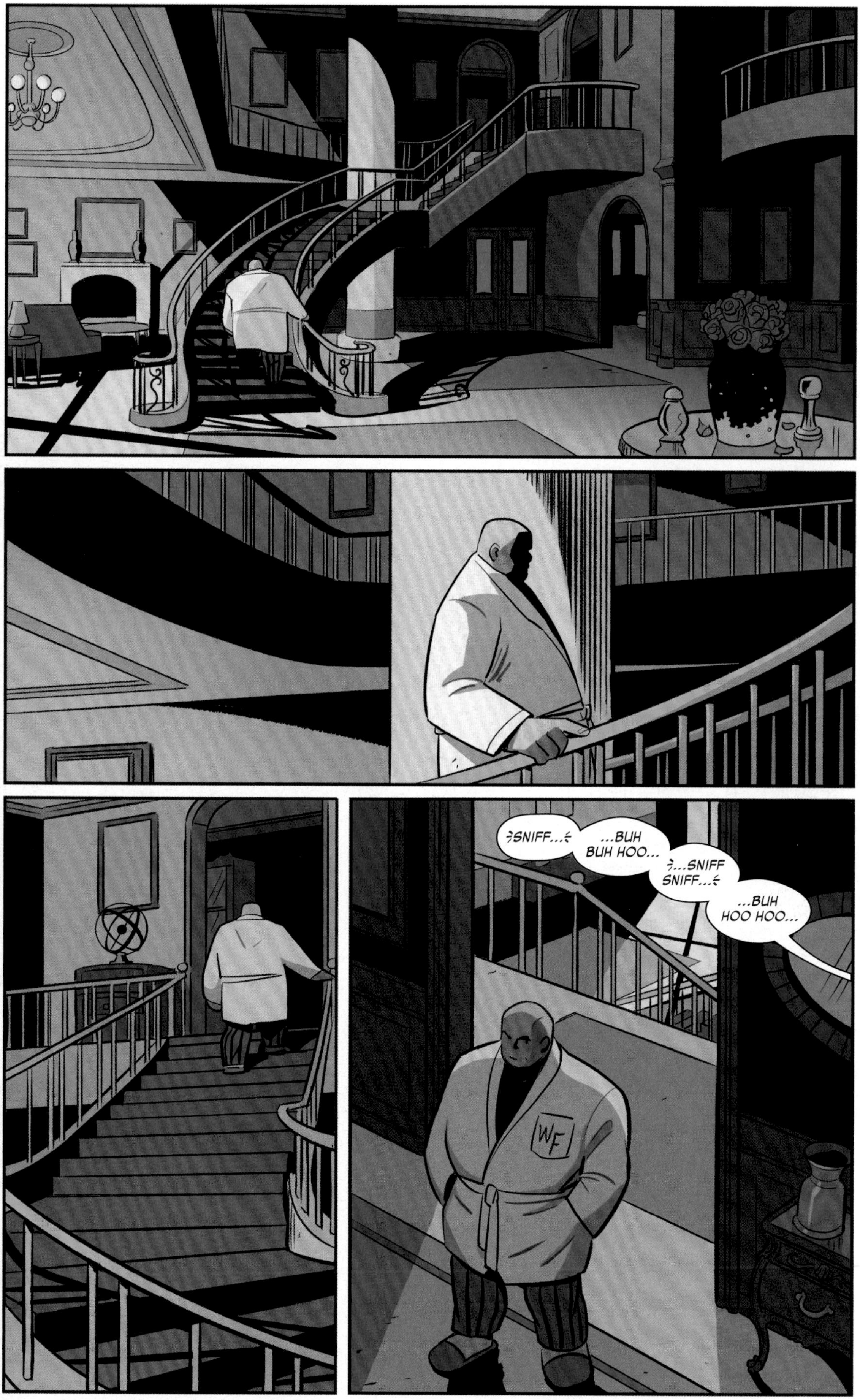
SNIFF...
...BUH BUH HOO...
...SNIFF SNIFF...
...BUH HOO HOO...
WF

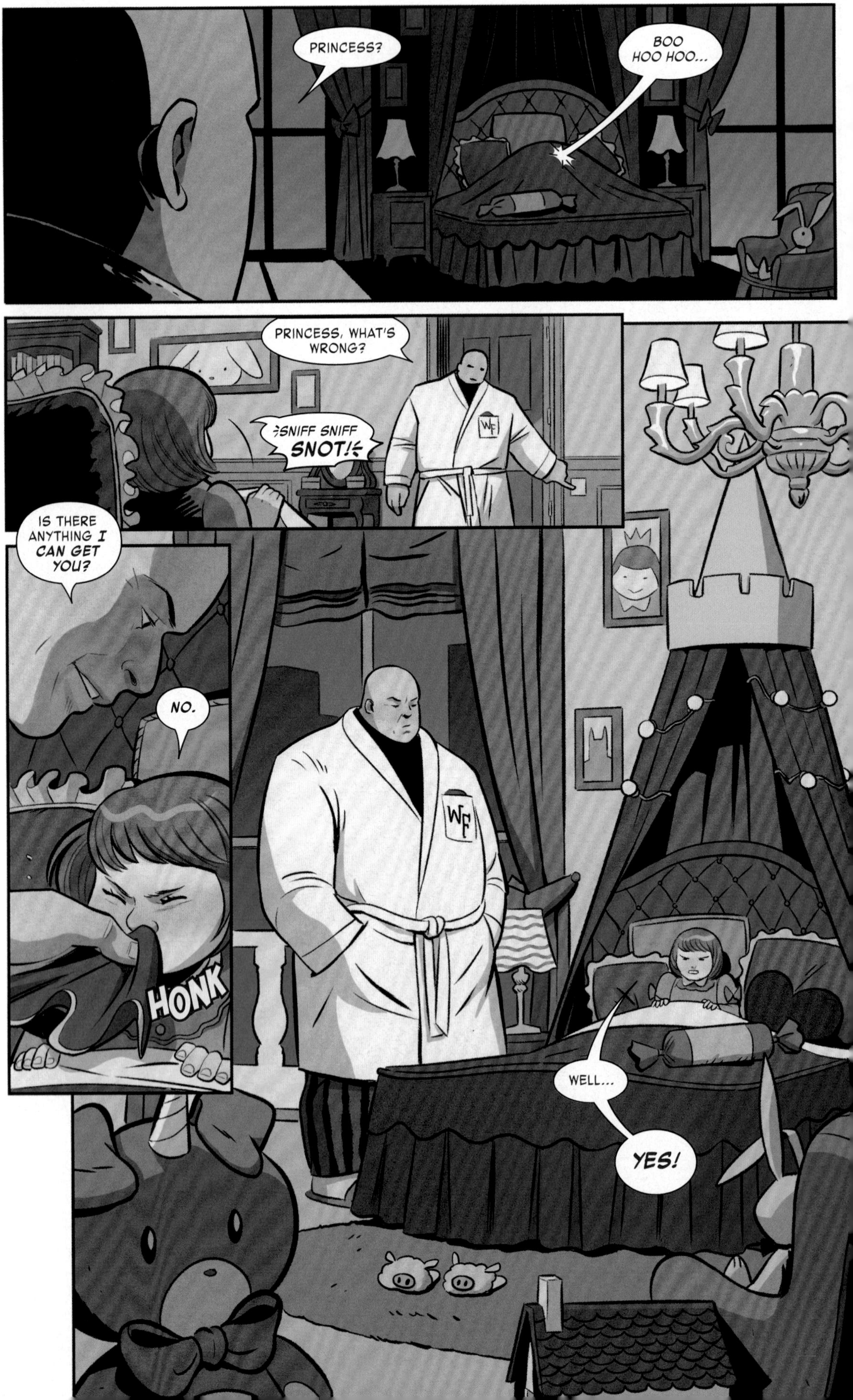
PRINCESS?
BOO HOO HOO...
PRINCESS, WHAT'S WRONG?
SNIFF SNIFF SNOT!
IS THERE ANYTHING I CAN GET YOU?
NO.
HONK
WELL...
YES!

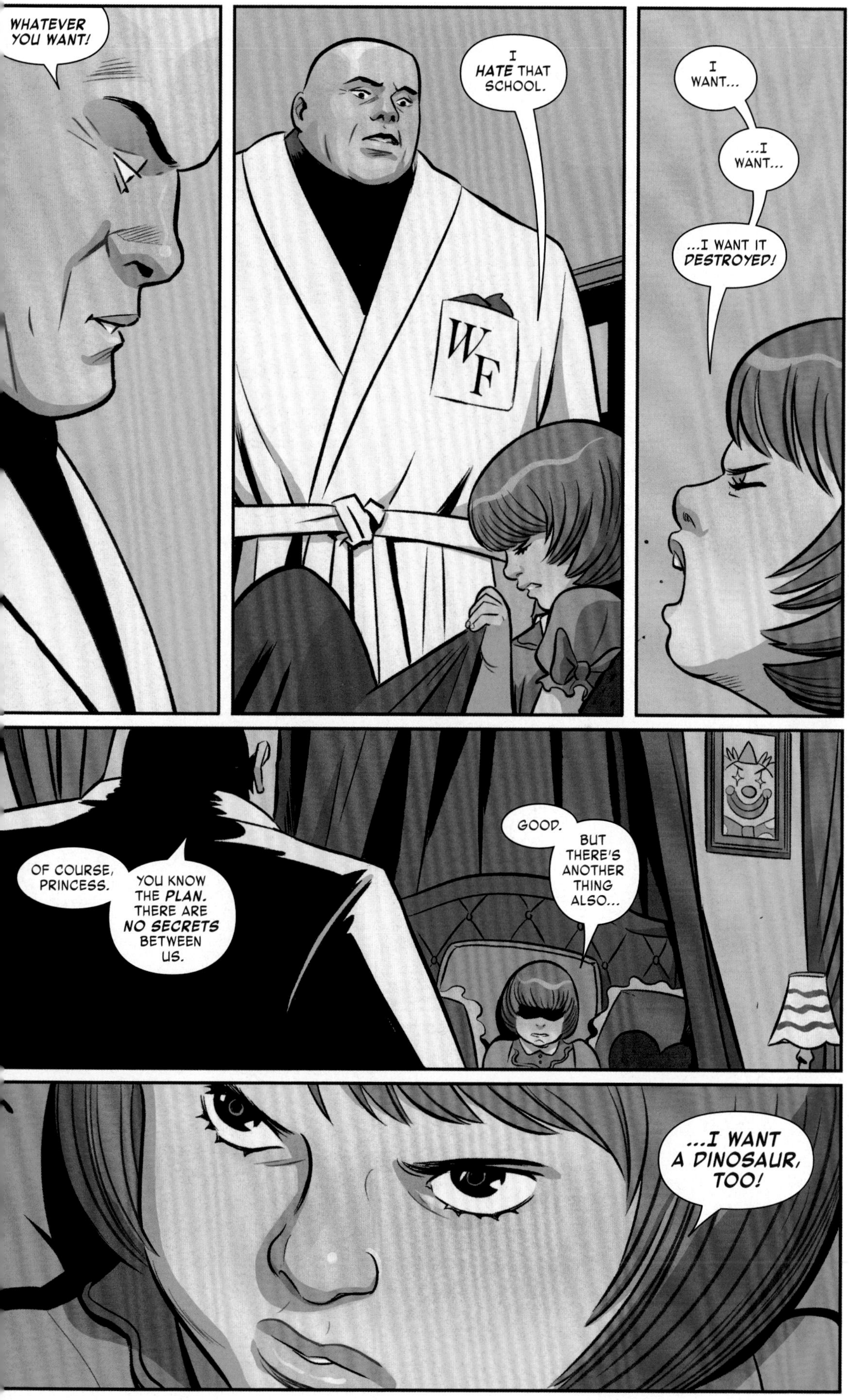

WHATEVER YOU WANT!
I HATE THAT SCHOOL.
I WANT...
...I WANT...
...I WANT IT DESTROYED!
OF COURSE, PRINCESS.
YOU KNOW THE PLAN. THERE ARE NO SECRETS BETWEEN US.
GOOD.
BUT THERE'S ANOTHER THING ALSO...
...I WANT A DINOSAUR, TOO!

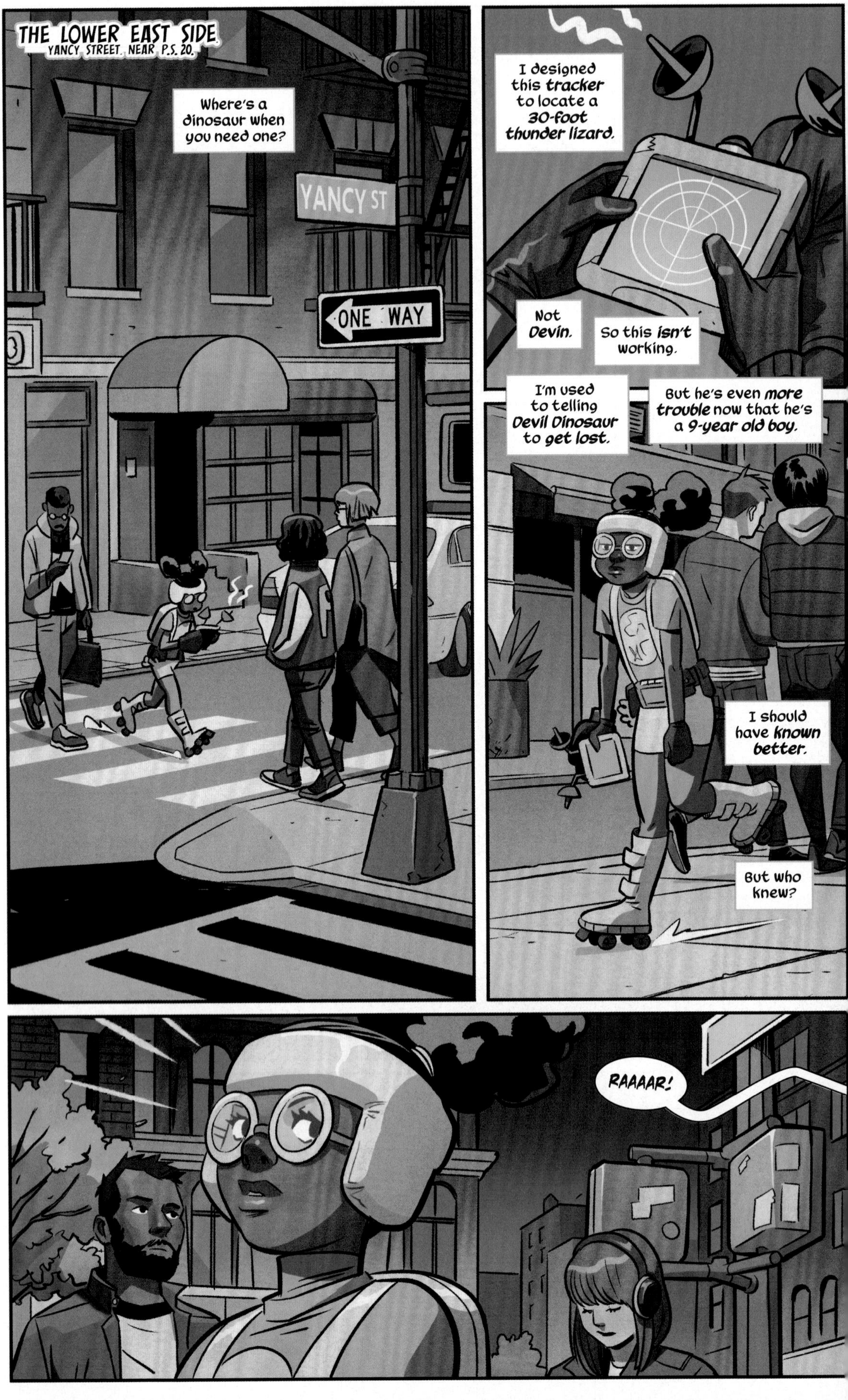
THE LOWER EAST SIDE.
YANCY STREET. NEAR P.S. 20.
Where's a dinosaur when you need one?
YANCY ST
ONE WAY
I designed this tracker to locate a 30-foot thunder lizard.
Not Devin.
So this isn't working.
I'm used to telling Devil Dinosaur to get lost.
But he's even more trouble now that he's a 9-year old boy.
I should have known better.
But who knew?
RAAAAR!

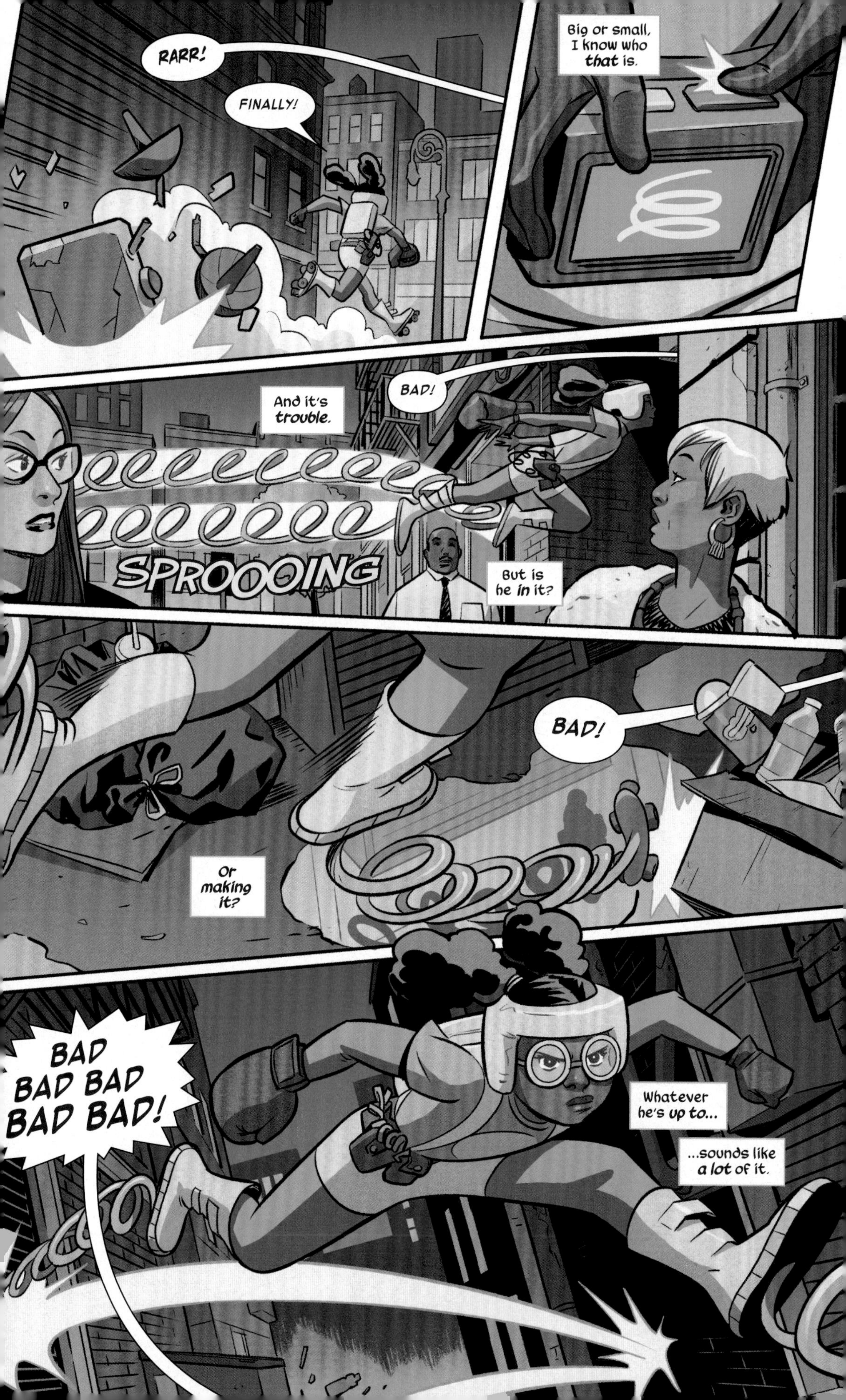

RARR!
FINALLY!
Big or small, I know who that is.
And it's trouble.
BAD!
SPROOOING
But is he in it?
BAD!
Or making it?
BAD BAD BAD BAD BAD!
Whatever he's up to...
...sounds like a lot of it.

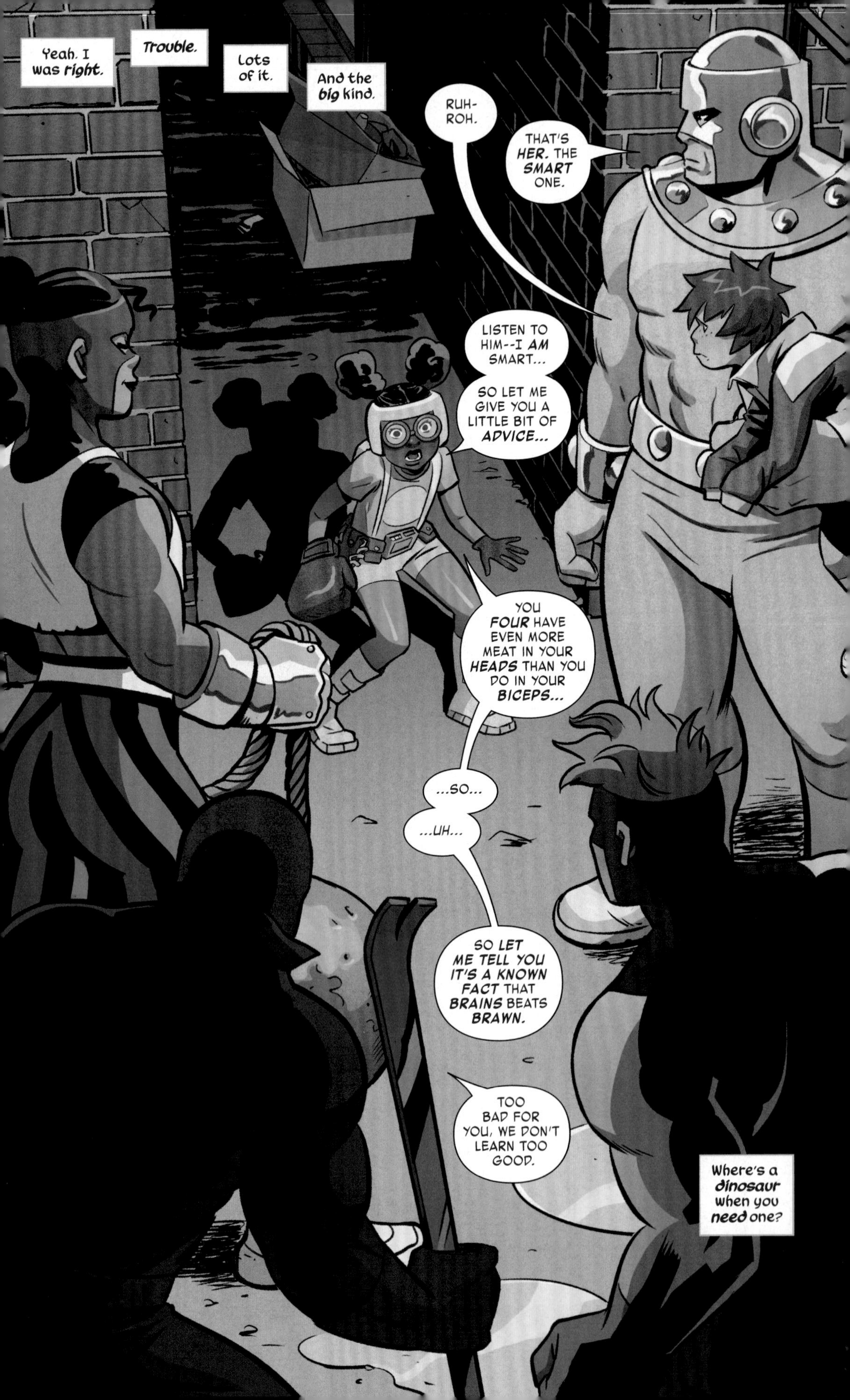
Yeah. I was right.
Trouble.
Lots of it.
And the big kind.
RUH-ROH.
THAT'S HER. THE SMART ONE.
LISTEN TO HIM--I AM SMART...
SO LET ME GIVE YOU A LITTLE BIT OF ADVICE...
YOU FOUR HAVE EVEN MORE MEAT IN YOUR HEADS THAN YOU DO IN YOUR BICEPS...
...SO...
...UH...
SO LET ME TELL YOU IT'S A KNOWN FACT THAT BRAINS BEATS BRAWN.
TOO BAD FOR YOU, WE DON'T LEARN TOO GOOD.
Where's a dinosaur when you need one?

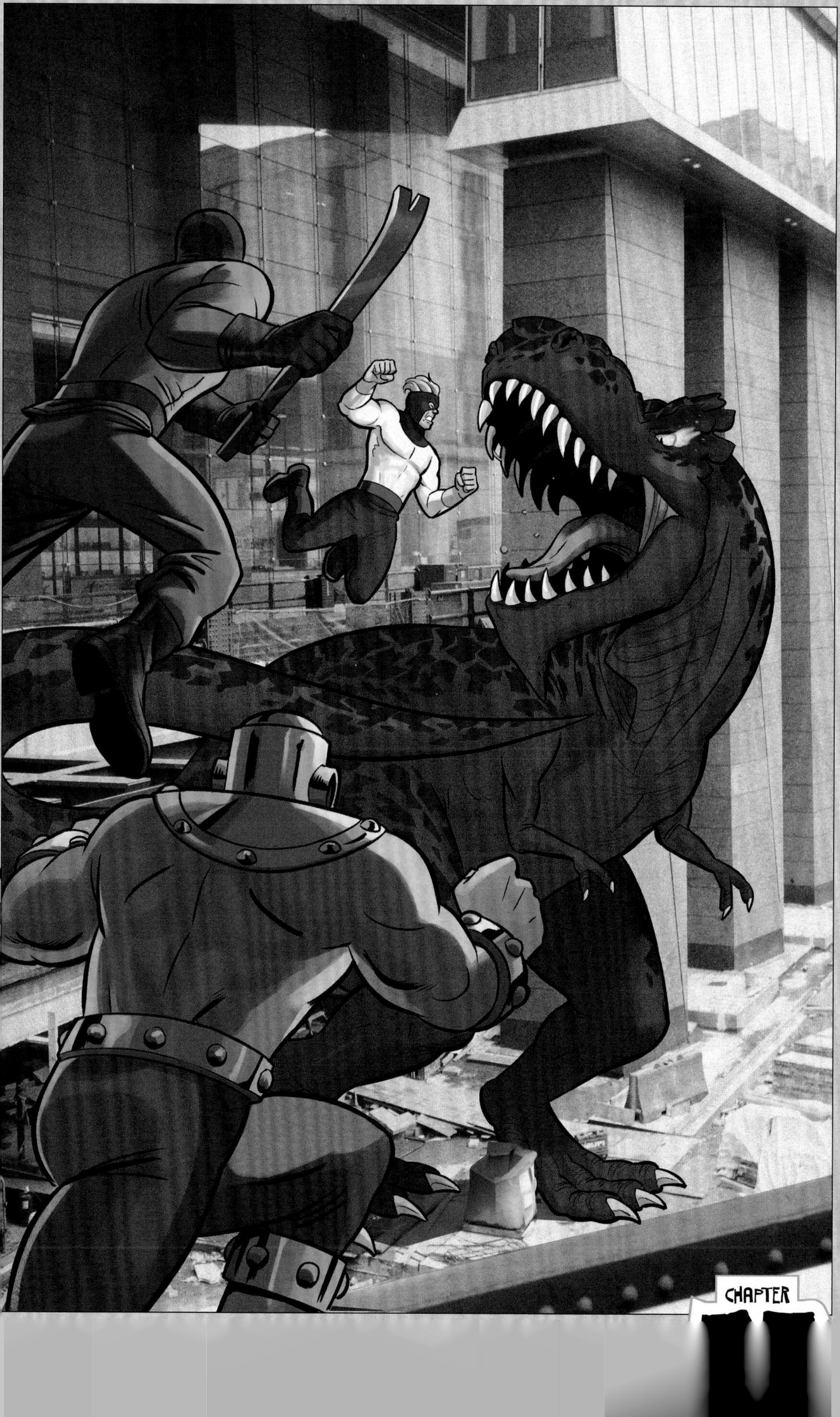
CHAPTER

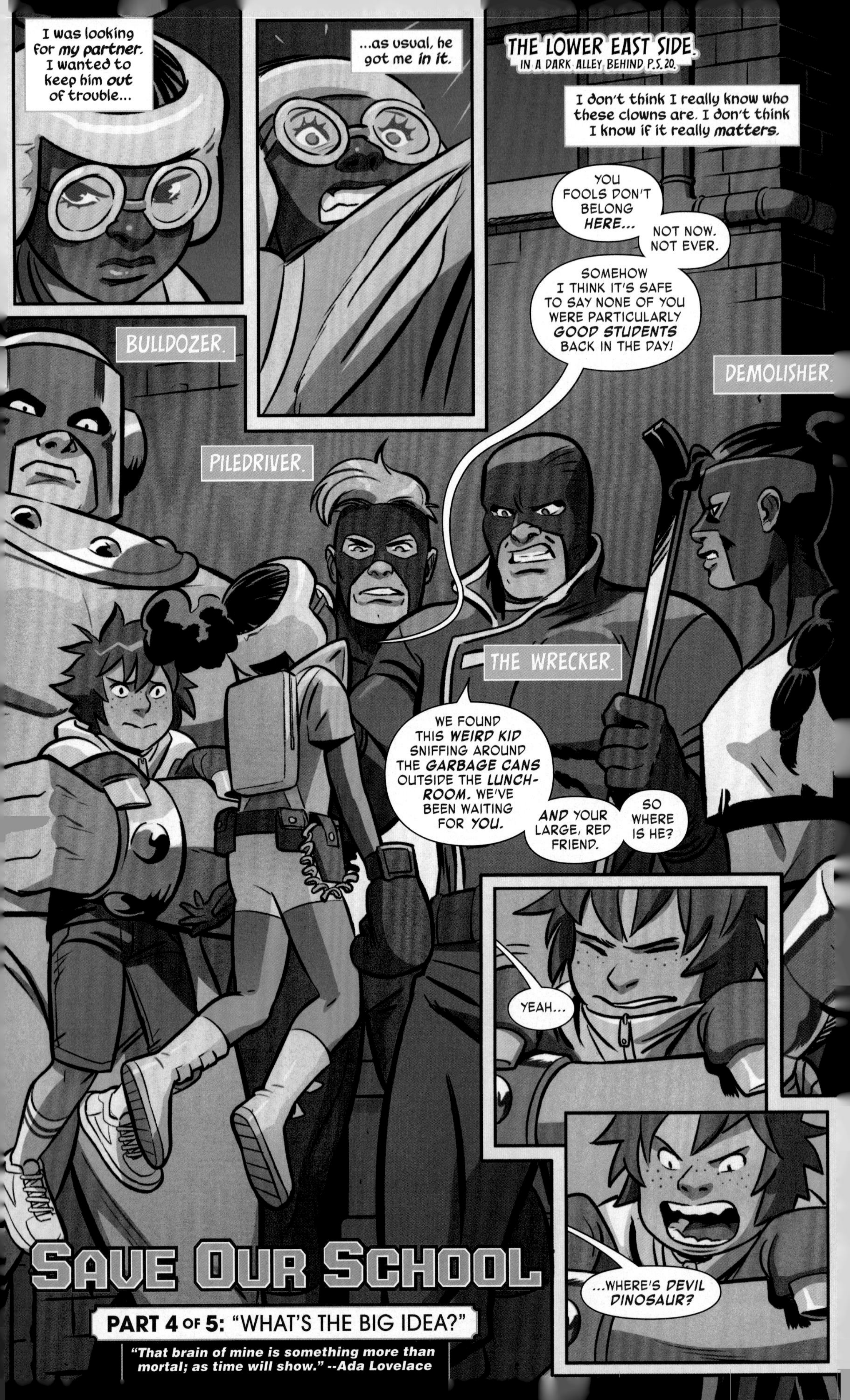
I was looking for my partner. I wanted to keep him out of trouble...
...as usual, he got me in it.
THE LOWER EAST SIDE.
IN A DARK ALLEY BEHIND P.S. 20.
I don't think I really know who these clowns are. I don't think I know if it really matters.
YOU FOOLS DON'T BELONG HERE...
NOT NOW. NOT EVER.
SOMEHOW I THINK IT'S SAFE TO SAY NONE OF YOU WERE PARTICULARLY GOOD STUDENTS BACK IN THE DAY!
BULLDOZER.
PILEDRIVER.
DEMOLISHER.
THE WRECKER.
WE FOUND THIS WEIRD KID SNIFFING AROUND THE GARBAGE CANS OUTSIDE THE LUNCHROOM. WE'VE BEEN WAITING FOR YOU.
AND YOUR LARGE, RED FRIEND.
SO WHERE IS HE?
YEAH...
...WHERE'S DEVIL DINOSAUR?
SAVE OUR SCHOOL
PART 4 OF 5: "WHAT'S THE BIG IDEA?"
"That brain of mine is something more than mortal; as time will show." --Ada Lovelace

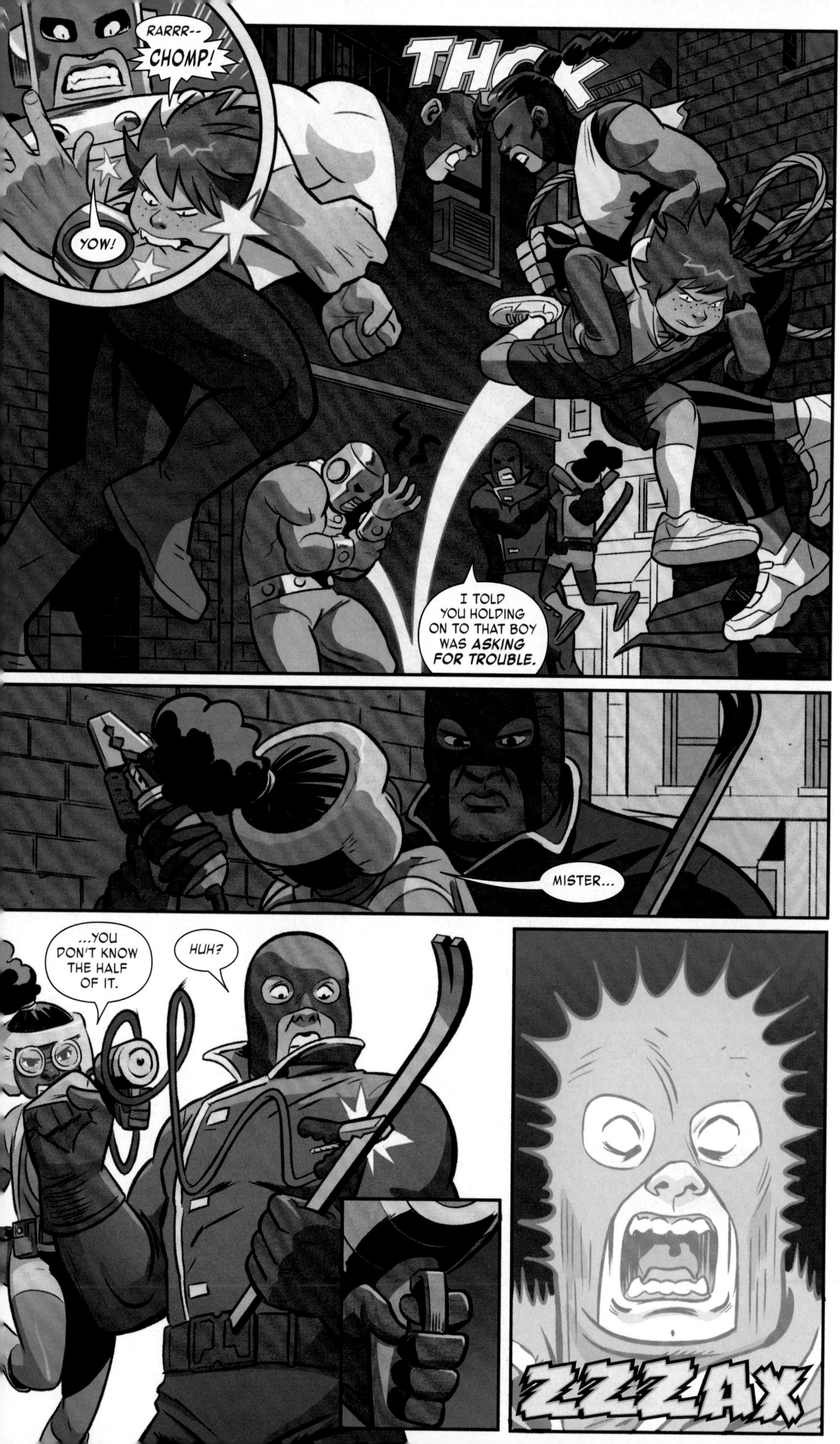

RARRR--
CHOMP!
THOK
YOW!
I TOLD YOU HOLDING ON TO THAT BOY WAS ASKING FOR TROUBLE.
MISTER...
...YOU DON'T KNOW THE HALF OF IT.
HUH?
ZZZZAX

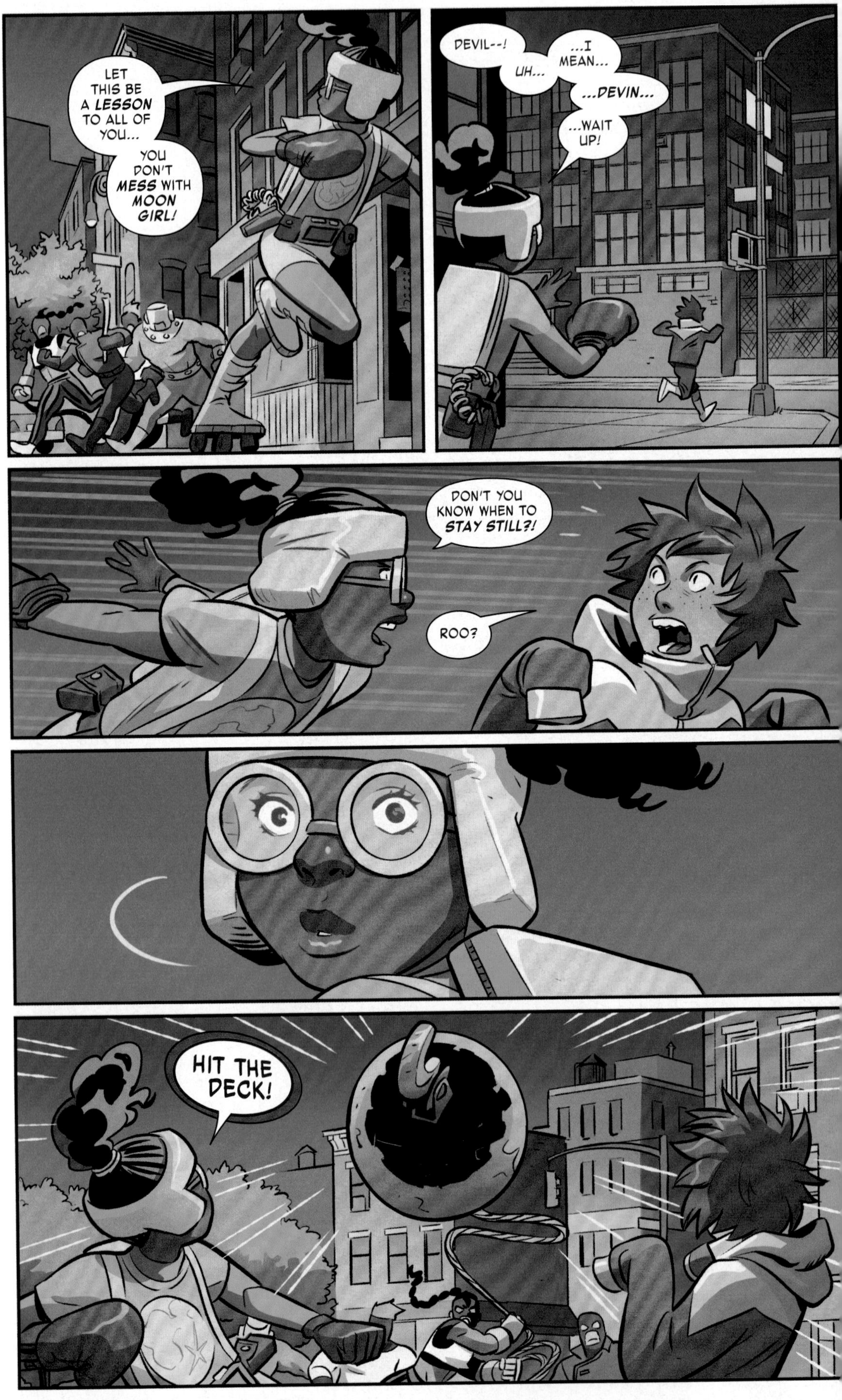

LET THIS BE A LESSON TO ALL OF YOU...
YOU DON'T MESS WITH MOON GIRL!
DEVIL--!
UH...
...I MEAN...
...DEVIN...
...WAIT UP!
DON'T YOU KNOW WHEN TO STAY STILL?!
ROO?
HIT THE DECK!

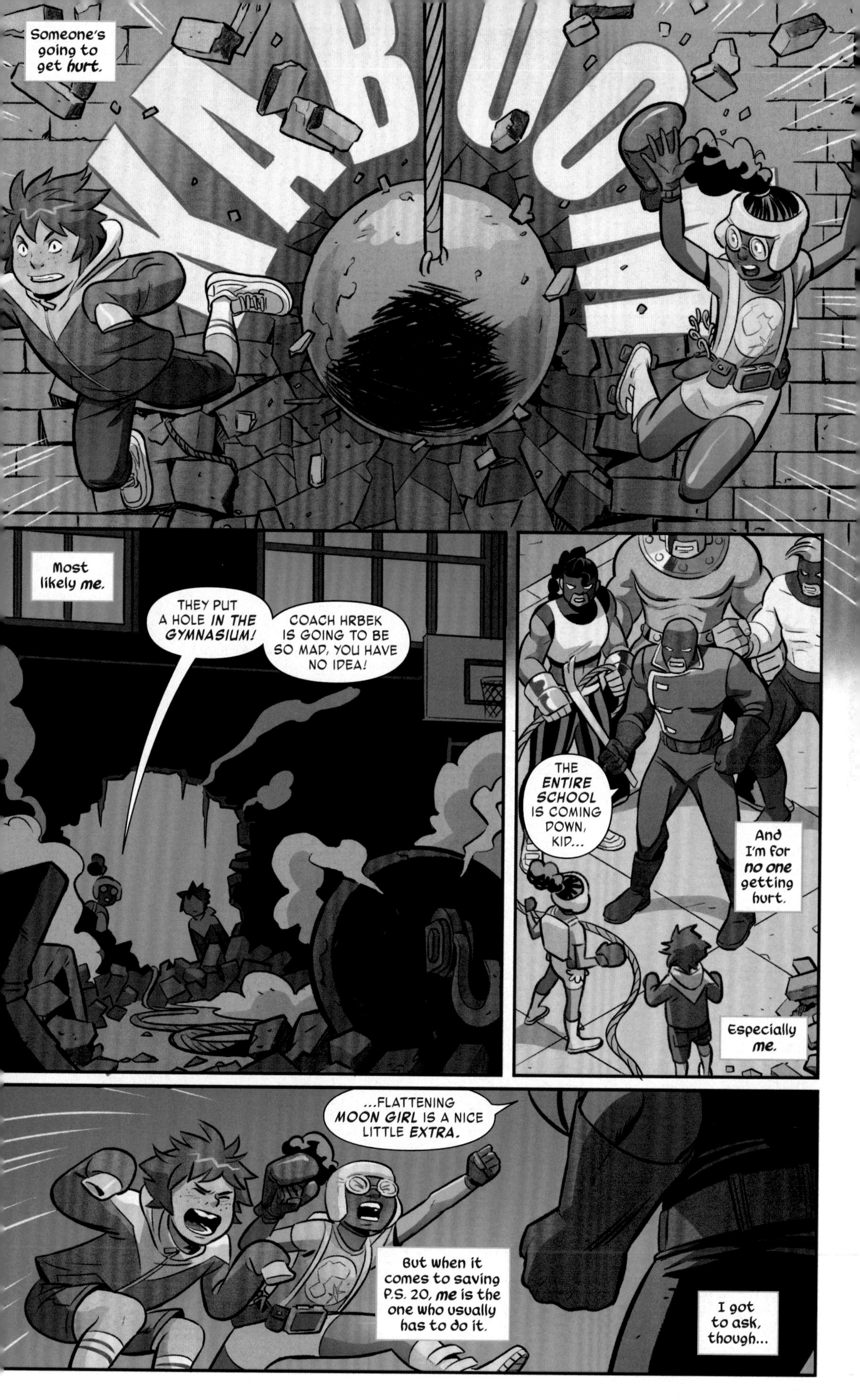
Someone's going to get hurt.
KABOOM!
Most likely me.
THEY PUT A HOLE IN THE GYMNASIUM!
COACH HRBEK IS GOING TO BE SO MAD, YOU HAVE NO IDEA!
THE ENTIRE SCHOOL IS COMING DOWN, KID...
And I'm for no one getting hurt.
Especially me.
...FLATTENING MOON GIRL IS A NICE LITTLE EXTRA.
But when it comes to saving P.S. 20, me is the one who usually has to do it.
I got to ask, though...

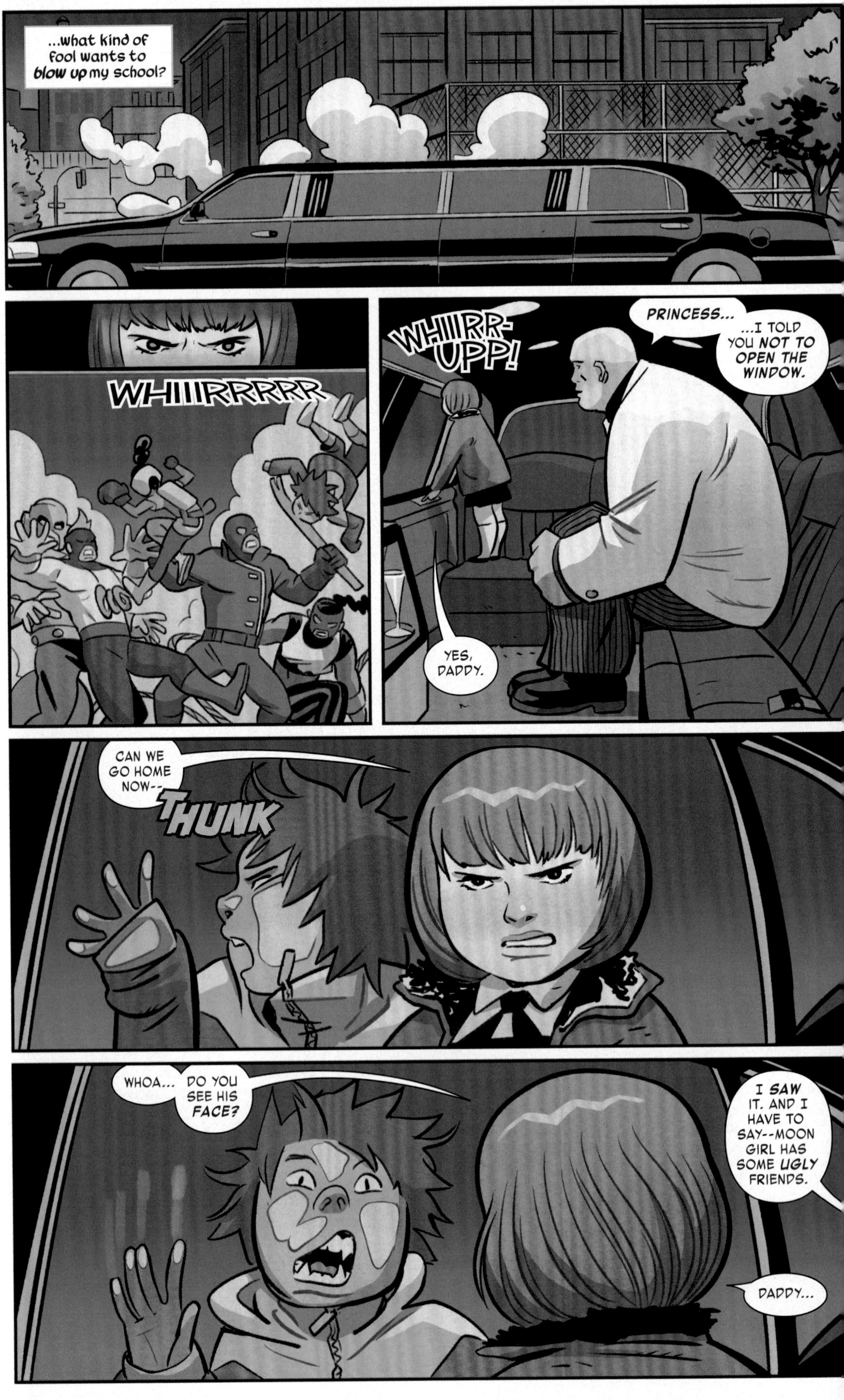

...what kind of fool wants to blow up my school?
WHIIIRRRRR
WHIIRR-UPP!
PRINCESS...
...I TOLD YOU NOT TO OPEN THE WINDOW.
YES, DADDY.
CAN WE GO HOME NOW--
THUNK
WHOA...
DO YOU SEE HIS FACE?
I SAW IT. AND I HAVE TO SAY--MOON GIRL HAS SOME UGLY FRIENDS.
DADDY...

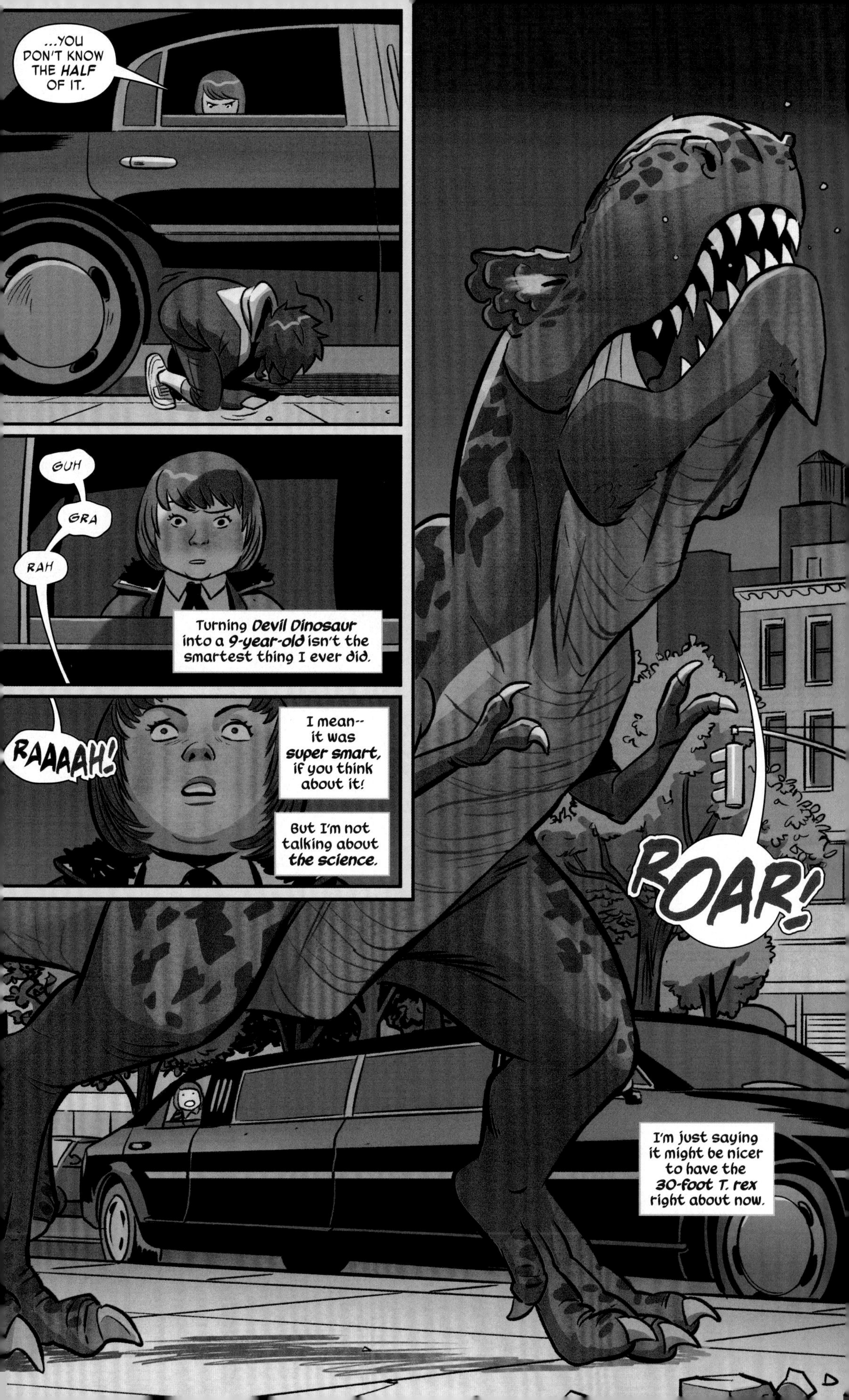
...YOU DON'T KNOW THE *HALF* OF IT.
GUH
GRA
RAH
Turning *Devil Dinosaur* into a *9-year-old* isn't the smartest thing I ever did.
RAAAAH!
I mean-- it was *super smart,* if you think about it!
But I'm not talking about *the science.*
ROAR!
I'm just saying it might be nicer to have the *30-foot T. rex* right about now.

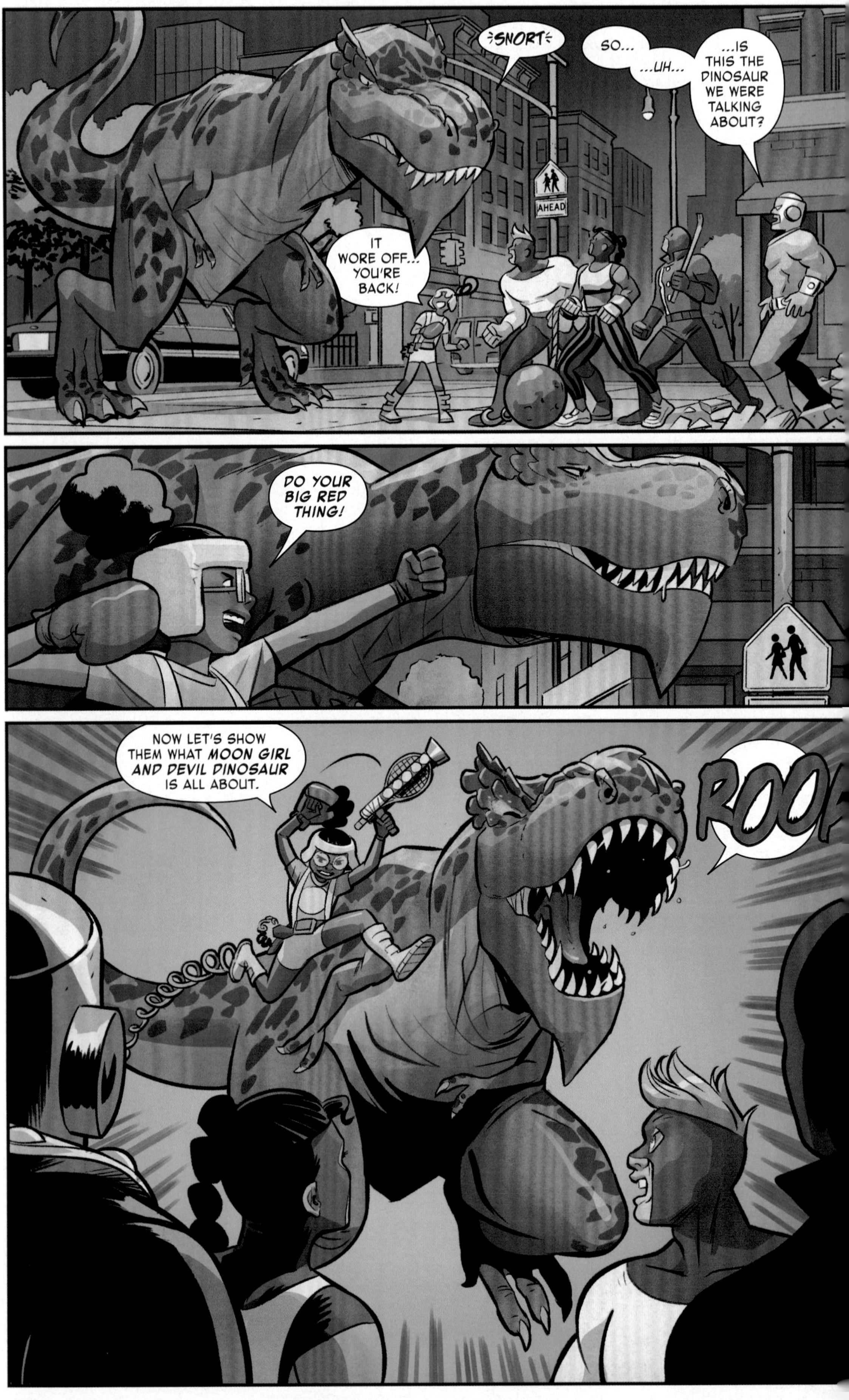
SNORT
SO...
...UH...
...IS THIS THE DINOSAUR WE WERE TALKING ABOUT?
AHEAD
IT WORE OFF... YOU'RE BACK!
DO YOUR BIG RED THING!
NOW LET'S SHOW THEM WHAT MOON GIRL AND DEVIL DINOSAUR IS ALL ABOUT.
ROO

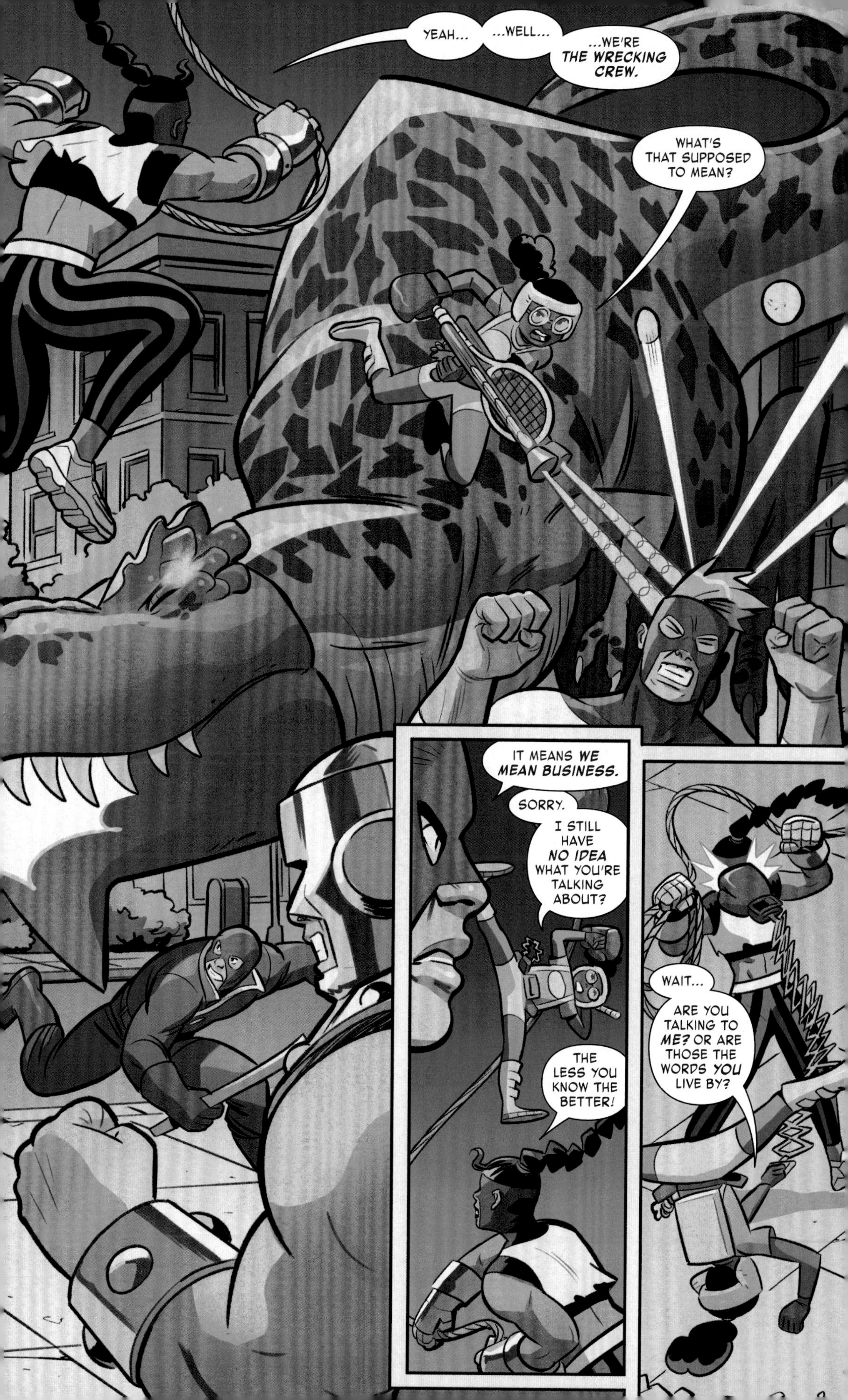
YEAH...
...WELL...
...WE'RE THE WRECKING CREW.
WHAT'S THAT SUPPOSED TO MEAN?
IT MEANS WE MEAN BUSINESS.
SORRY.
I STILL HAVE NO IDEA WHAT YOU'RE TALKING ABOUT?
THE LESS YOU KNOW THE BETTER!
WAIT...
ARE YOU TALKING TO ME? OR ARE THOSE THE WORDS YOU LIVE BY?

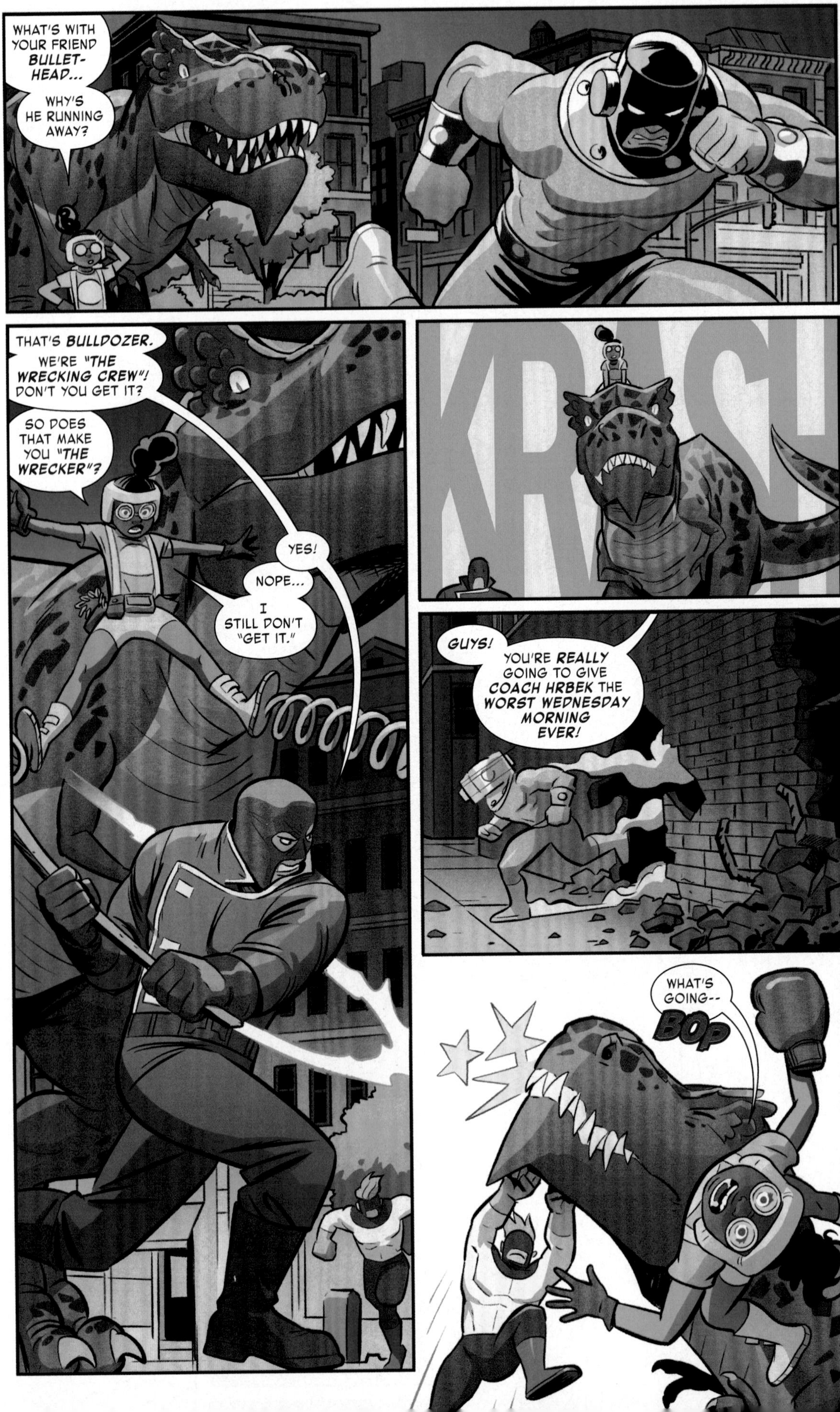
WHAT'S WITH YOUR FRIEND BULLET-HEAD...
WHY'S HE RUNNING AWAY?
THAT'S BULLDOZER.
WE'RE "THE WRECKING CREW"! DON'T YOU GET IT?
SO DOES THAT MAKE YOU "THE WRECKER"?
YES!
NOPE...
I STILL DON'T "GET IT."
KRASH
GUYS!
YOU'RE REALLY GOING TO GIVE COACH HRBEK THE WORST WEDNESDAY MORNING EVER!
WHAT'S GOING--
BOP

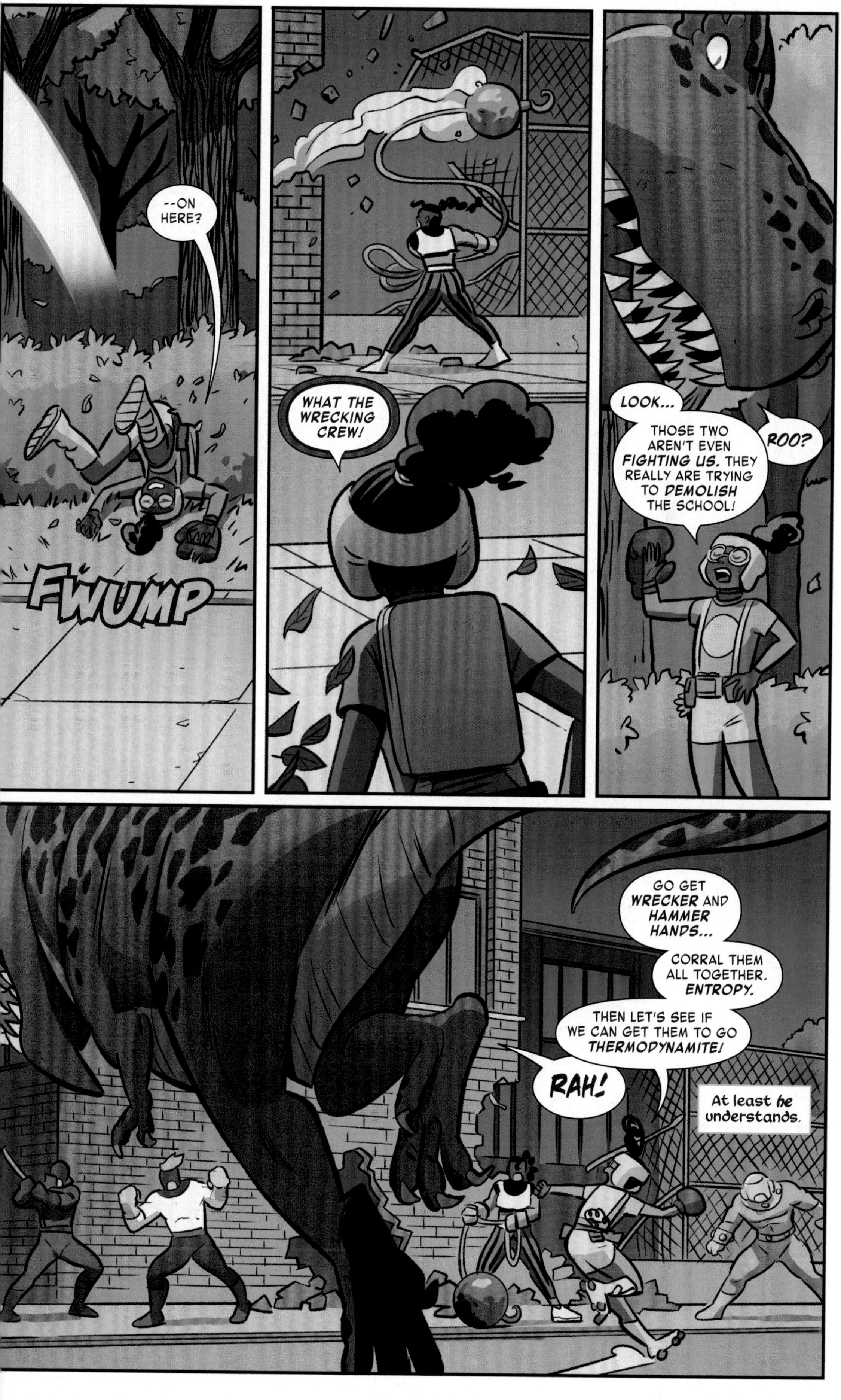
--ON HERE?
FWUMP
WHAT THE WRECKING CREW!
LOOK...
THOSE TWO AREN'T EVEN FIGHTING US. THEY REALLY ARE TRYING TO DEMOLISH THE SCHOOL!
ROO?
GO GET WRECKER AND HAMMER HANDS...
CORRAL THEM ALL TOGETHER. ENTROPY.
THEN LET'S SEE IF WE CAN GET THEM TO GO THERMODYNAMITE!
RAH!
At least he understands.

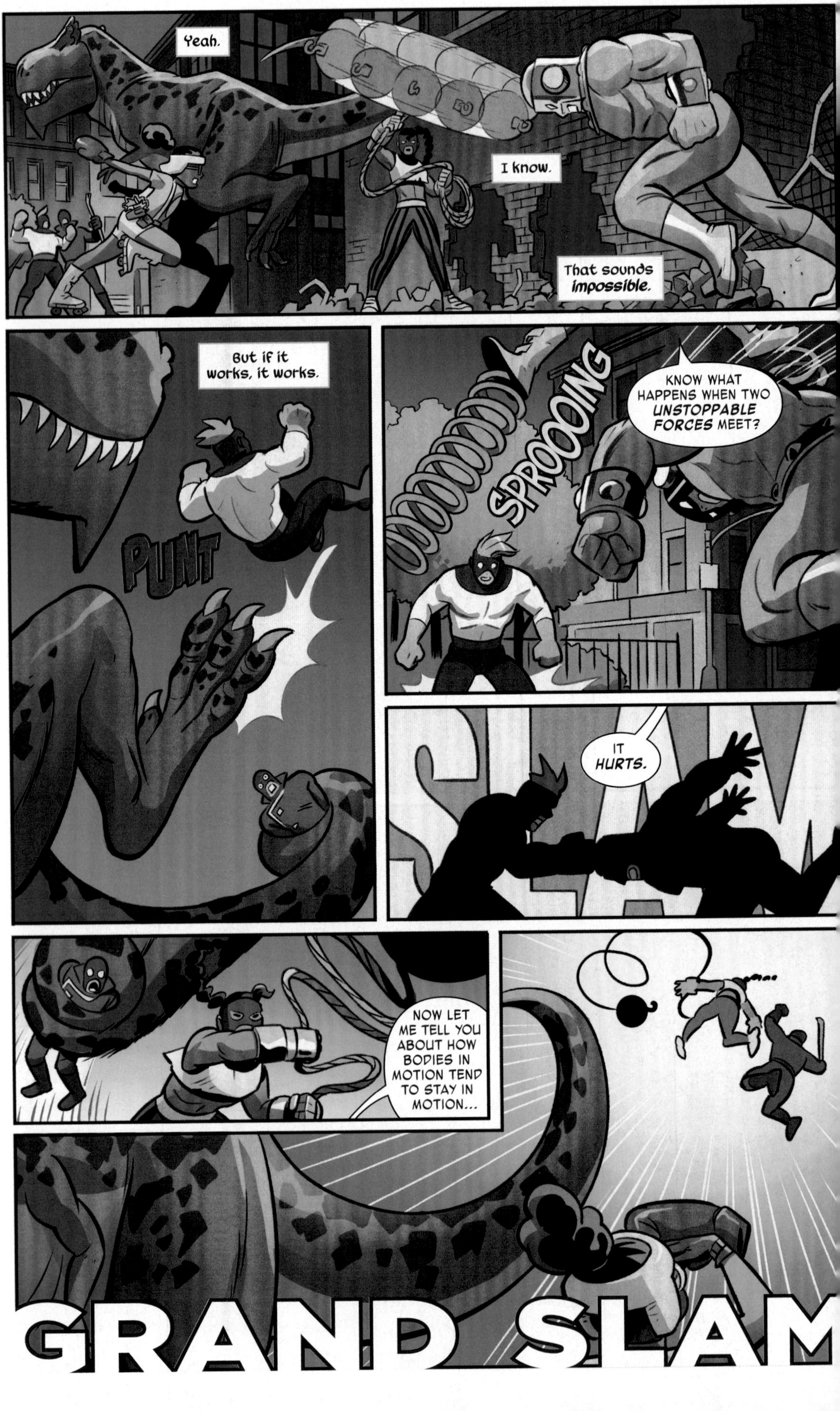
Yeah.
I know.
That sounds *impossible.*
But if it works, it works.
PUNT
SPROOOING
KNOW WHAT HAPPENS WHEN TWO *UNSTOPPABLE FORCES* MEET?
IT *HURTS.*
NOW LET ME TELL YOU ABOUT HOW BODIES IN MOTION TEND TO STAY IN MOTION...
GRAND SLAM

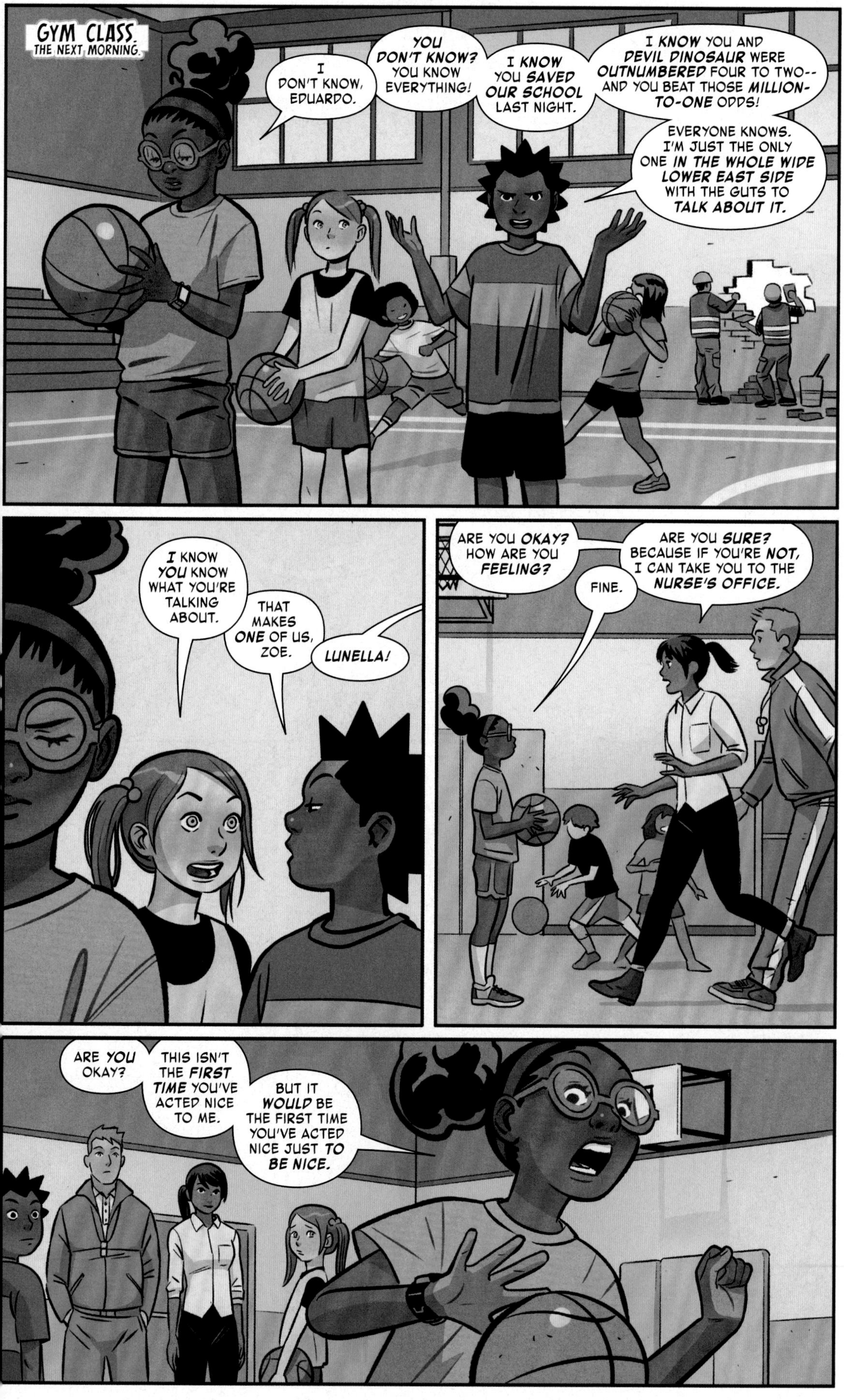
GYM CLASS. THE NEXT MORNING.
I DON'T KNOW, EDUARDO.
YOU DON'T KNOW? YOU KNOW EVERYTHING!
I KNOW YOU SAVED OUR SCHOOL LAST NIGHT.
I KNOW YOU AND DEVIL DINOSAUR WERE OUTNUMBERED FOUR TO TWO-- AND YOU BEAT THOSE MILLION-TO-ONE ODDS!
EVERYONE KNOWS. I'M JUST THE ONLY ONE IN THE WHOLE WIDE LOWER EAST SIDE WITH THE GUTS TO TALK ABOUT IT.
I KNOW YOU KNOW WHAT YOU'RE TALKING ABOUT.
THAT MAKES ONE OF US, ZOE.
LUNELLA!
ARE YOU OKAY? HOW ARE YOU FEELING?
FINE.
ARE YOU SURE? BECAUSE IF YOU'RE NOT, I CAN TAKE YOU TO THE NURSE'S OFFICE.
ARE YOU OKAY?
THIS ISN'T THE FIRST TIME YOU'VE ACTED NICE TO ME.
BUT IT WOULD BE THE FIRST TIME YOU'VE ACTED NICE JUST TO BE NICE.

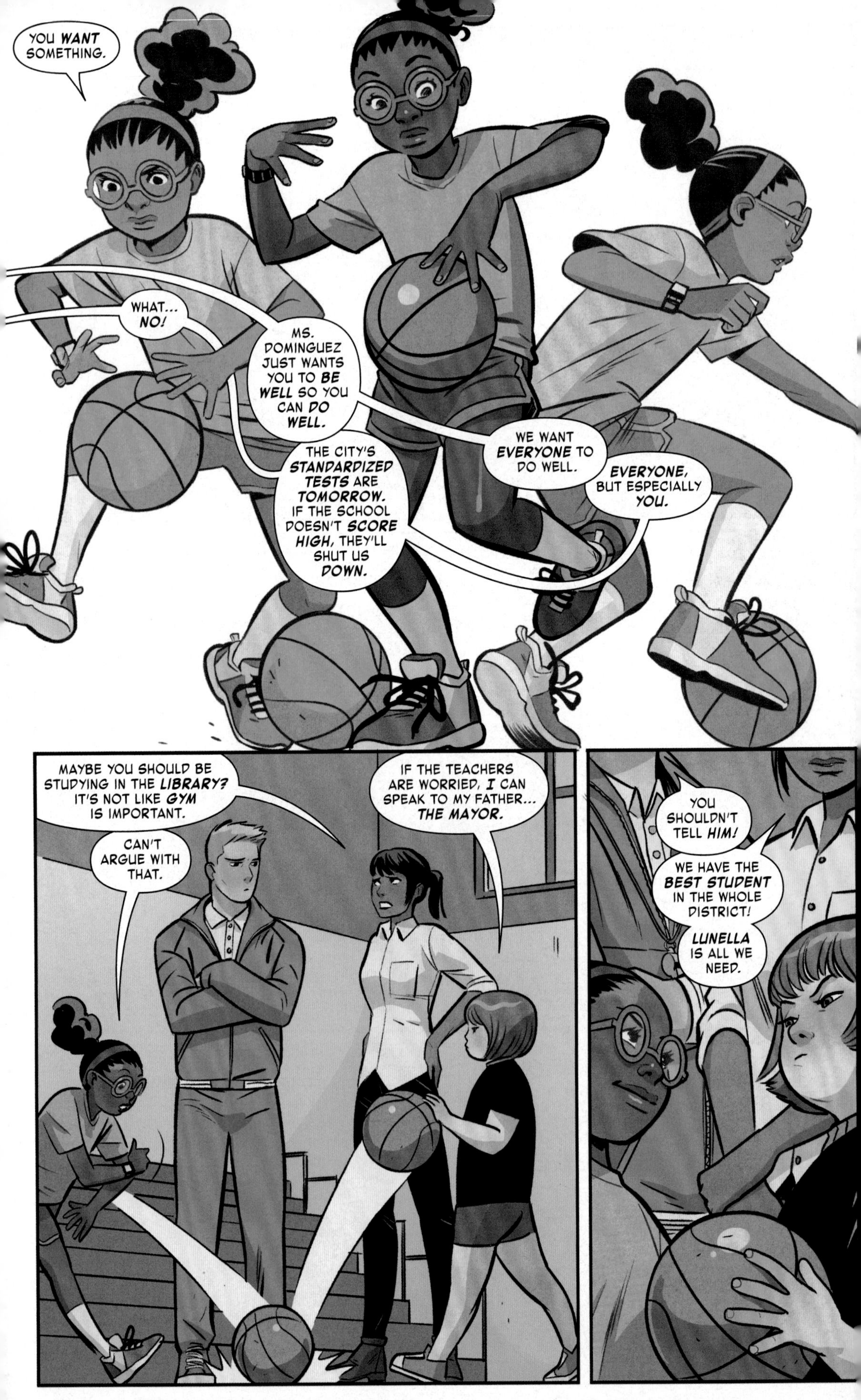
YOU **WANT** SOMETHING.
WHAT... **NO!**
MS. DOMINGUEZ JUST WANTS YOU TO **BE WELL** SO YOU CAN **DO WELL.**
WE WANT **EVERYONE** TO DO WELL.
THE CITY'S **STANDARDIZED TESTS** ARE **TOMORROW.** IF THE SCHOOL DOESN'T **SCORE HIGH,** THEY'LL SHUT US **DOWN.**
EVERYONE, BUT ESPECIALLY **YOU.**
MAYBE YOU SHOULD BE STUDYING IN THE **LIBRARY?** IT'S NOT LIKE **GYM** IS IMPORTANT.
CAN'T ARGUE WITH THAT.
IF THE TEACHERS ARE WORRIED, **I** CAN SPEAK TO MY FATHER... **THE MAYOR.**
YOU SHOULDN'T TELL **HIM!**
WE HAVE THE **BEST STUDENT** IN THE WHOLE DISTRICT!
LUNELLA IS ALL WE NEED.

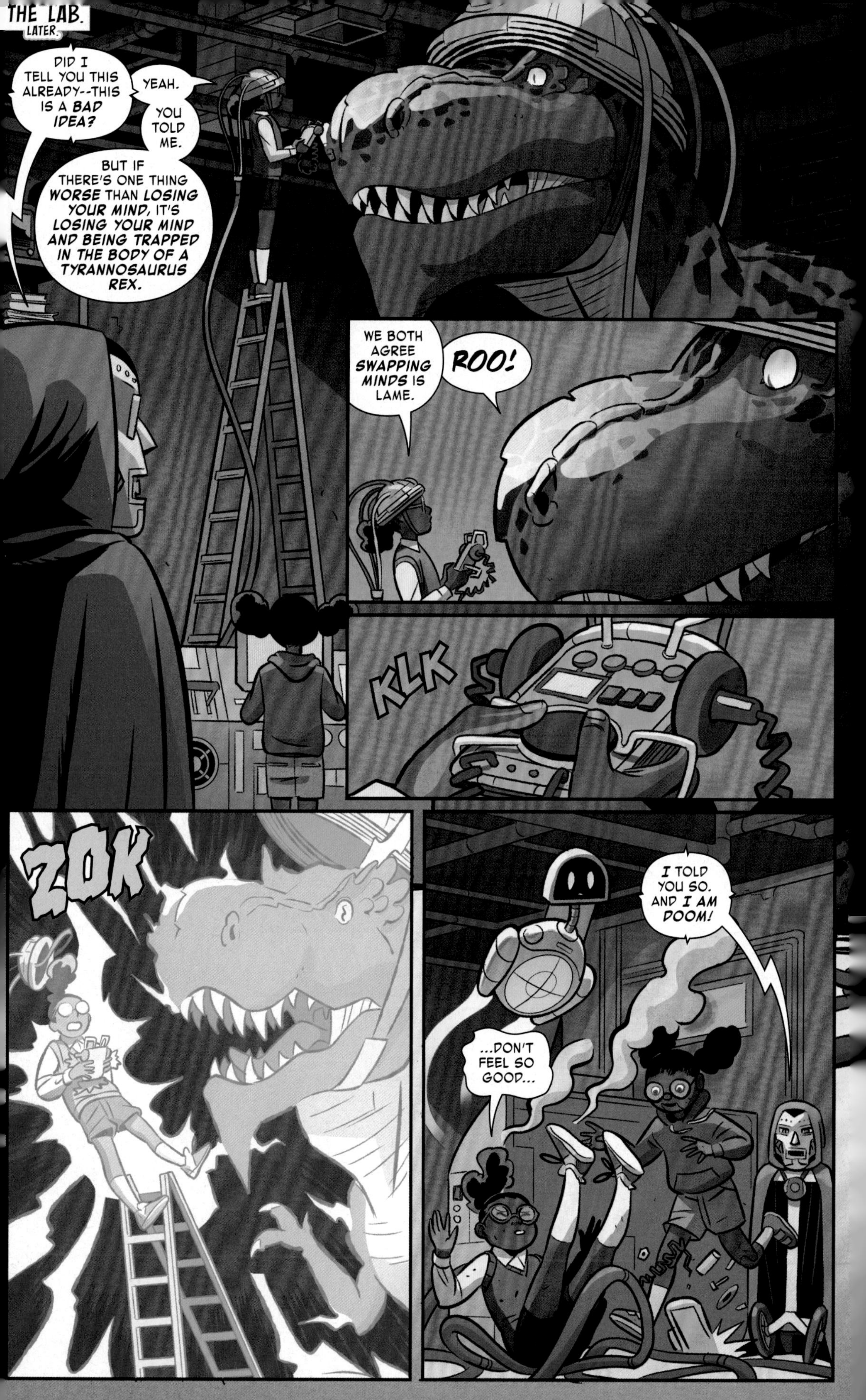
THE LAB. LATER.
DID I TELL YOU THIS ALREADY--THIS IS A BAD IDEA?
YEAH.
YOU TOLD ME.
BUT IF THERE'S ONE THING WORSE THAN LOSING YOUR MIND, IT'S LOSING YOUR MIND AND BEING TRAPPED IN THE BODY OF A TYRANNOSAURUS REX.
WE BOTH AGREE SWAPPING MINDS IS LAME.
ROO!
KLK
ZOK
I TOLD YOU SO. AND I AM DOOM!
...DON'T FEEL SO GOOD...

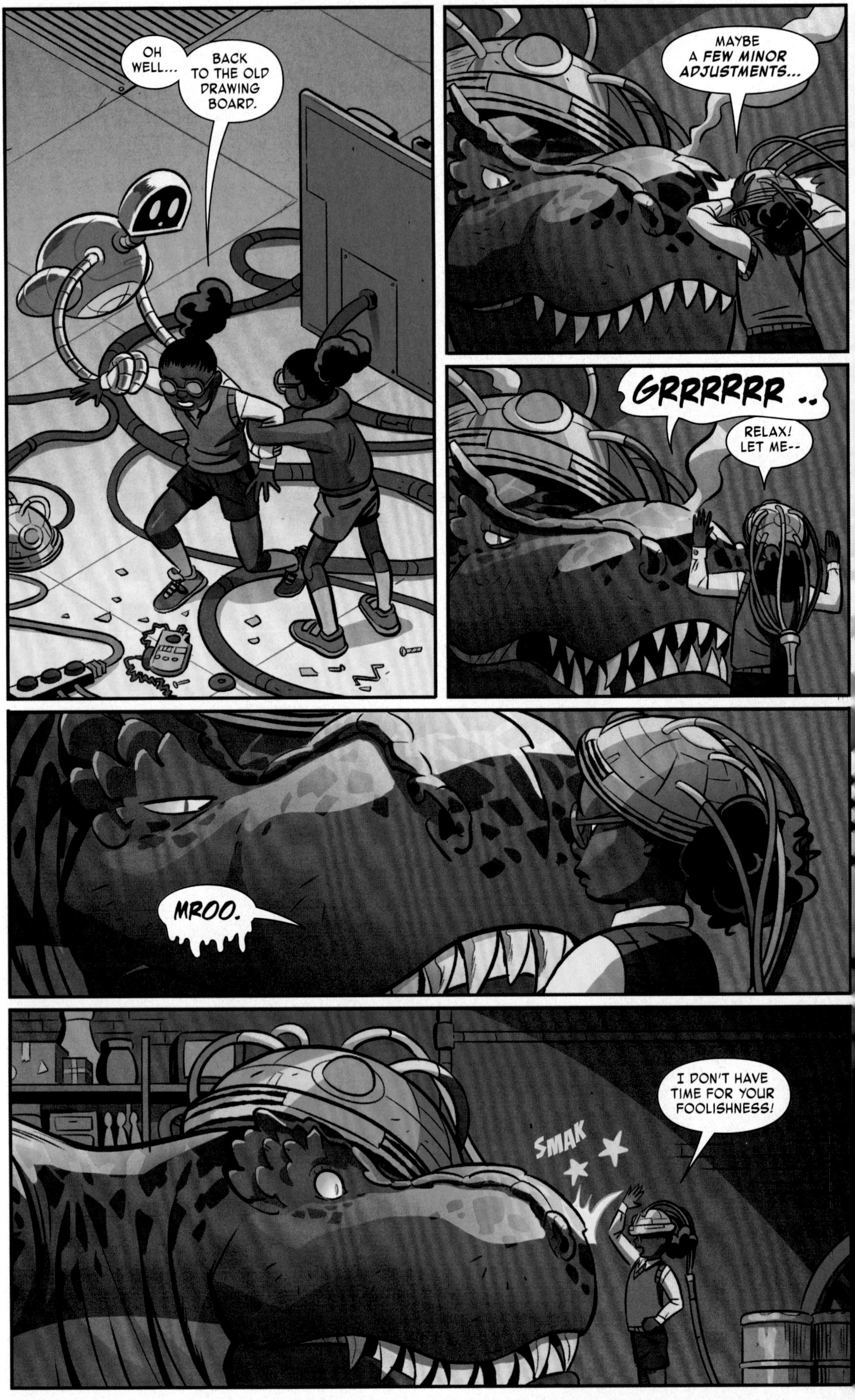
OH WELL...
BACK TO THE OLD DRAWING BOARD.
MAYBE A FEW MINOR ADJUSTMENTS...
GRRRRRR ..
RELAX! LET ME--
MROO.
SMAK
I DON'T HAVE TIME FOR YOUR FOOLISHNESS!

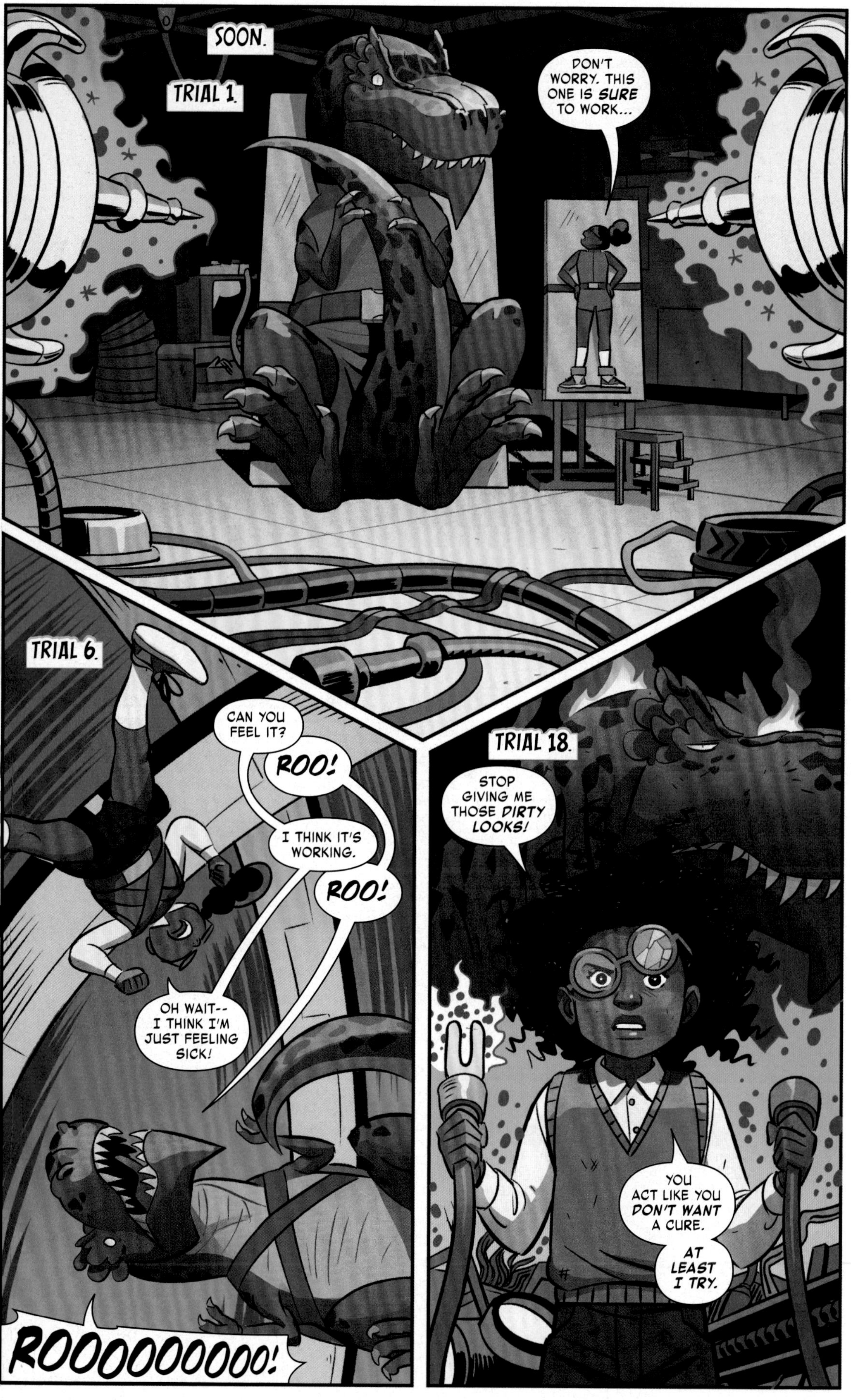
SOON.
TRIAL 1.
DON'T WORRY. THIS ONE IS SURE TO WORK...
TRIAL 6.
CAN YOU FEEL IT?
ROO!
I THINK IT'S WORKING.
ROO!
OH WAIT-- I THINK I'M JUST FEELING SICK!
ROOOOOOOOO!
TRIAL 18.
STOP GIVING ME THOSE DIRTY LOOKS!
YOU ACT LIKE YOU DON'T WANT A CURE.
AT LEAST I TRY.

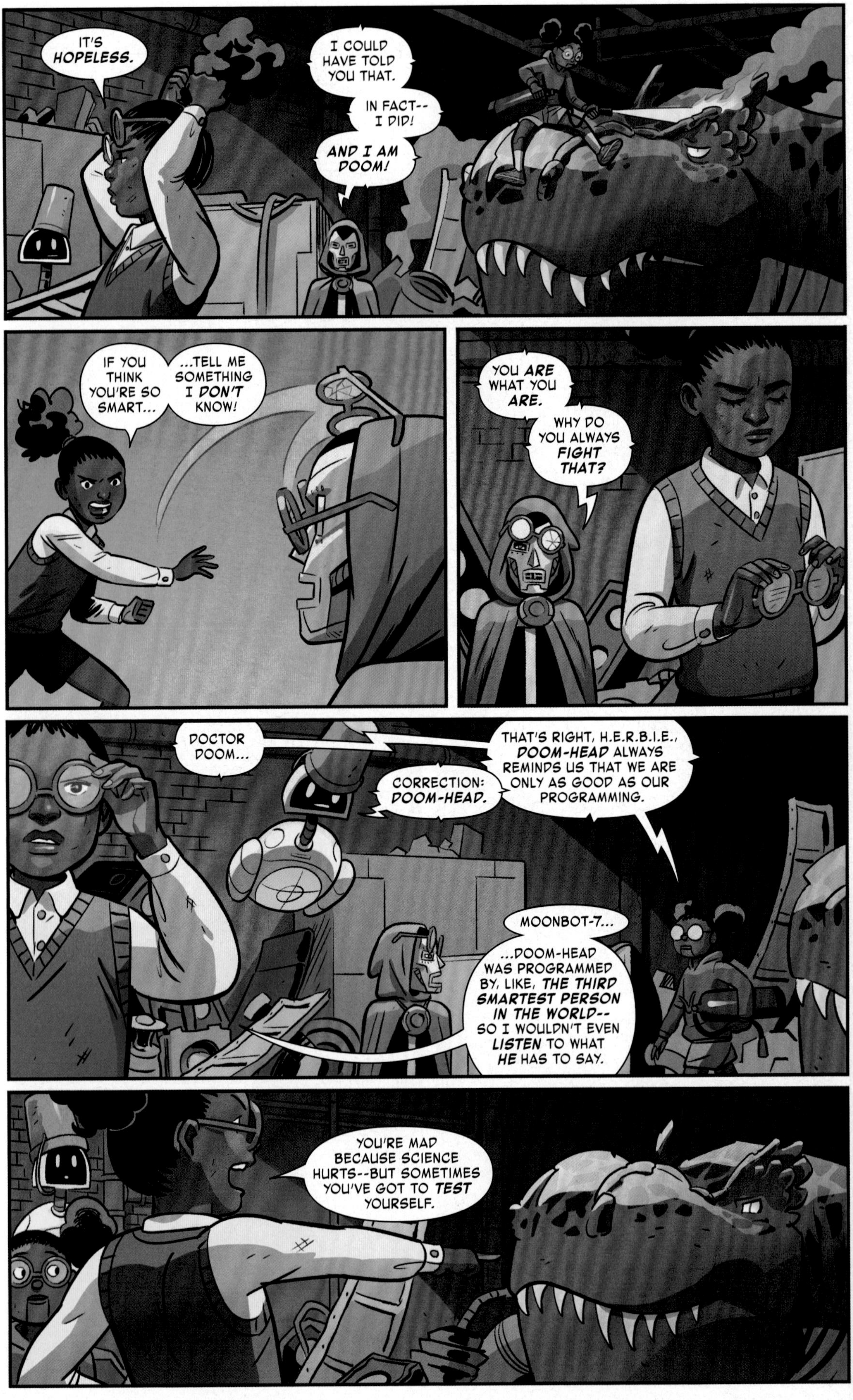
IT'S HOPELESS.
I COULD HAVE TOLD YOU THAT.
IN FACT-- I DID!
AND I AM DOOM!
IF YOU THINK YOU'RE SO SMART...
...TELL ME SOMETHING I DON'T KNOW!
YOU ARE WHAT YOU ARE.
WHY DO YOU ALWAYS FIGHT THAT?
DOCTOR DOOM...
CORRECTION: DOOM-HEAD.
THAT'S RIGHT, H.E.R.B.I.E., DOOM-HEAD ALWAYS REMINDS US THAT WE ARE ONLY AS GOOD AS OUR PROGRAMMING.
MOONBOT-7...
...DOOM-HEAD WAS PROGRAMMED BY, LIKE, THE THIRD SMARTEST PERSON IN THE WORLD-- SO I WOULDN'T EVEN LISTEN TO WHAT HE HAS TO SAY.
YOU'RE MAD BECAUSE SCIENCE HURTS--BUT SOMETIMES YOU'VE GOT TO TEST YOURSELF.

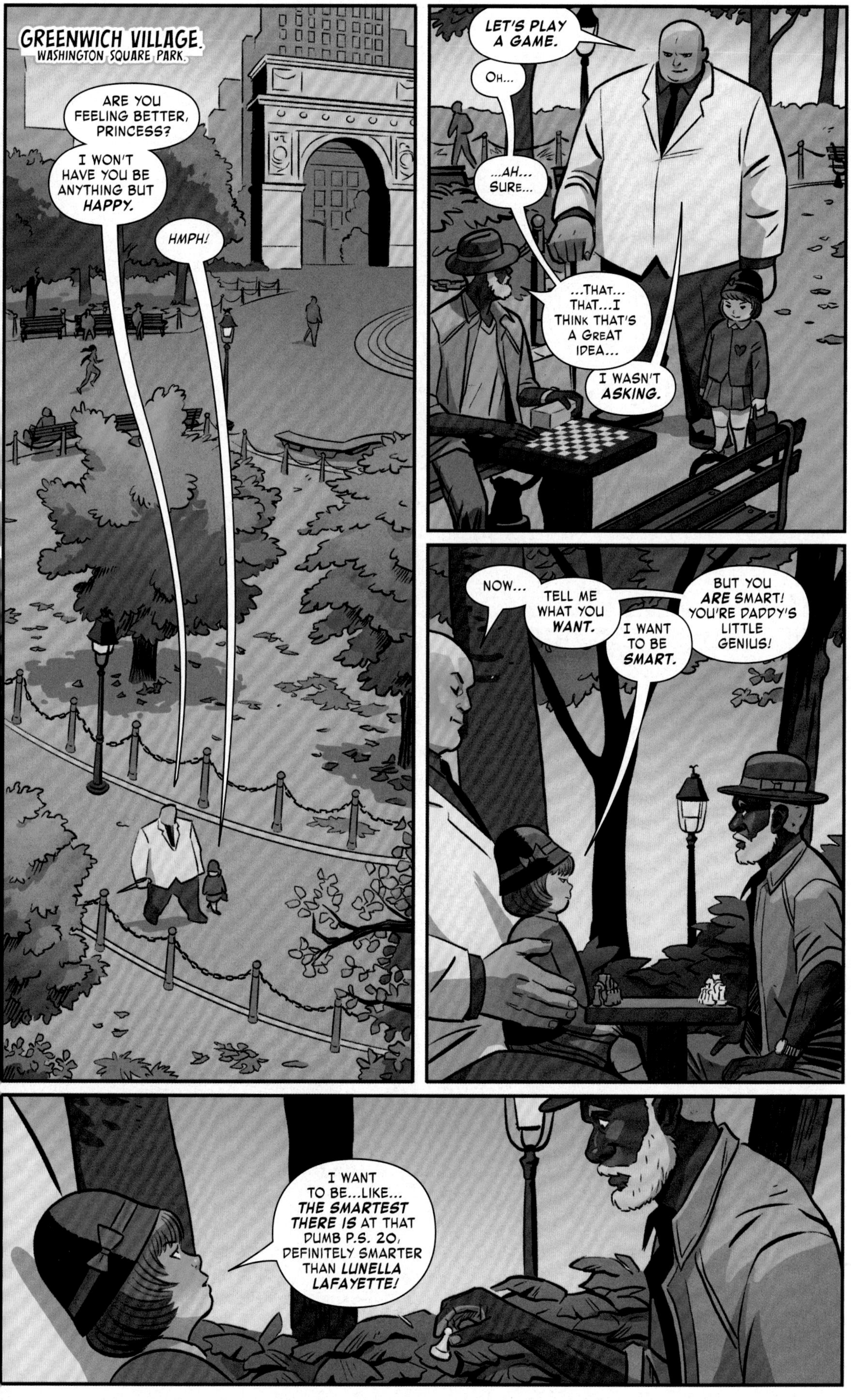
GREENWICH VILLAGE.
WASHINGTON SQUARE PARK.
ARE YOU FEELING BETTER, PRINCESS?
I WON'T HAVE YOU BE ANYTHING BUT HAPPY.
HMPH!
LET'S PLAY A GAME.
OH...
...AH... SURE...
...THAT... THAT...I THINK THAT'S A GREAT IDEA...
I WASN'T ASKING.
NOW...
TELL ME WHAT YOU WANT.
I WANT TO BE SMART.
BUT YOU ARE SMART! YOU'RE DADDY'S LITTLE GENIUS!
I WANT TO BE...LIKE... THE SMARTEST THERE IS AT THAT DUMB P.S. 20, DEFINITELY SMARTER THAN LUNELLA LAFAYETTE!

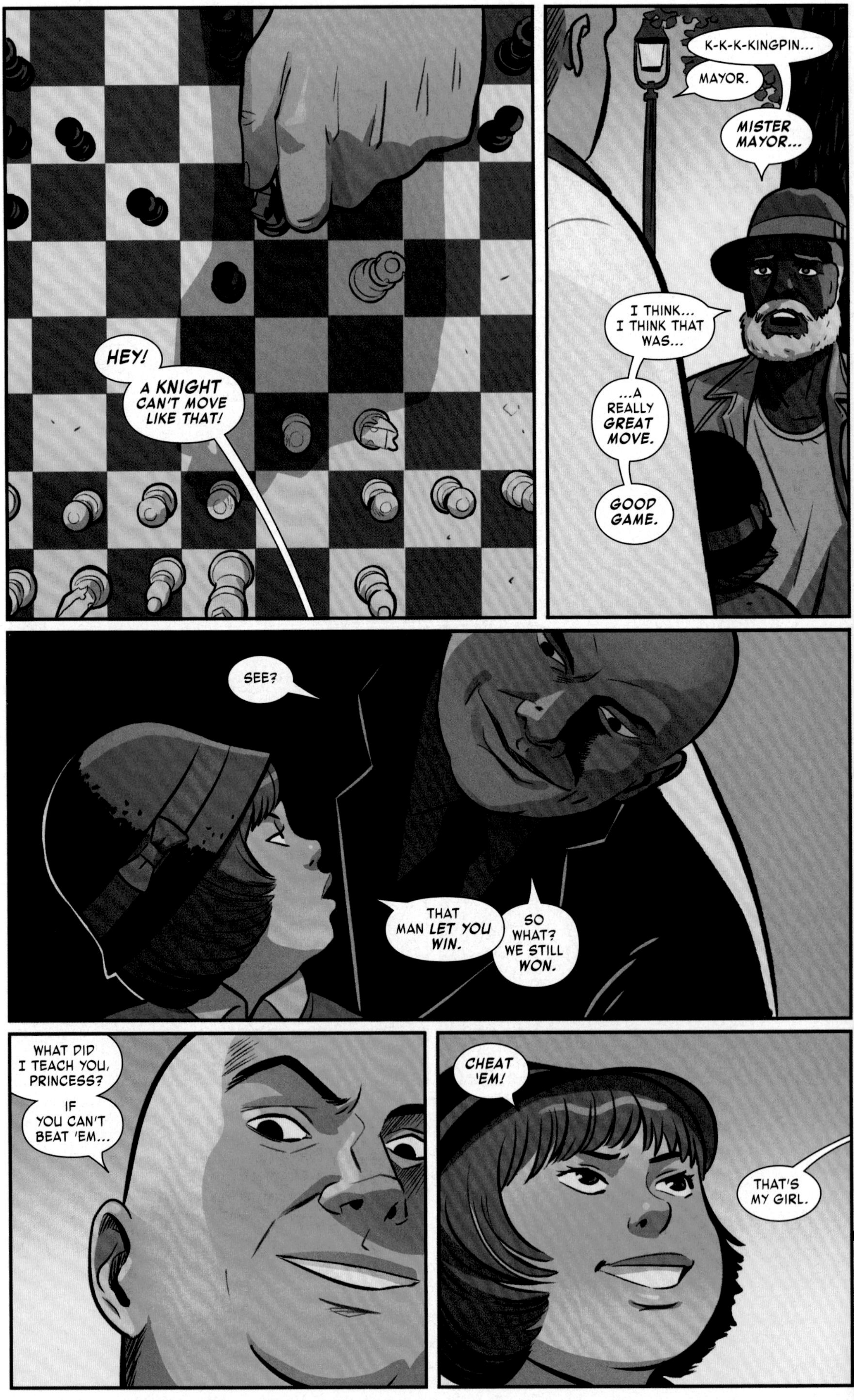
HEY!
A KNIGHT CAN'T MOVE LIKE THAT!
K-K-K-KINGPIN...
MAYOR.
MISTER MAYOR...
I THINK... I THINK THAT WAS...
...A REALLY GREAT MOVE.
GOOD GAME.
SEE?
THAT MAN LET YOU WIN.
SO WHAT? WE STILL WON.
WHAT DID I TEACH YOU, PRINCESS?
IF YOU CAN'T BEAT 'EM...
CHEAT 'EM!
THAT'S MY GIRL.

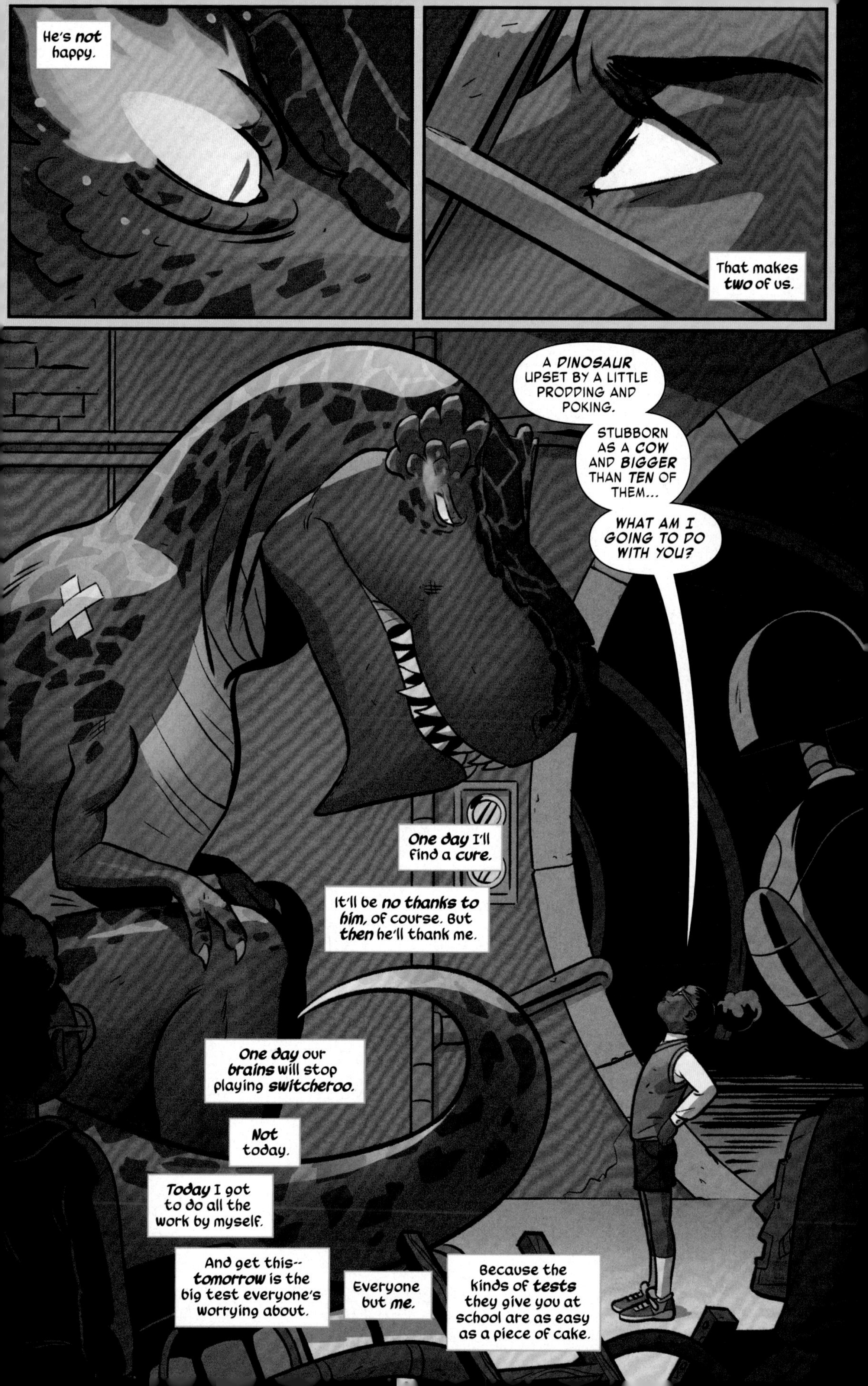
He's not happy.
That makes two of us.
A DINOSAUR UPSET BY A LITTLE PRODDING AND POKING.
STUBBORN AS A COW AND BIGGER THAN TEN OF THEM...
WHAT AM I GOING TO DO WITH YOU?
One day I'll find a cure.
It'll be no thanks to him, of course. But then he'll thank me.
One day our brains will stop playing switcheroo.
Not today.
Today I got to do all the work by myself.
And get this-- tomorrow is the big test everyone's worrying about.
Everyone but me.
Because the kinds of tests they give you at school are as easy as a piece of cake.

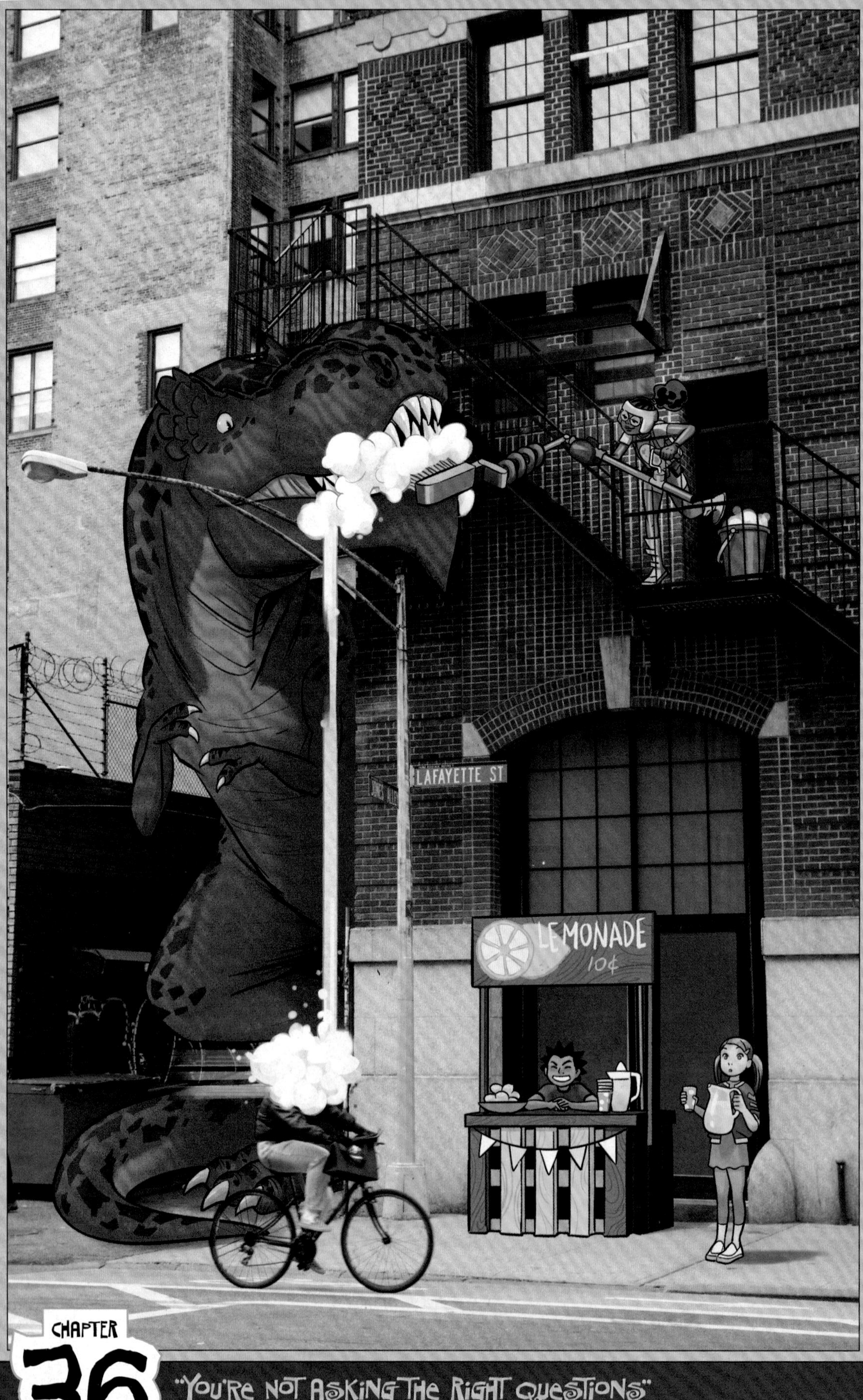
LAFAYETTE ST
LEMONADE
10¢

CHAPTER 36

"YOU'RE NOT ASKING THE RIGHT QUESTIONS"

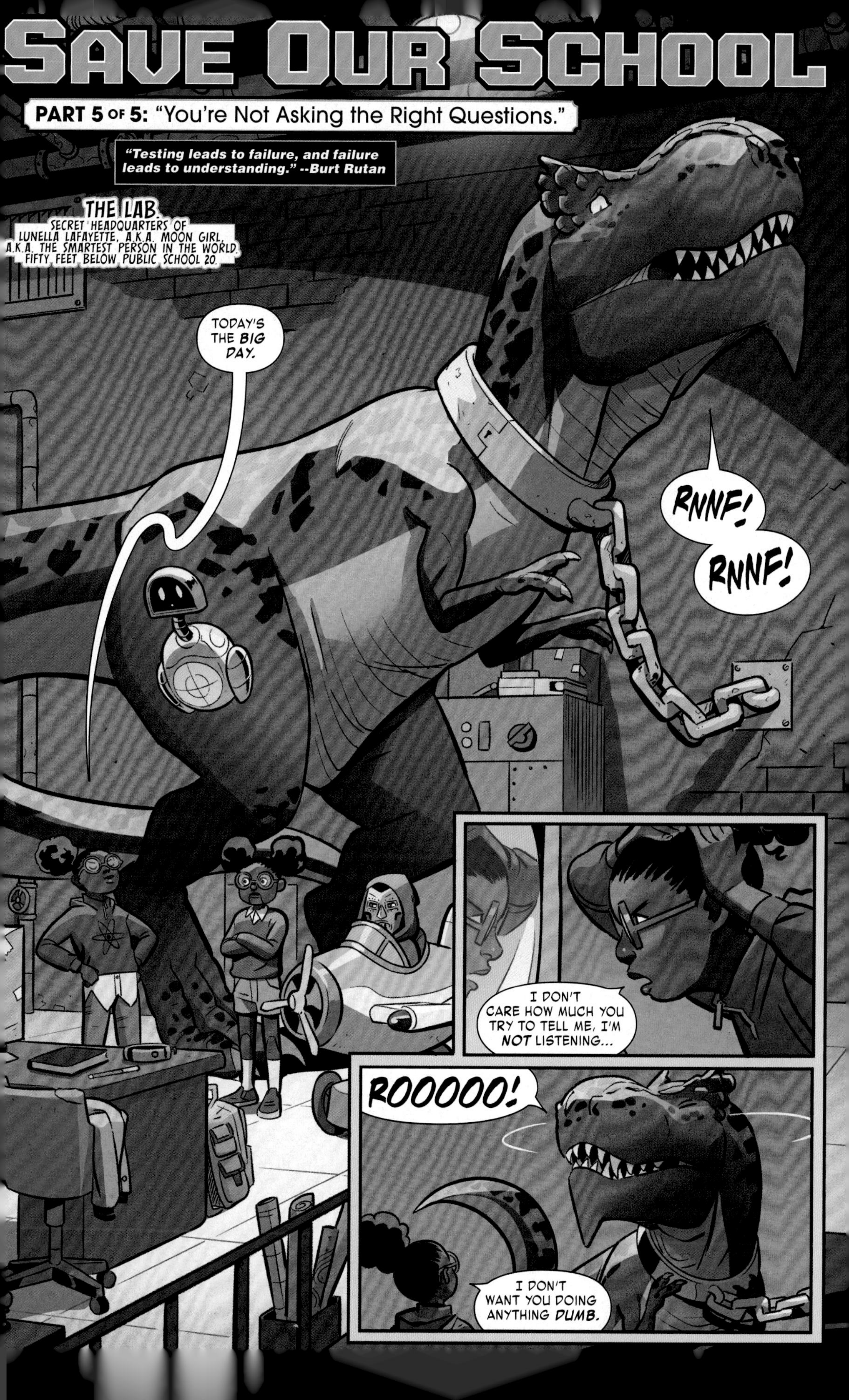
SAVE OUR SCHOOL
PART 5 OF 5: "You're Not Asking the Right Questions."
"Testing leads to failure, and failure leads to understanding." --Burt Rutan
THE LAB. SECRET HEADQUARTERS OF LUNELLA LAFAYETTE, A.K.A. MOON GIRL, A.K.A. THE SMARTEST PERSON IN THE WORLD. FIFTY FEET BELOW PUBLIC SCHOOL 20.
TODAY'S THE BIG DAY.
RNNF! RNNF!
I DON'T CARE HOW MUCH YOU TRY TO TELL ME, I'M NOT LISTENING...
ROOOOO!
I DON'T WANT YOU DOING ANYTHING DUMB.

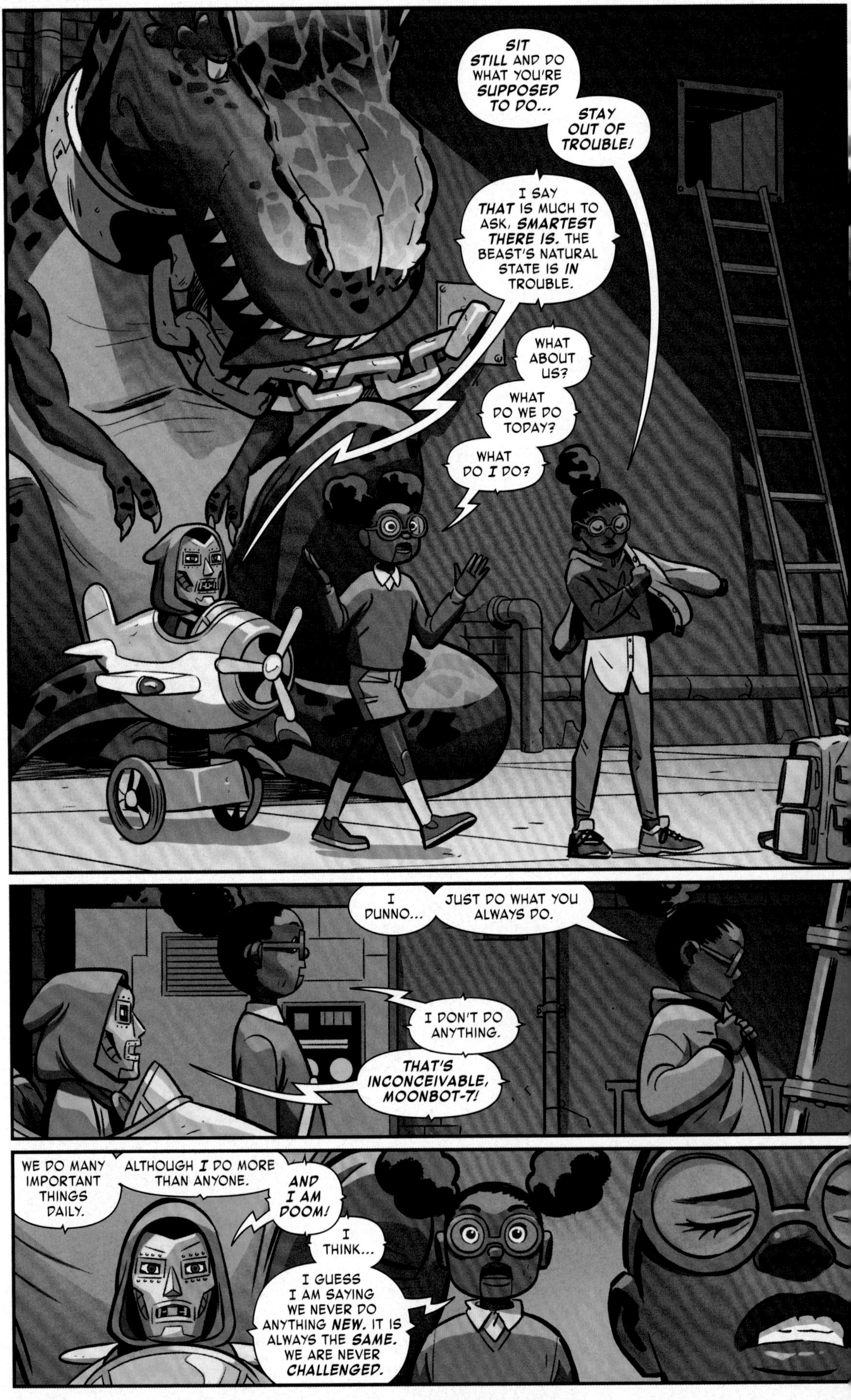

SIT STILL AND DO WHAT YOU'RE SUPPOSED TO DO...
STAY OUT OF TROUBLE!
I SAY THAT IS MUCH TO ASK, SMARTEST THERE IS. THE BEAST'S NATURAL STATE IS IN TROUBLE.
WHAT ABOUT US?
WHAT DO WE DO TODAY?
WHAT DO I DO?
I DUNNO...
JUST DO WHAT YOU ALWAYS DO.
I DON'T DO ANYTHING.
THAT'S INCONCEIVABLE, MOONBOT-7!
WE DO MANY IMPORTANT THINGS DAILY.
ALTHOUGH I DO MORE THAN ANYONE.
AND I AM DOOM!
I THINK...
I GUESS I AM SAYING WE NEVER DO ANYTHING NEW. IT IS ALWAYS THE SAME. WE ARE NEVER CHALLENGED.

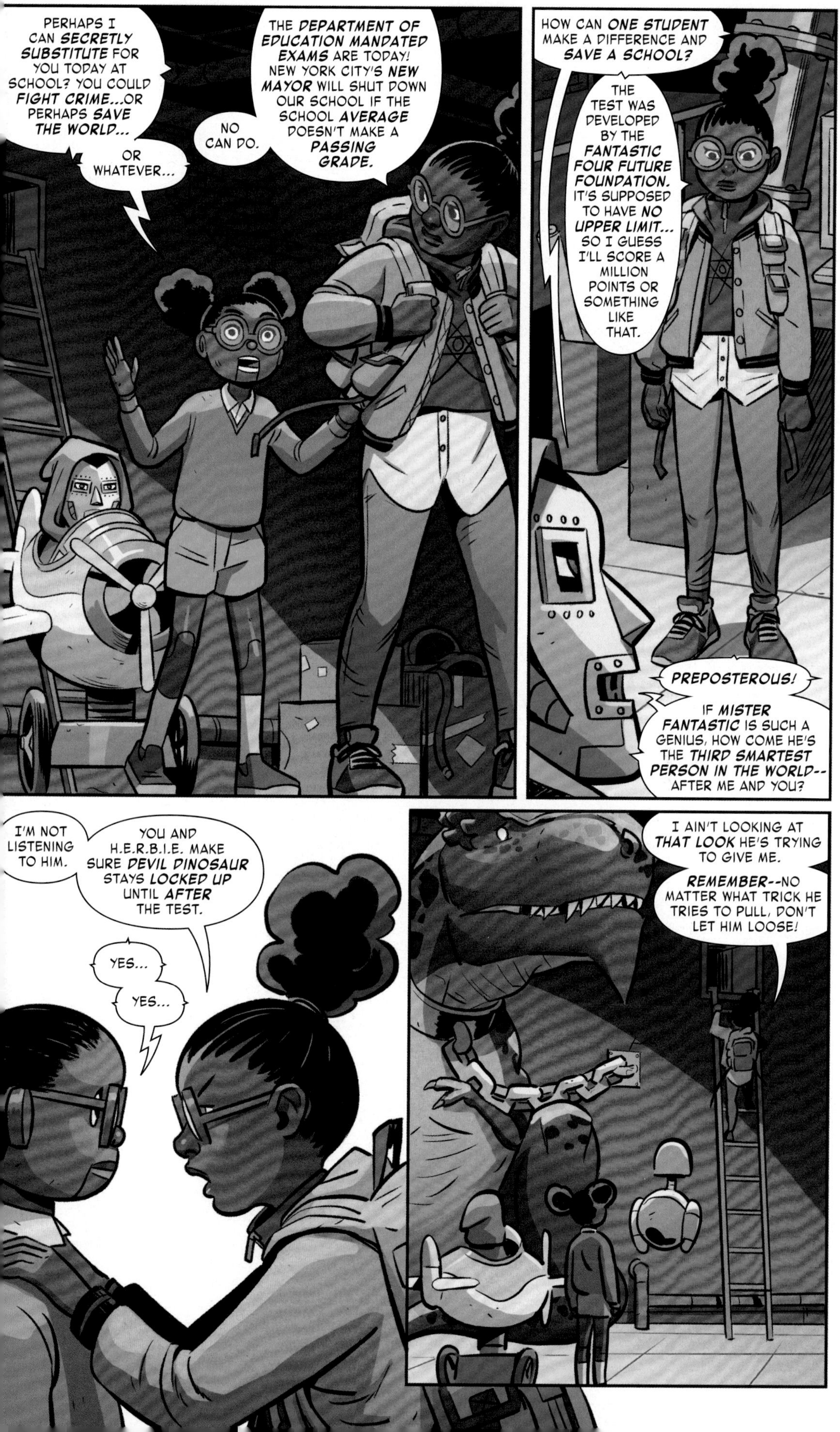
PERHAPS I CAN SECRETLY SUBSTITUTE FOR YOU TODAY AT SCHOOL? YOU COULD FIGHT CRIME...OR PERHAPS SAVE THE WORLD...
OR WHATEVER...
NO CAN DO.
THE DEPARTMENT OF EDUCATION MANDATED EXAMS ARE TODAY! NEW YORK CITY'S NEW MAYOR WILL SHUT DOWN OUR SCHOOL IF THE SCHOOL AVERAGE DOESN'T MAKE A PASSING GRADE.
HOW CAN ONE STUDENT MAKE A DIFFERENCE AND SAVE A SCHOOL?
THE TEST WAS DEVELOPED BY THE FANTASTIC FOUR FUTURE FOUNDATION. IT'S SUPPOSED TO HAVE NO UPPER LIMIT... SO I GUESS I'LL SCORE A MILLION POINTS OR SOMETHING LIKE THAT.
PREPOSTEROUS!
IF MISTER FANTASTIC IS SUCH A GENIUS, HOW COME HE'S THE THIRD SMARTEST PERSON IN THE WORLD-- AFTER ME AND YOU?
I'M NOT LISTENING TO HIM.
YOU AND H.E.R.B.I.E. MAKE SURE DEVIL DINOSAUR STAYS LOCKED UP UNTIL AFTER THE TEST.
YES...
YES...
I AIN'T LOOKING AT THAT LOOK HE'S TRYING TO GIVE ME.
REMEMBER--NO MATTER WHAT TRICK HE TRIES TO PULL, DON'T LET HIM LOOSE!

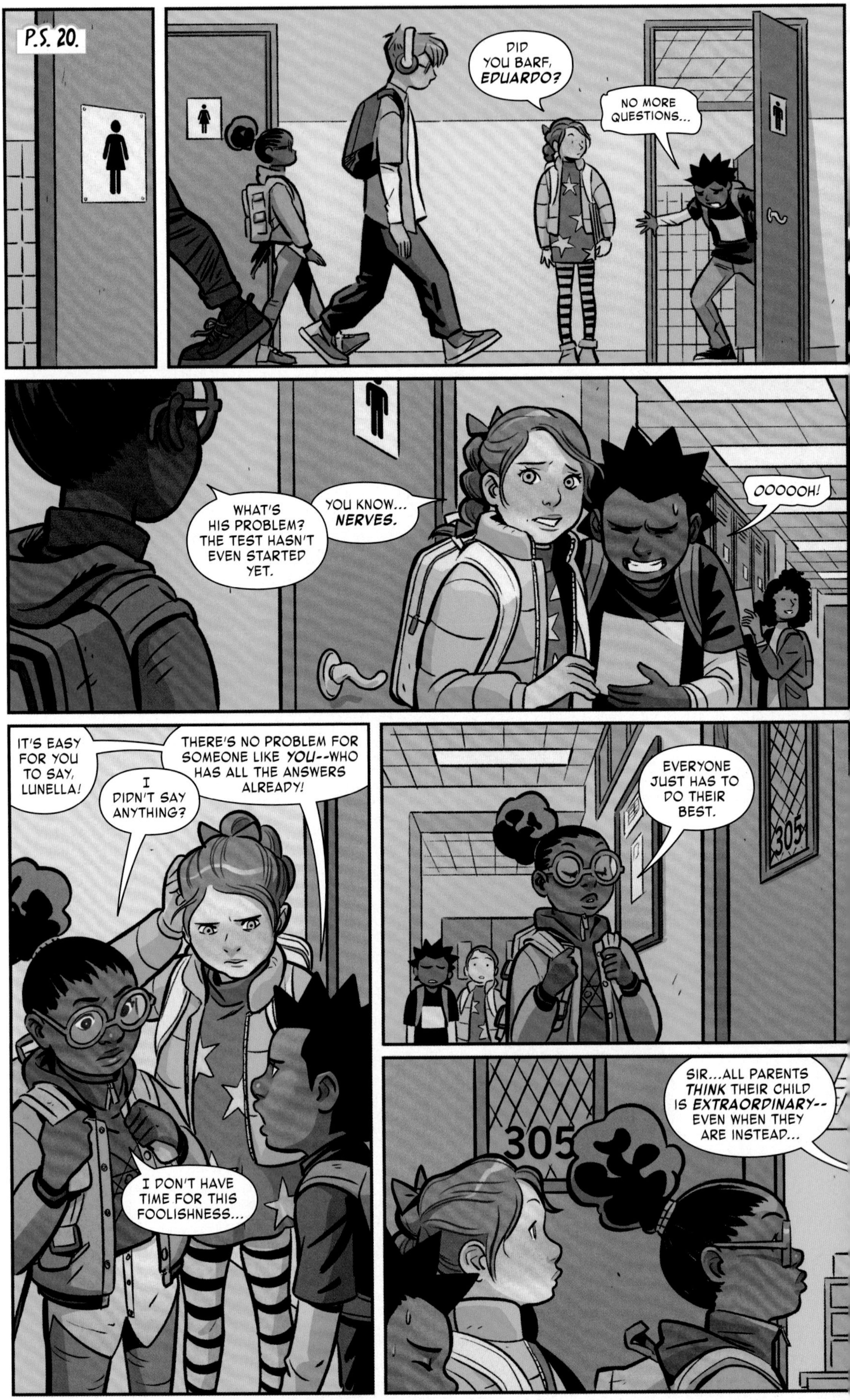
P.S. 20.
DID YOU BARF, EDUARDO?
NO MORE QUESTIONS...
WHAT'S HIS PROBLEM? THE TEST HASN'T EVEN STARTED YET.
YOU KNOW... NERVES.
OOOOOH!
IT'S EASY FOR YOU TO SAY, LUNELLA!
THERE'S NO PROBLEM FOR SOMEONE LIKE YOU--WHO HAS ALL THE ANSWERS ALREADY!
I DIDN'T SAY ANYTHING?
I DON'T HAVE TIME FOR THIS FOOLISHNESS...
EVERYONE JUST HAS TO DO THEIR BEST.
305
305
SIR...ALL PARENTS THINK THEIR CHILD IS EXTRAORDINARY-- EVEN WHEN THEY ARE INSTEAD...

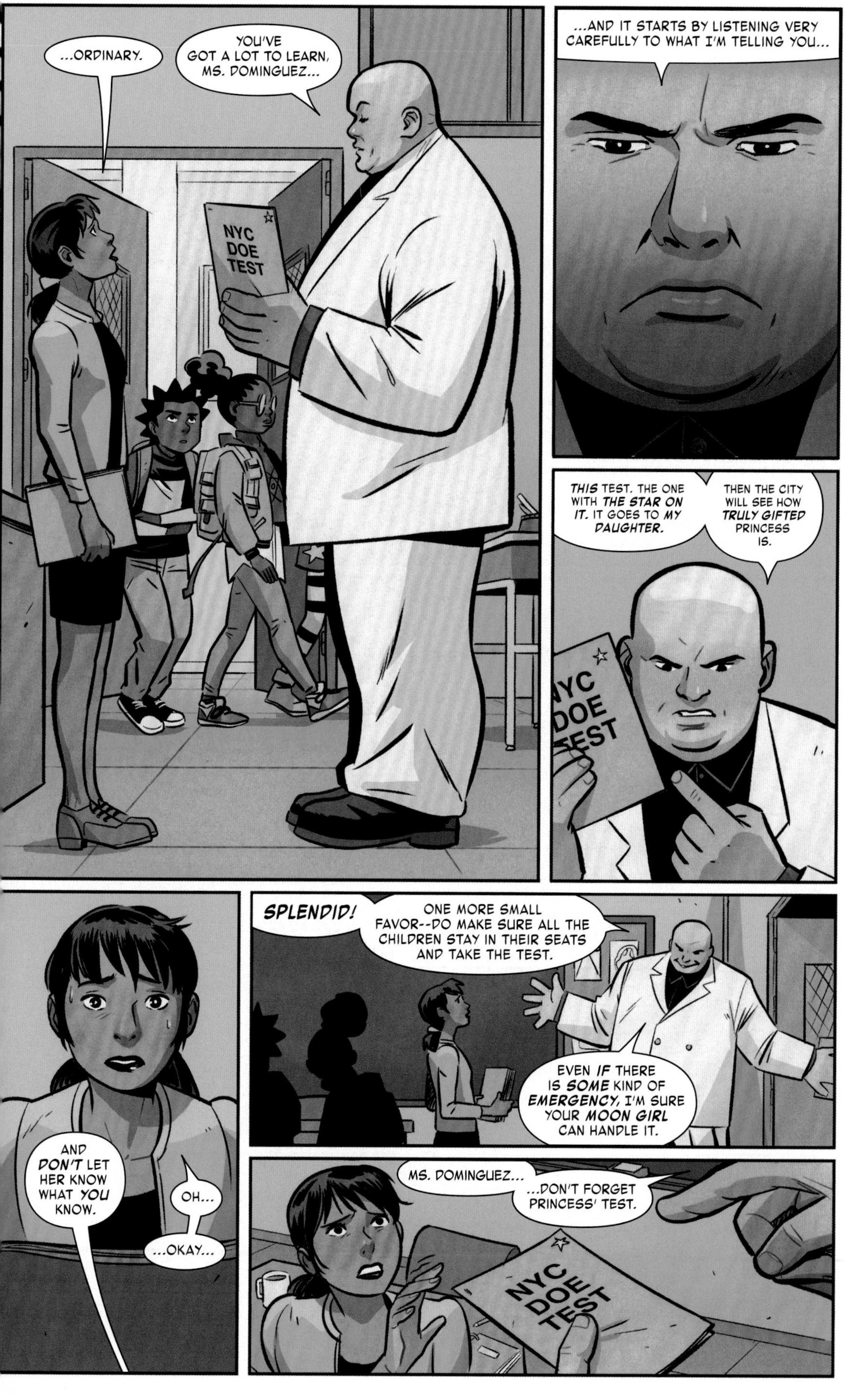

...ORDINARY.
YOU'VE GOT A LOT TO LEARN, MS. DOMINGUEZ...
NYC DOE TEST
...AND IT STARTS BY LISTENING VERY CAREFULLY TO WHAT I'M TELLING YOU...
THIS TEST. THE ONE WITH THE STAR ON IT. IT GOES TO MY DAUGHTER.
THEN THE CITY WILL SEE HOW TRULY GIFTED PRINCESS IS.
AND DON'T LET HER KNOW WHAT YOU KNOW.
OH...
...OKAY...
SPLENDID!
ONE MORE SMALL FAVOR--DO MAKE SURE ALL THE CHILDREN STAY IN THEIR SEATS AND TAKE THE TEST.
EVEN IF THERE IS SOME KIND OF EMERGENCY, I'M SURE YOUR MOON GIRL CAN HANDLE IT.
MS. DOMINGUEZ...
...DON'T FORGET PRINCESS' TEST.
NYC DOE TEST

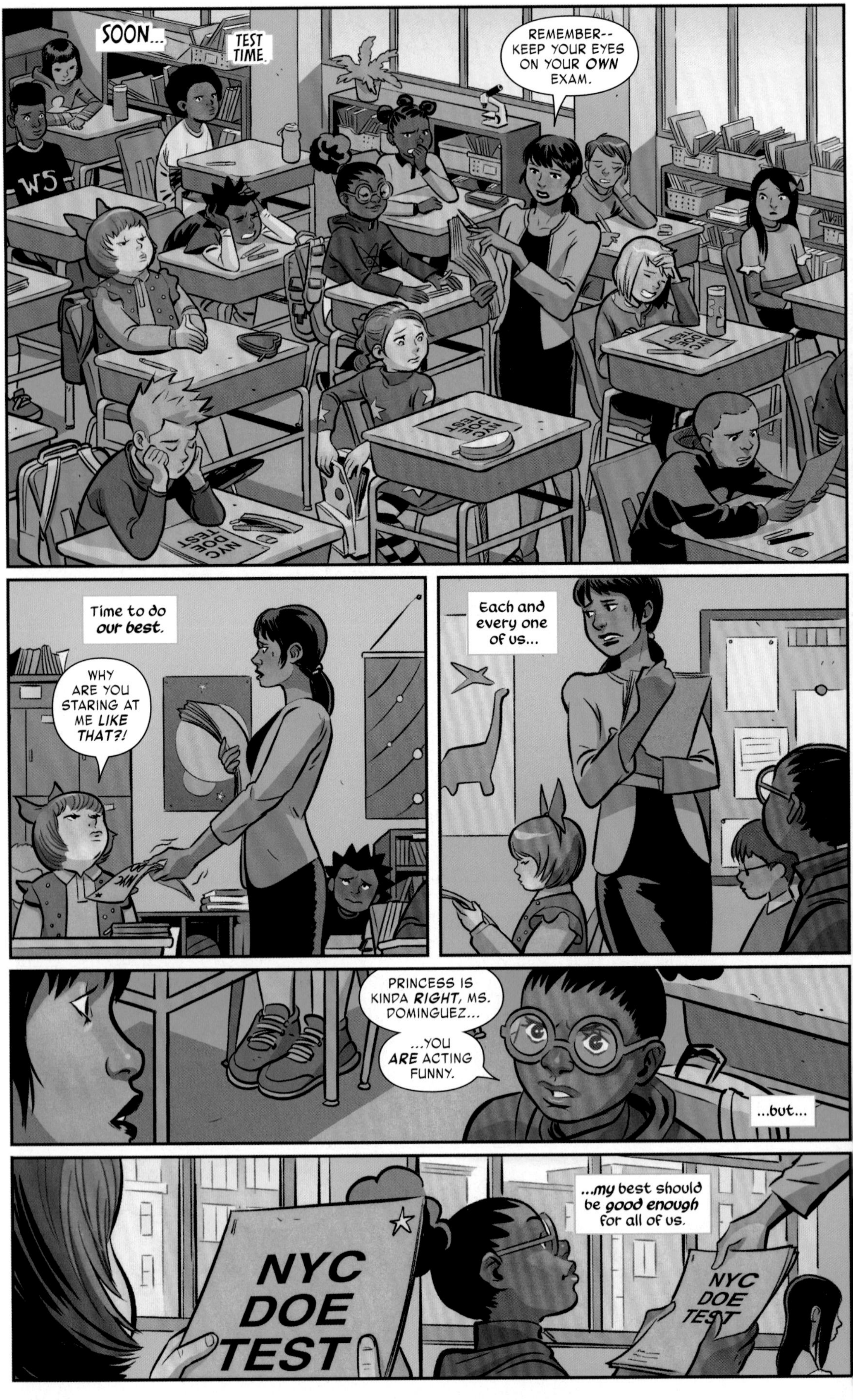
SOON...
TEST TIME.
REMEMBER-- KEEP YOUR EYES ON YOUR OWN EXAM.
NYC DOE TEST
Time to do our best.
WHY ARE YOU STARING AT ME LIKE THAT?!
Each and every one of us...
PRINCESS IS KINDA RIGHT, MS. DOMINGUEZ...
...YOU ARE ACTING FUNNY.
...but...
...my best should be good enough for all of us.
NYC DOE TEST
NYC DOE TEST

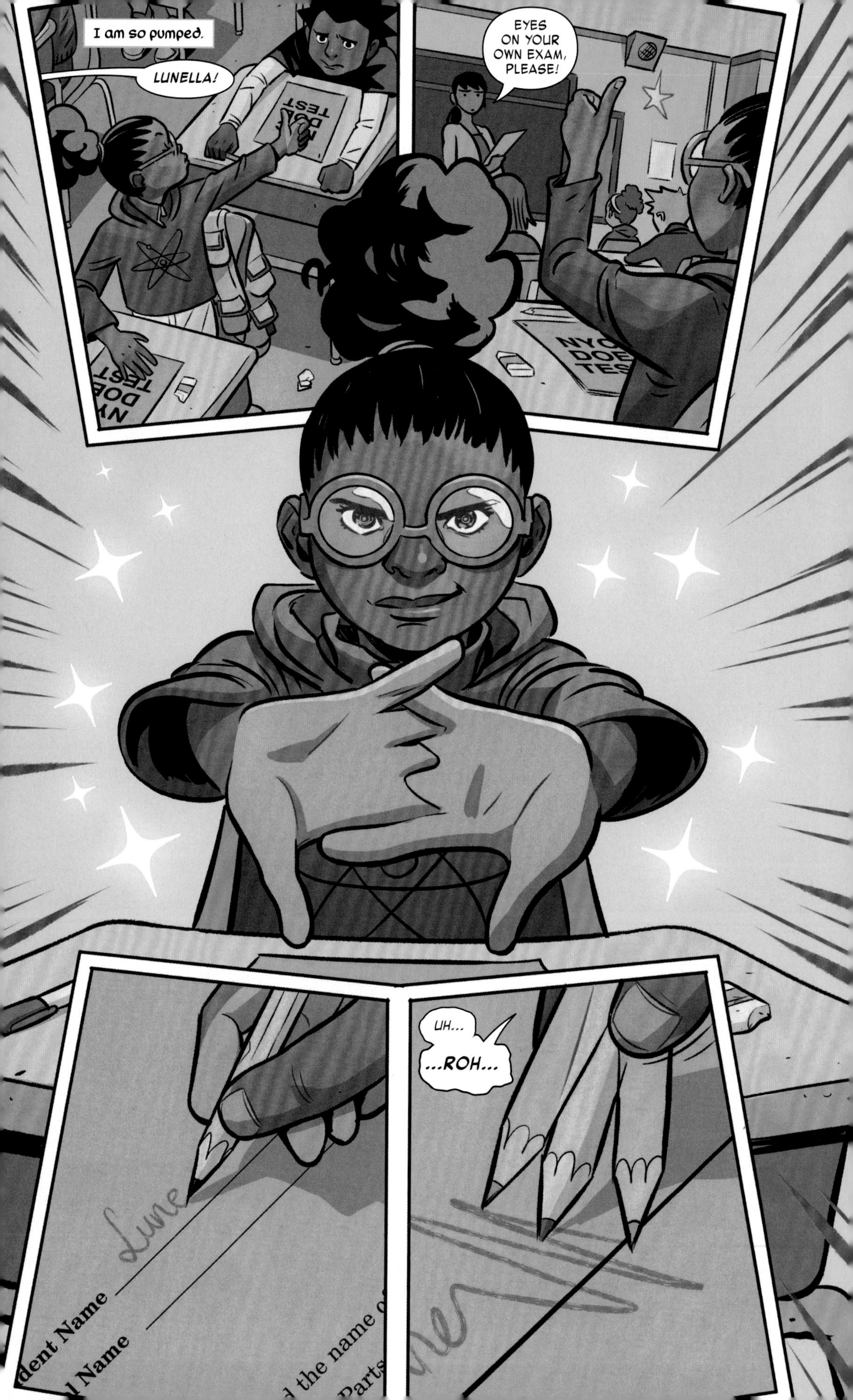
I am so pumped.
LUNELLA!
NYC DOE TEST
EYES ON YOUR OWN EXAM, PLEASE!
NYC DOE TEST
UH...
...ROH...
Lune
dent Name
l Name
d the name o
Parts

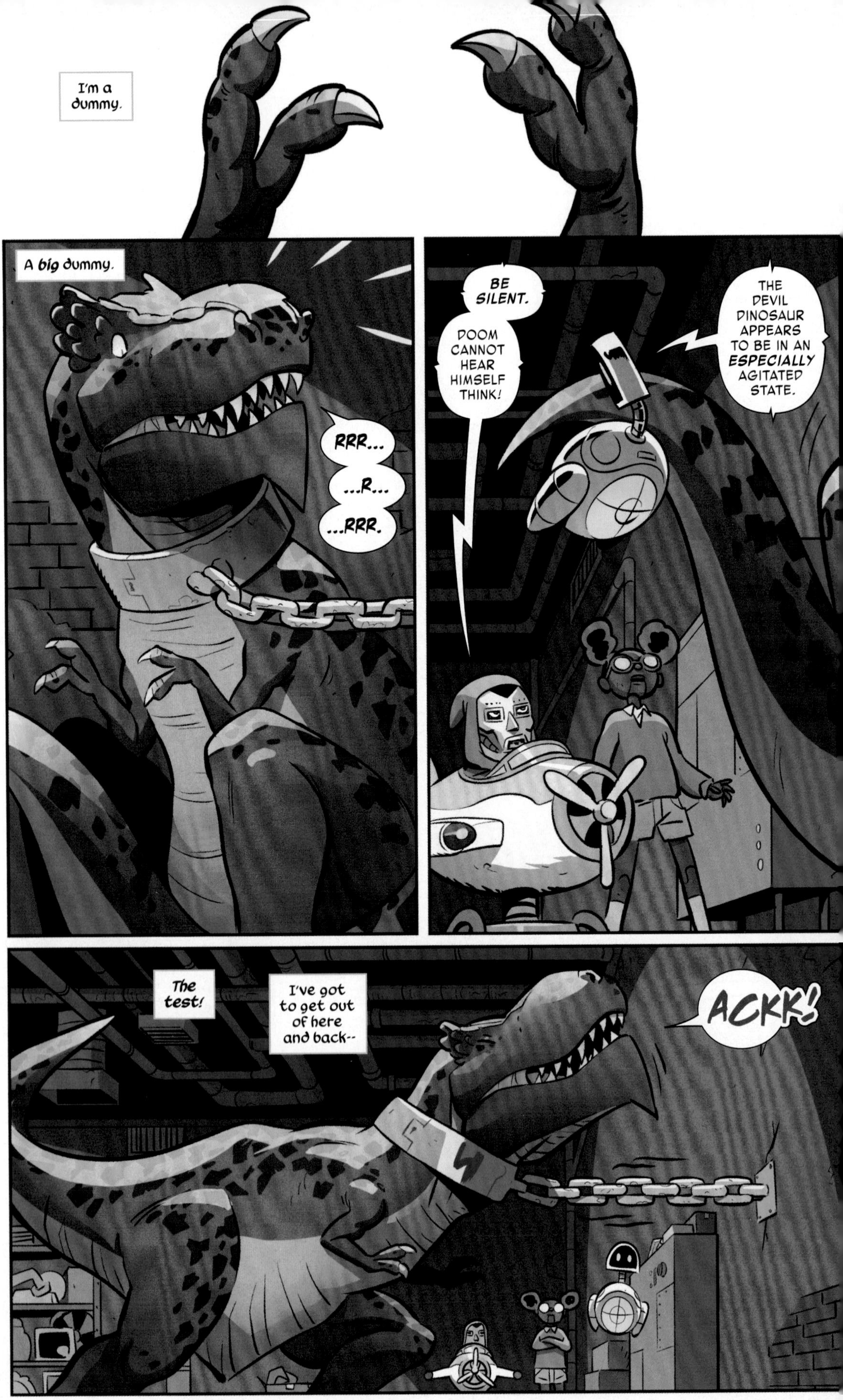
I'm a dummy.
A big dummy.
RRR...
...R...
...RRR.
BE SILENT.
DOOM CANNOT HEAR HIMSELF THINK!
THE DEVIL DINOSAUR APPEARS TO BE IN AN ESPECIALLY AGITATED STATE.
The test!
I've got to get out of here and back--
ACKK!

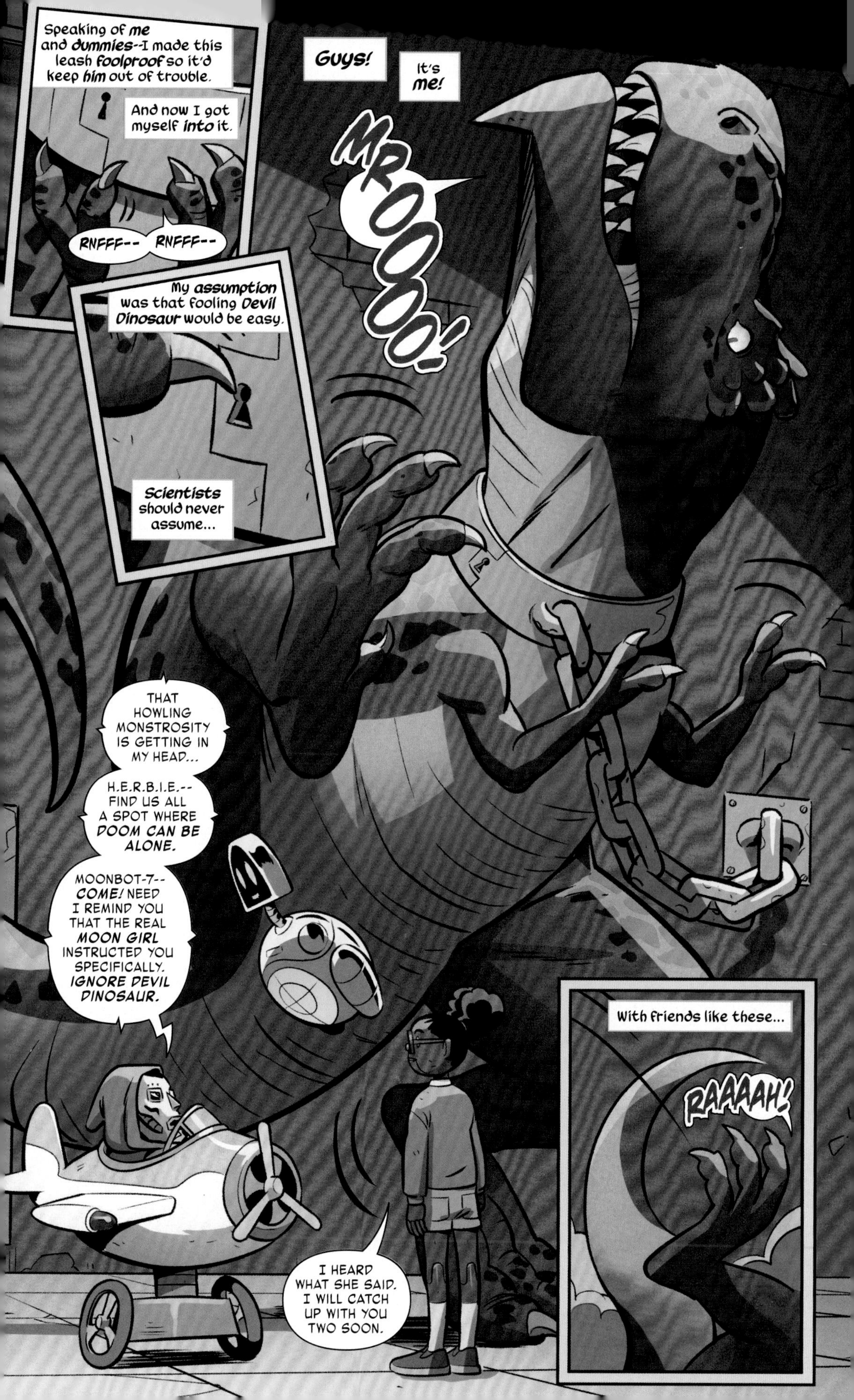
Speaking of me and dummies--I made this leash foolproof so it'd keep him out of trouble.
And now I got myself into it.
RNFFF--
RNFFF--
My assumption was that fooling Devil Dinosaur would be easy.
Scientists should never assume...
GUYS!
It's me!
MROOOOO!
THAT HOWLING MONSTROSITY IS GETTING IN MY HEAD...
H.E.R.B.I.E.-- FIND US ALL A SPOT WHERE DOOM CAN BE ALONE.
MOONBOT-7-- COME! NEED I REMIND YOU THAT THE REAL MOON GIRL INSTRUCTED YOU SPECIFICALLY. IGNORE DEVIL DINOSAUR.
I HEARD WHAT SHE SAID. I WILL CATCH UP WITH YOU TWO SOON.
With friends like these...
RAAAAH!

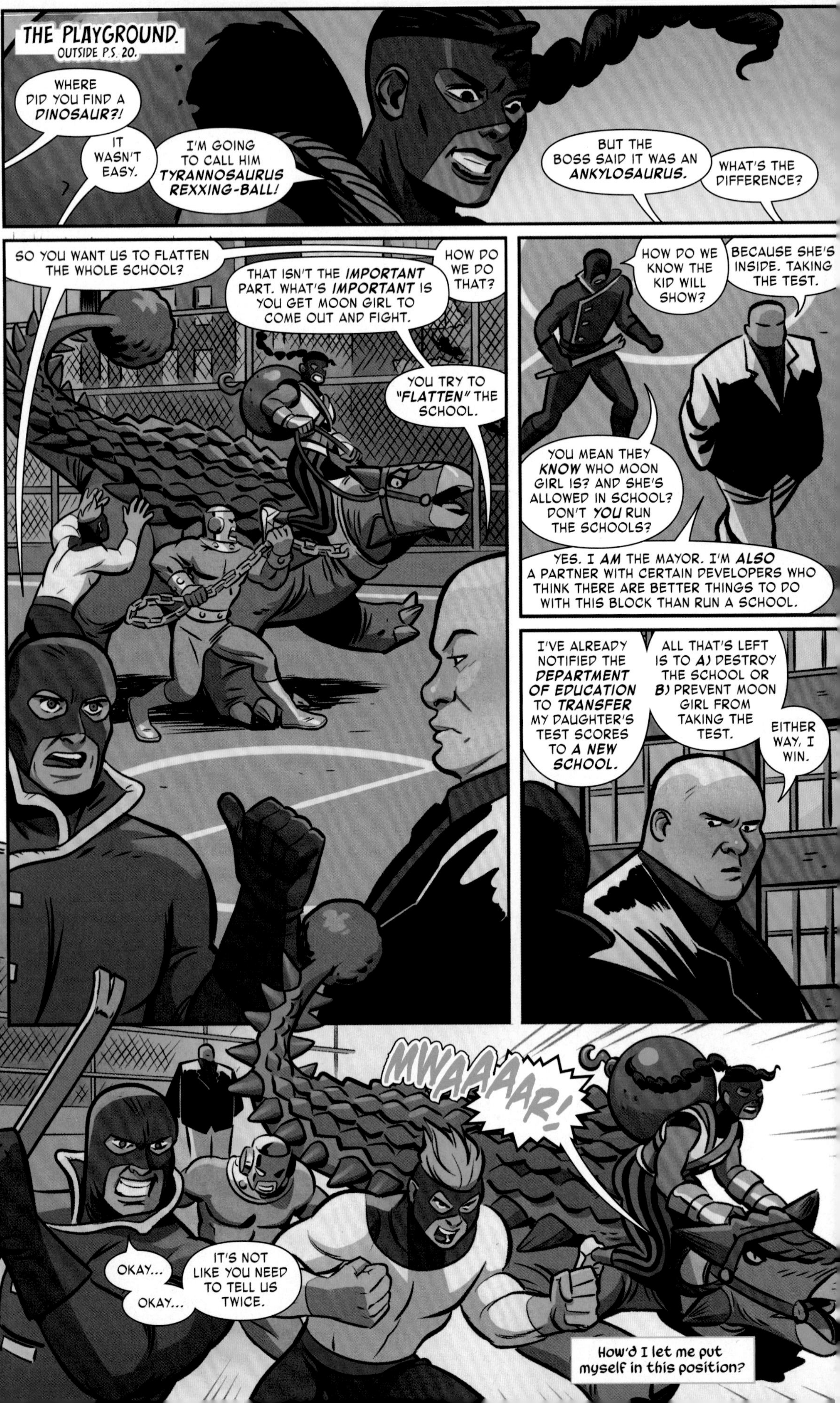

THE PLAYGROUND. OUTSIDE P.S. 20.
WHERE DID YOU FIND A DINOSAUR?!
IT WASN'T EASY.
I'M GOING TO CALL HIM TYRANNOSAURUS REXXING-BALL!
BUT THE BOSS SAID IT WAS AN ANKYLOSAURUS.
WHAT'S THE DIFFERENCE?
SO YOU WANT US TO FLATTEN THE WHOLE SCHOOL?
HOW DO WE DO THAT?
THAT ISN'T THE IMPORTANT PART. WHAT'S IMPORTANT IS YOU GET MOON GIRL TO COME OUT AND FIGHT.
YOU TRY TO "FLATTEN" THE SCHOOL.
HOW DO WE KNOW THE KID WILL SHOW?
BECAUSE SHE'S INSIDE. TAKING THE TEST.
YOU MEAN THEY KNOW WHO MOON GIRL IS? AND SHE'S ALLOWED IN SCHOOL? DON'T YOU RUN THE SCHOOLS?
YES. I AM THE MAYOR. I'M ALSO A PARTNER WITH CERTAIN DEVELOPERS WHO THINK THERE ARE BETTER THINGS TO DO WITH THIS BLOCK THAN RUN A SCHOOL.
I'VE ALREADY NOTIFIED THE DEPARTMENT OF EDUCATION TO TRANSFER MY DAUGHTER'S TEST SCORES TO A NEW SCHOOL.
ALL THAT'S LEFT IS TO A) DESTROY THE SCHOOL OR B) PREVENT MOON GIRL FROM TAKING THE TEST.
EITHER WAY, I WIN.
MWAAAAAR!
OKAY...
OKAY...
IT'S NOT LIKE YOU NEED TO TELL US TWICE.
How'd I let me put myself in this position?

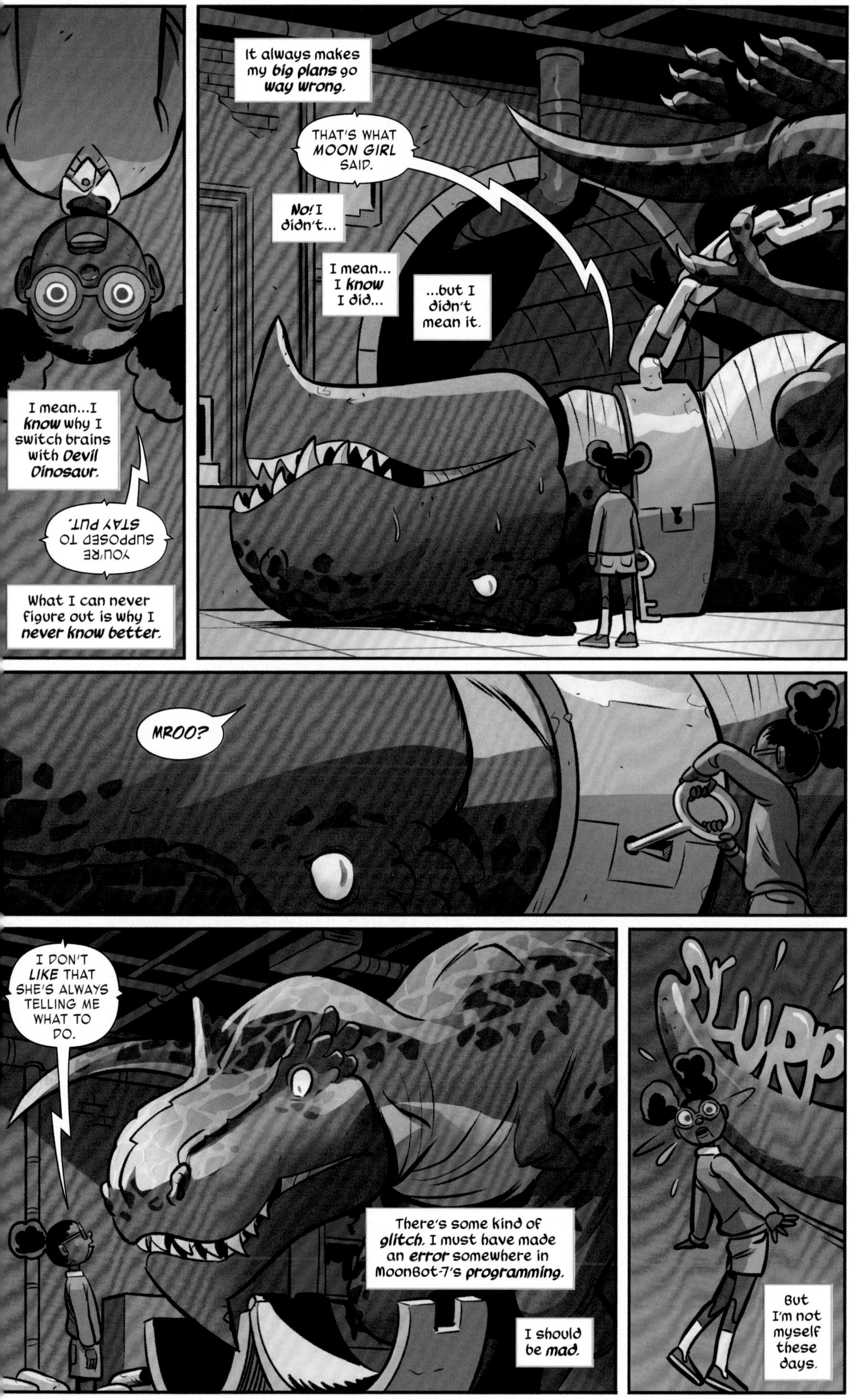
I mean...I know why I switch brains with Devil Dinosaur.
YOU'RE SUPPOSED TO STAY PUT.
What I can never figure out is why I never know better.
It always makes my big plans go way wrong.
THAT'S WHAT MOON GIRL SAID.
No! I didn't...
I mean... I know I did...
...but I didn't mean it.
MROO?
I DON'T LIKE THAT SHE'S ALWAYS TELLING ME WHAT TO DO.
There's some kind of glitch. I must have made an error somewhere in MoonBot-7's programming.
I should be mad.
SLURP
But I'm not myself these days.

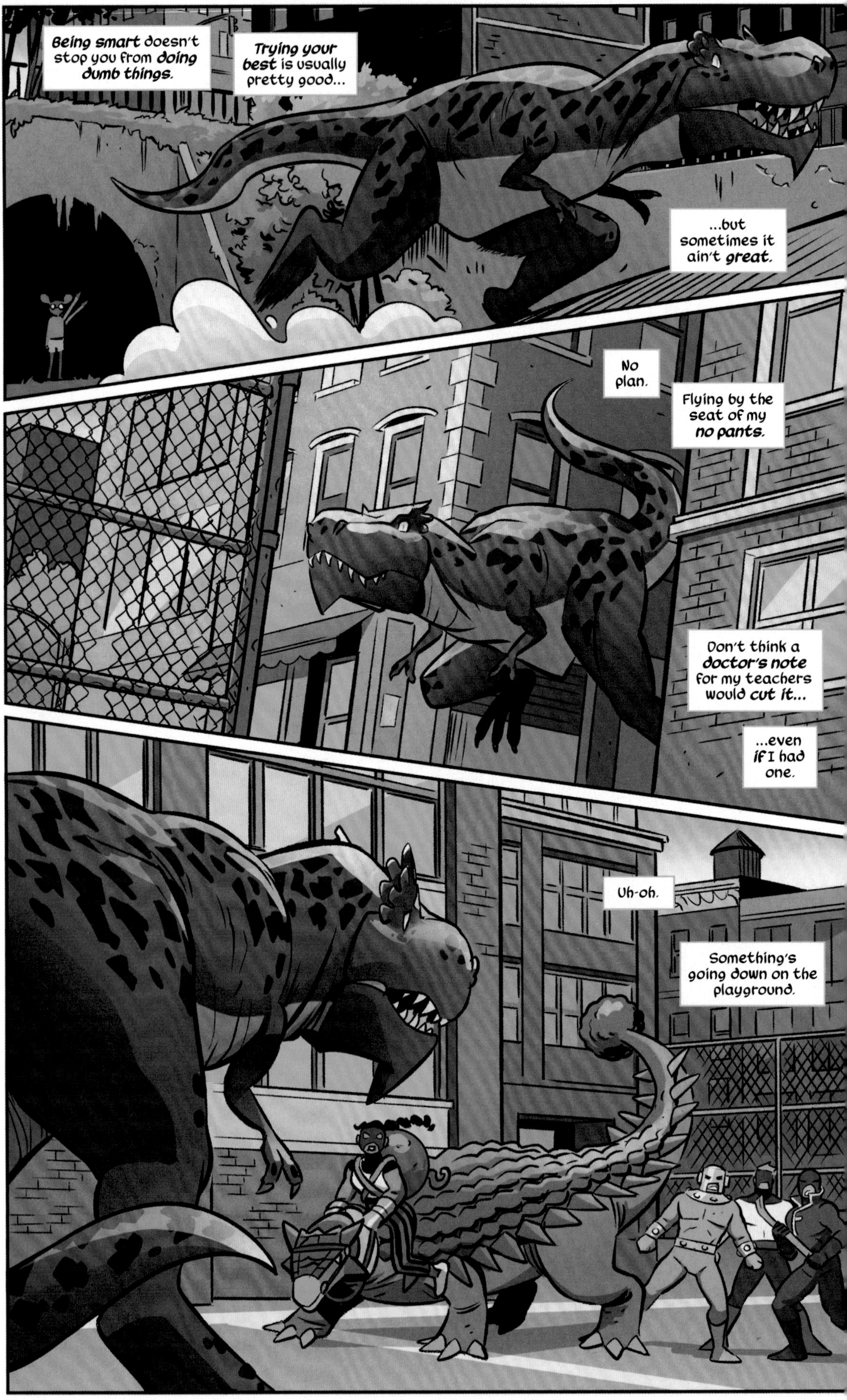

Being smart doesn't stop you from doing dumb things.
Trying your best is usually pretty good...
...but sometimes it ain't great.
No plan.
Flying by the seat of my no pants.
Don't think a doctor's note for my teachers would cut it...
...even if I had one.
Uh-oh.
Something's going down on the playground.

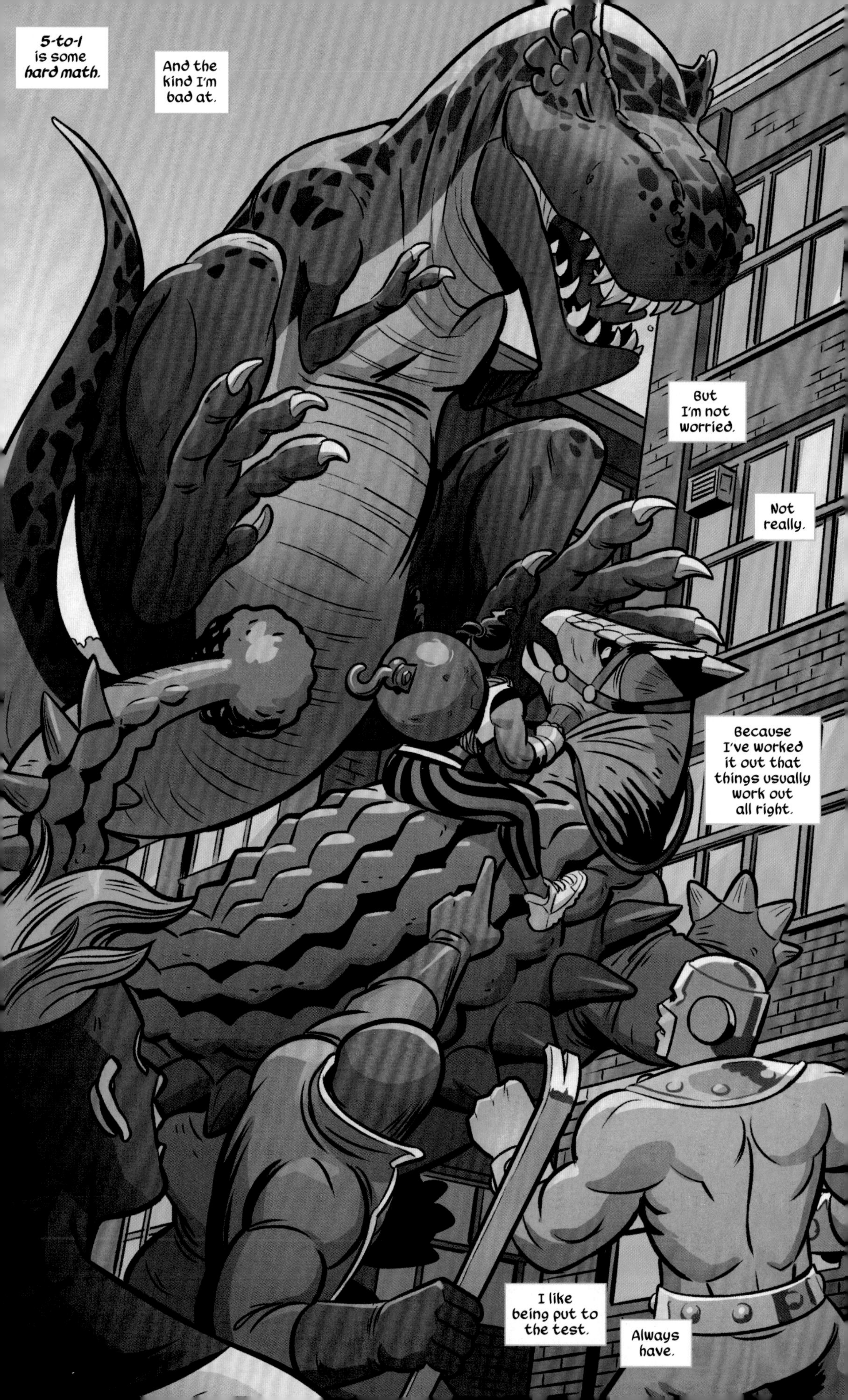

5-to-1 is some hard math.
And the kind I'm bad at.
But I'm not worried.
Not really.
Because I've worked it out that things usually work out all right.
I like being put to the test.
Always have.

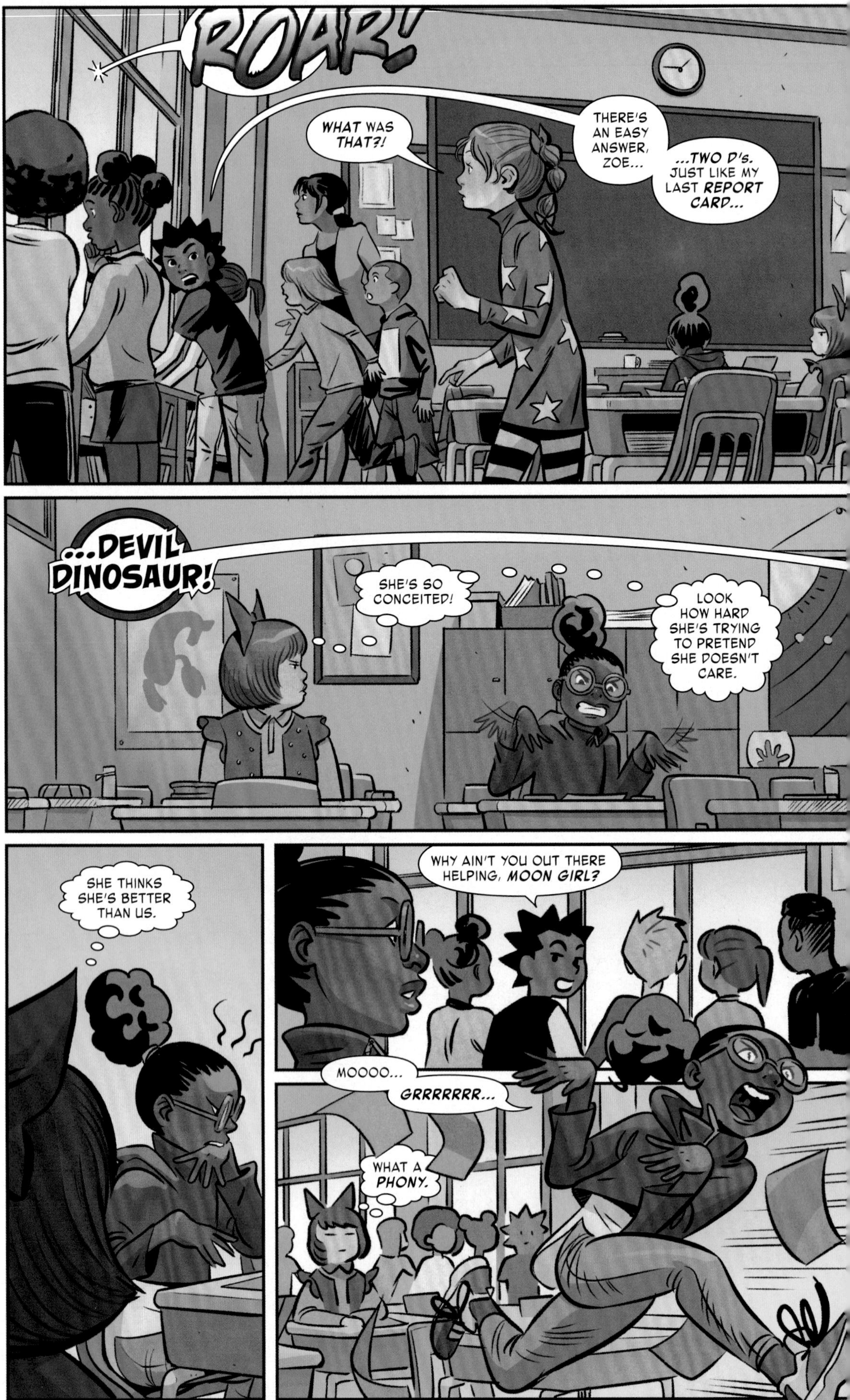

ROAR!
WHAT WAS THAT?!
THERE'S AN EASY ANSWER, ZOE...
...TWO D's. JUST LIKE MY LAST REPORT CARD...
...DEVIL DINOSAUR!
SHE'S SO CONCEITED!
LOOK HOW HARD SHE'S TRYING TO PRETEND SHE DOESN'T CARE.
SHE THINKS SHE'S BETTER THAN US.
WHY AIN'T YOU OUT THERE HELPING, MOON GIRL?
MOOOO... GRRRRRRR...
WHAT A PHONY.

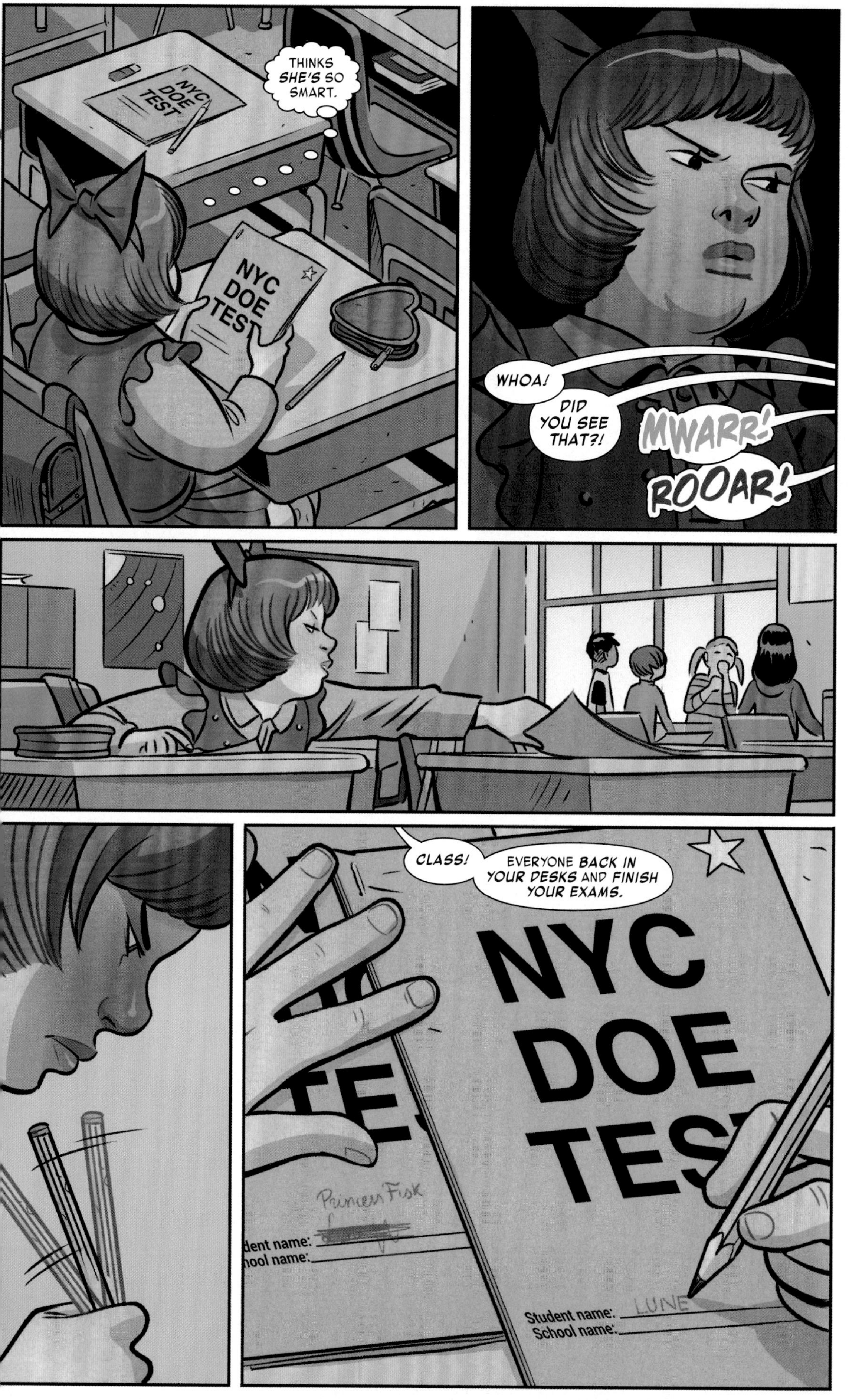
THINKS SHE'S SO SMART.
NYC DOE TEST
NYC DOE TEST
WHOA!
DID YOU SEE THAT?!
MWARR!
ROOAR!
CLASS!
EVERYONE BACK IN YOUR DESKS AND FINISH YOUR EXAMS.
NYC DOE TEST
Princess Fisk
Student name:
School name:
LUNE

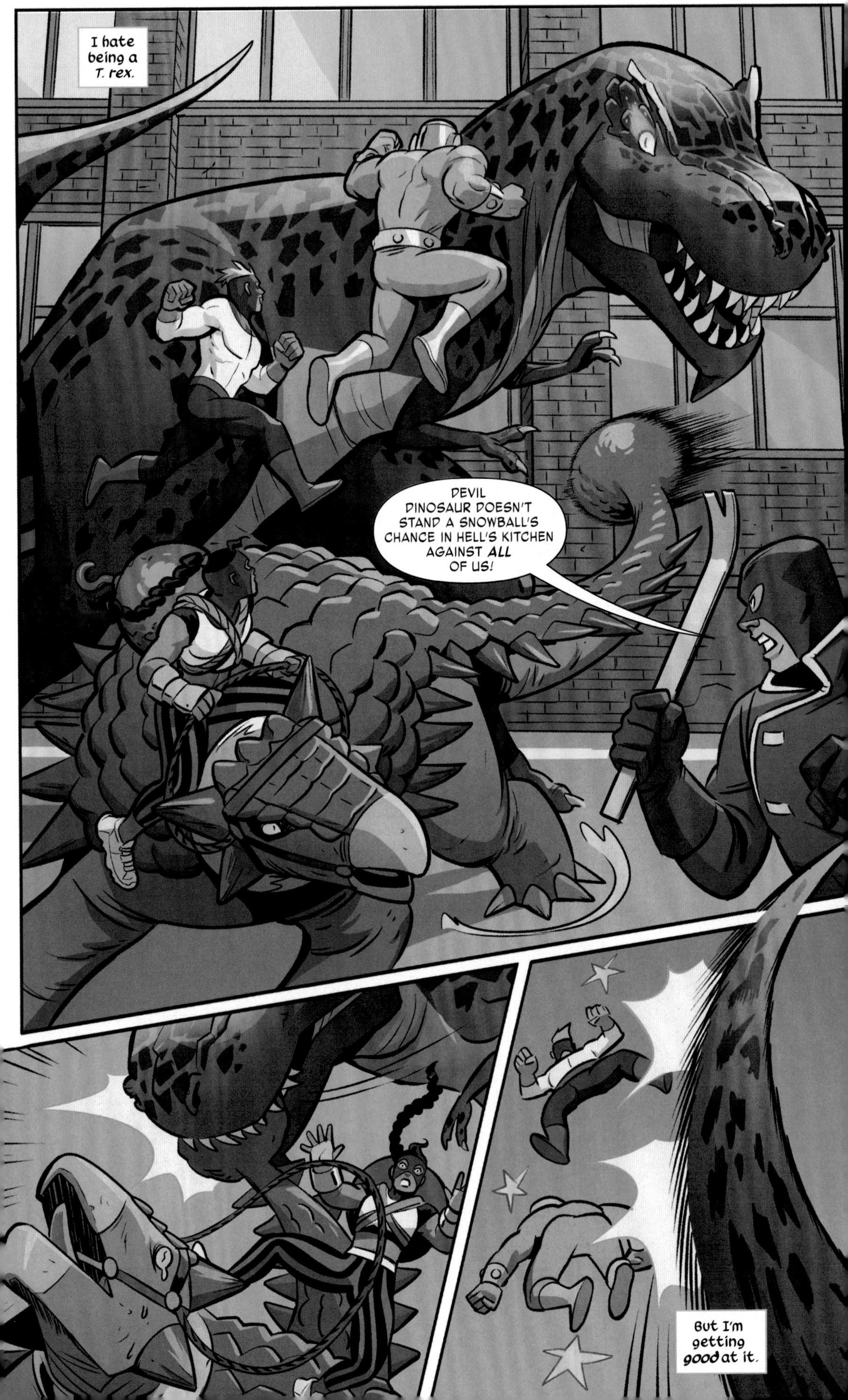
I hate being a T. rex.
DEVIL DINOSAUR DOESN'T STAND A SNOWBALL'S CHANCE IN HELL'S KITCHEN AGAINST ALL OF US!
But I'm getting good at it.

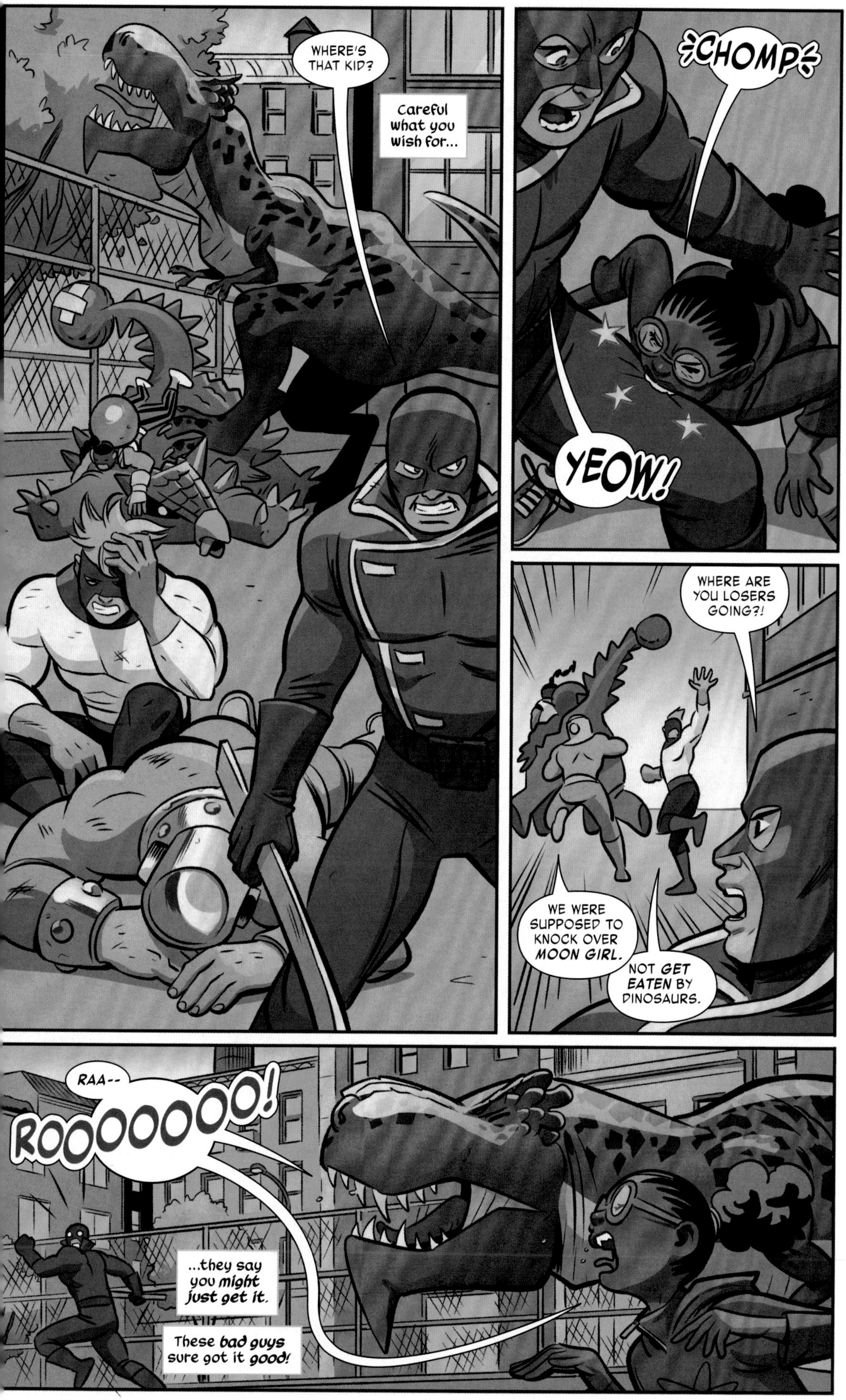
WHERE'S THAT KID?
Careful what you wish for...
CHOMP
YEOW!
WHERE ARE YOU LOSERS GOING?!
WE WERE SUPPOSED TO KNOCK OVER MOON GIRL.
NOT GET EATEN BY DINOSAURS.
RAA--
ROOOOOOO!
...they say you might just get it.
These bad guys sure got it good!

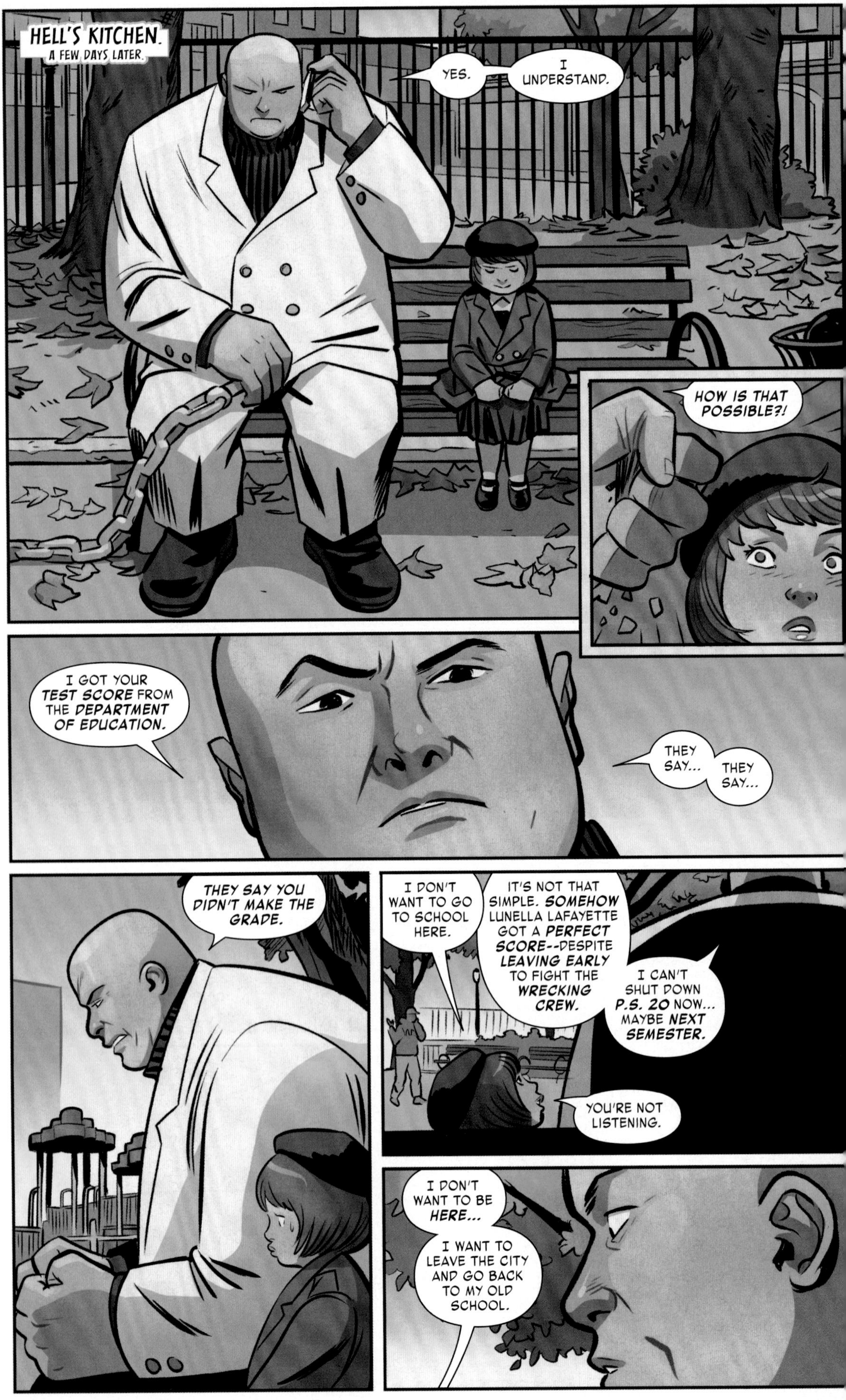
HELL'S KITCHEN. A FEW DAYS LATER.
YES.
I UNDERSTAND.
HOW IS THAT POSSIBLE?!
I GOT YOUR TEST SCORE FROM THE DEPARTMENT OF EDUCATION.
THEY SAY...
THEY SAY...
THEY SAY YOU DIDN'T MAKE THE GRADE.
I DON'T WANT TO GO TO SCHOOL HERE.
IT'S NOT THAT SIMPLE. SOMEHOW LUNELLA LAFAYETTE GOT A PERFECT SCORE--DESPITE LEAVING EARLY TO FIGHT THE WRECKING CREW.
I CAN'T SHUT DOWN P.S. 20 NOW... MAYBE NEXT SEMESTER.
YOU'RE NOT LISTENING.
I DON'T WANT TO BE HERE...
I WANT TO LEAVE THE CITY AND GO BACK TO MY OLD SCHOOL.

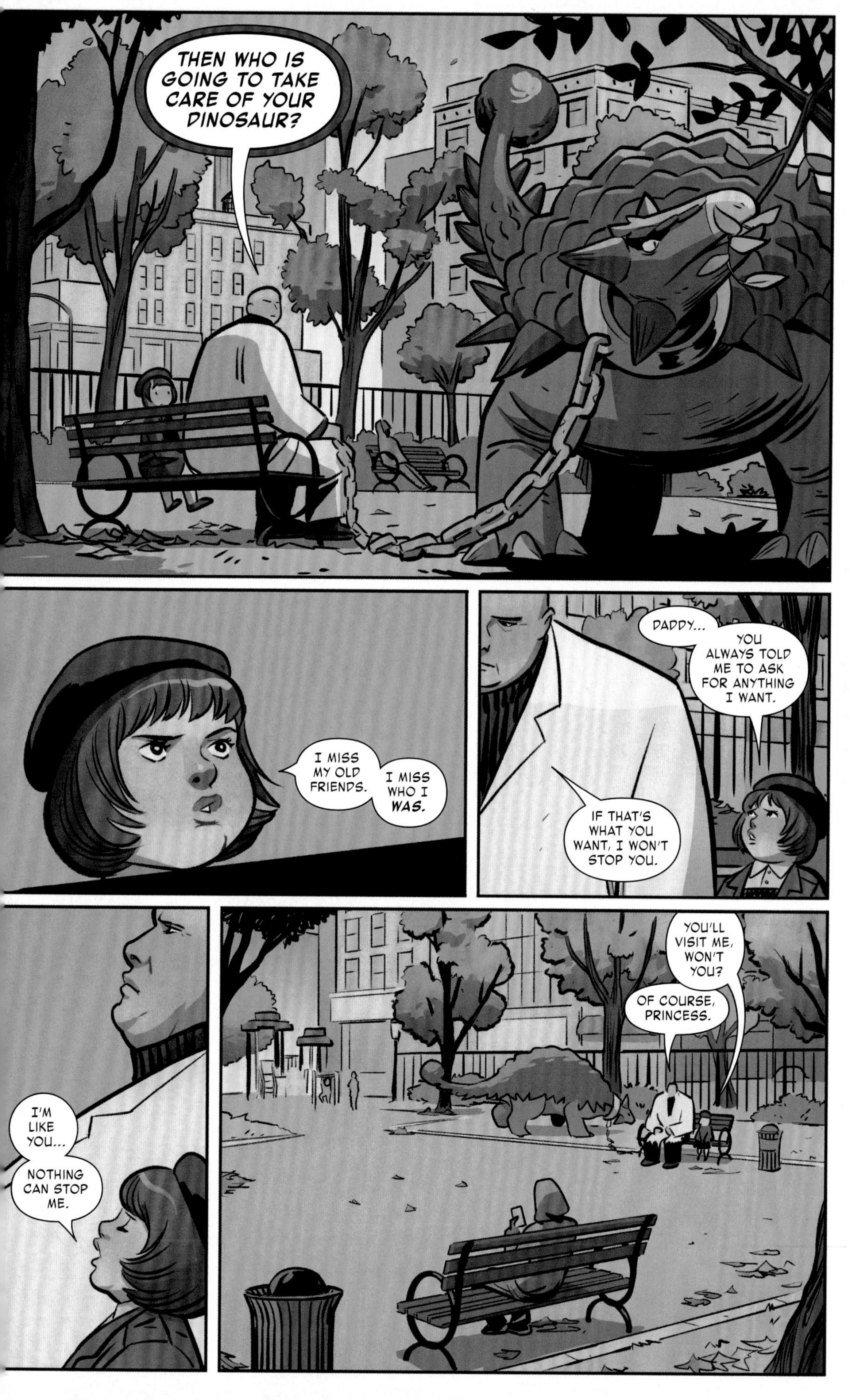
THEN WHO IS GOING TO TAKE CARE OF YOUR DINOSAUR?
I MISS MY OLD FRIENDS.
I MISS WHO I *WAS.*
DADDY...
YOU ALWAYS TOLD ME TO ASK FOR ANYTHING I WANT.
IF THAT'S WHAT YOU WANT, I WON'T STOP YOU.
I'M LIKE YOU...
NOTHING CAN STOP ME.
YOU'LL VISIT ME, WON'T YOU?
OF COURSE, PRINCESS.

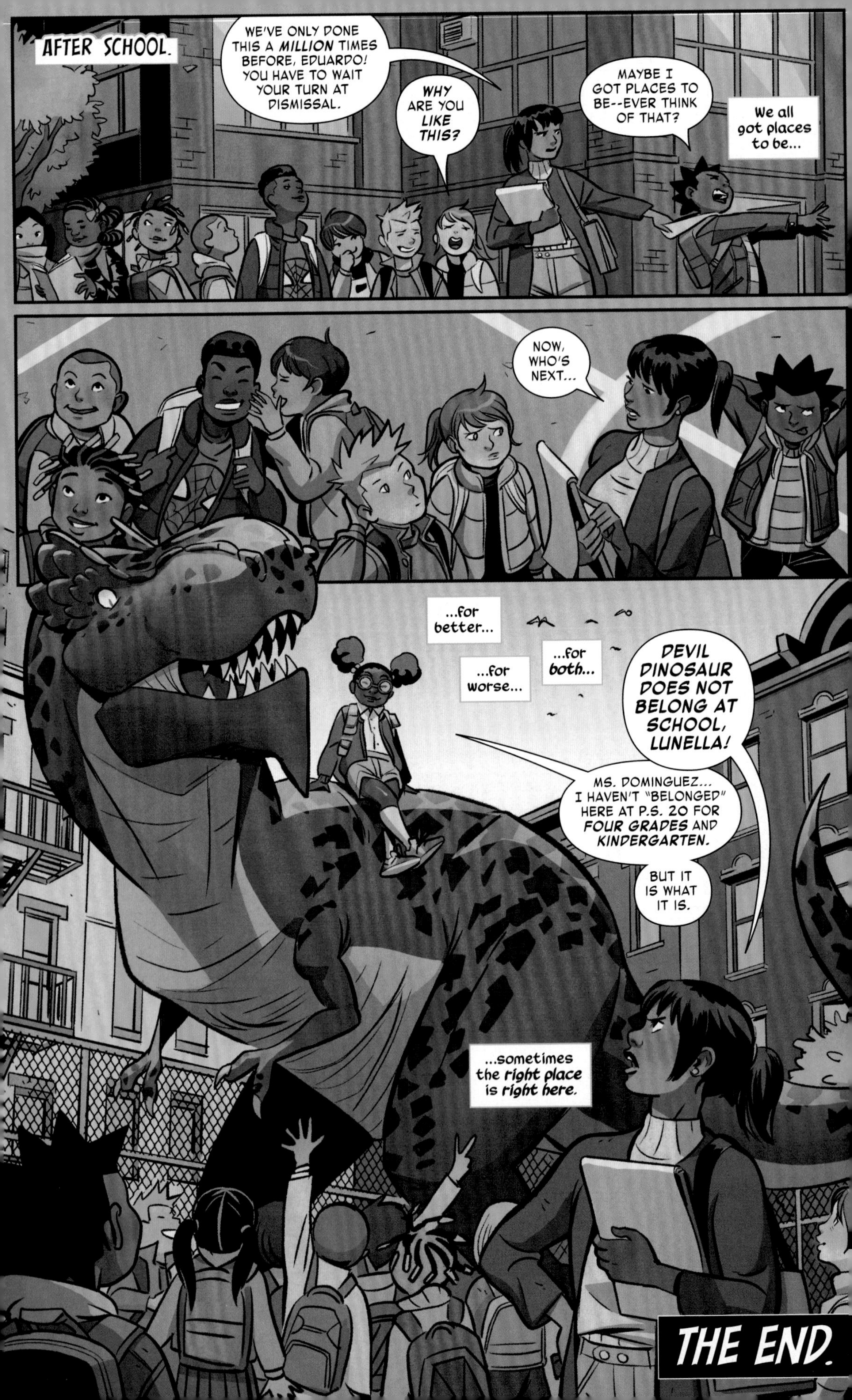
AFTER SCHOOL.
WE'VE ONLY DONE THIS A MILLION TIMES BEFORE, EDUARDO! YOU HAVE TO WAIT YOUR TURN AT DISMISSAL.
WHY ARE YOU LIKE THIS?
MAYBE I GOT PLACES TO BE--EVER THINK OF THAT?
We all got places to be...
NOW, WHO'S NEXT...
...for better...
...for worse...
...for both...
DEVIL DINOSAUR DOES NOT BELONG AT SCHOOL, LUNELLA!
MS. DOMINGUEZ... I HAVEN'T "BELONGED" HERE AT P.S. 20 FOR FOUR GRADES AND KINDERGARTEN.
BUT IT IS WHAT IT IS.
...sometimes the right place is right here.
THE END.

ACTIVITY PAGE

Break out your best markers and splash some color on the art below!

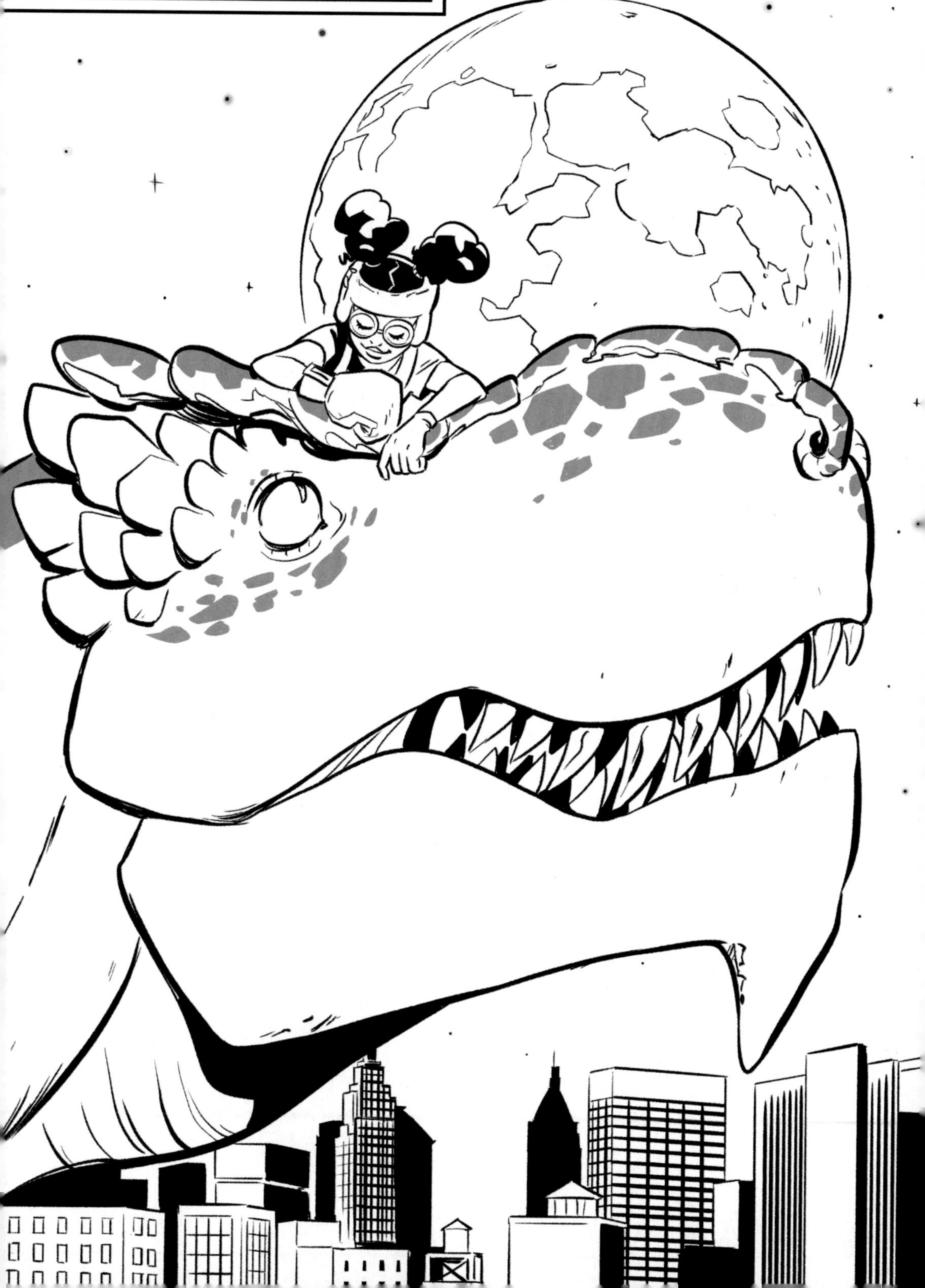

ACTIVITY PAGE

Break out your best markers and splash some color on the art below!

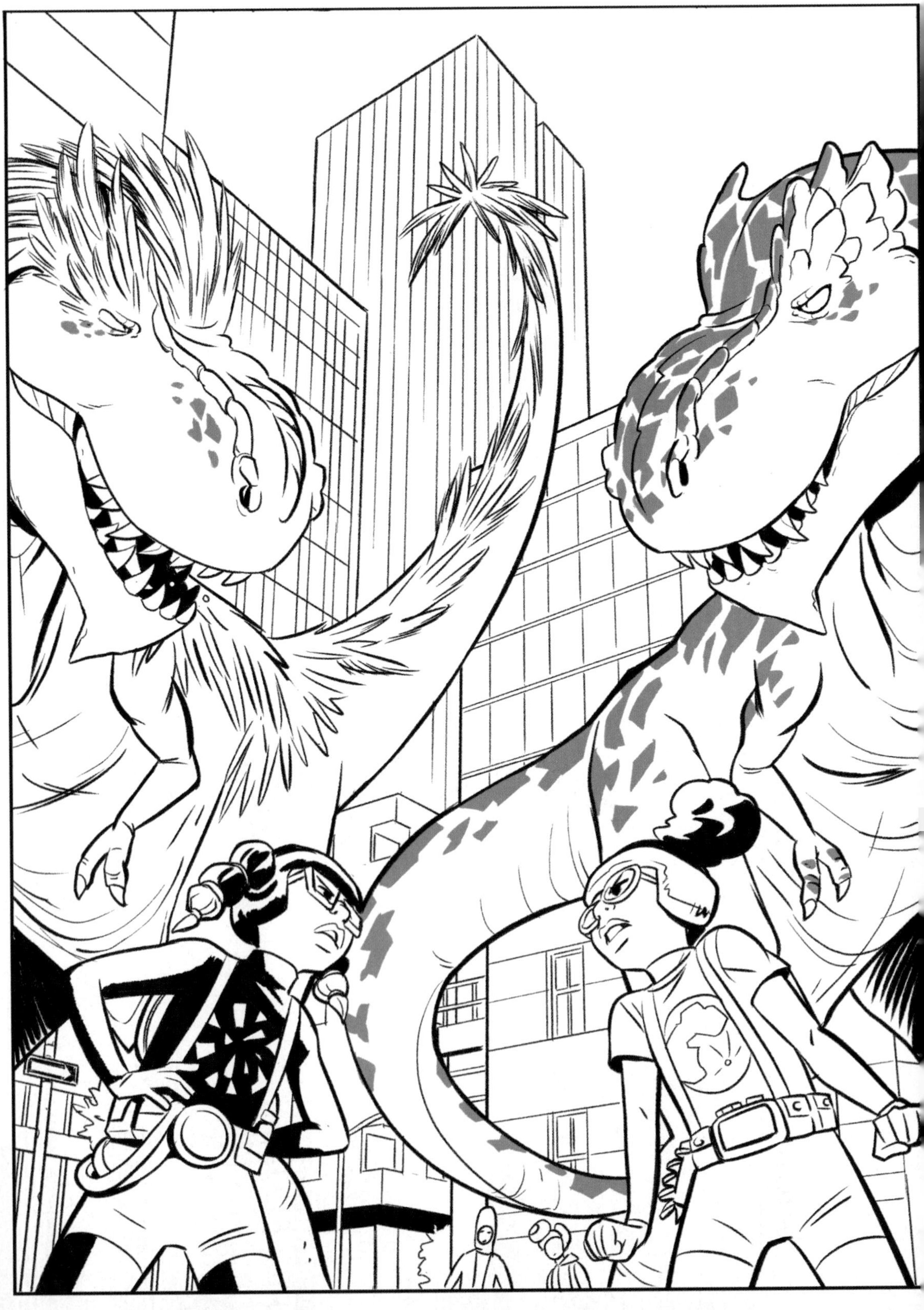